Living Space

Openness and Freedom through Spatial Awareness

Living Space

Openness and Freedom through Spatial Awareness

Paul Holman

BOOKS

Winchester, UK
Washington, USA

First published by O-Books, 2018
O-Books is an imprint of John Hunt Publishing Ltd., 3 East St., Alresford,
Hampshire SO24 9EE, UK
office1@jhpbooks.net
www.johnhuntpublishing.com

For distributor details and how to order please visit the 'Ordering' section on our website.

ISBN: 978 1 78535 609 4
978 1 78535 610 0 (ebook)
Library of Congress Control Number: 2017944840

A CIP catalogue record for this book is available from the British Library.

Design: Stuart Davies

UK: Printed and bound by CPI Group (UK) Ltd, Croydon, CR0 4YY
US: Printed and bound by Thomson Shore, 7300 West Joy Road, Dexter, MI 48130

Contents

Preface

We read every day, with astonishment, things which we see every day, without surprise.
Lord Chesterfield

This book is about space, not outer space particularly, just the space all around us, the openness which gets ignored in our fascination with the many things that space contains. The practice of becoming aware of space can quickly change the quality of our awareness, not only in simple beneficial ways, but also in a manner that can be transformative. A simple example can illustrate this idea.

As you continue reading, become aware that these words are printed on a blank sheet. This blank piece of paper supports the written words but plays no part in their formation. Yet all the spaces are absolutely necessary for the letters and words to be understood. What's more, you could probably read this whole book and never be consciously aware of this silent background.

Now become aware that as you read these words your whole body is present in a space, perhaps a room, and that you are able to pay attention to the space that both surrounds and suffuses you.

Notice, too, that as your attention moves to and fro between these instructions and feeling space, something special happens to the way you are attending. Now I am not going to say what that is of course, but I expect that you may have felt it already. Something happens when you start to become aware of the mystery of space, something that happens to you regularly, even though you may not have been consciously aware that space was involved.

The space that you are experiencing is the visual equivalent of silence, but more immediately accessible. Space, silence and awareness are the hidden matrix behind everything that arises and each is a door into its sibling.

And that, dear reader, is what this book is all about: the mystery of Space, which contains everything and is present inside everything, yet can only ever be defined in terms of the objects that float in it. It is truly a presence that is an absence, or is it an absence that is a presence? Well both, it seems, and at the same time a key to a freer form of personal presence that is physical, mental and spiritual.

This book is also an homage to many of my favourite authors and an opportunity to glimpse some modern 'classic' accounts of spiritual awakening. May these few shreds of wisdom be worth the price of the book.

In the first chapter, I introduce three modern accounts of sudden changes in the perception of Space. These examples will start us off on our journey of Seeing: seeing in a way that is always fresh and vital.

Please note that no part of this book should be taken as medical or psychological advice.

1

Experiencing Great Space

Now and then it is good to pause in our pursuit of happiness and just be happy.
Guillaume Apollinaire

In 1961 the British Buddhist Society published a remarkable book by Douglas Harding entitled *On Having No Head*. Diminutive in size and less than sixty pages in length, this small volume has subsequently been reprinted many times and has become a classic of modern spiritual literature. The book is based upon a very simple but revelatory experience that arose while Harding was walking in the Himalayas. This is how he describes it:

> What actually happened was something absurdly simple and unspectacular: I stopped thinking. A peculiar quiet, an odd kind of alert limpness or numbness came over me. Reason and imagination and all mental chatter died down. For once, words really failed me. Past and future dropped away. I forgot who and what I was, my name, manhood, animalhood, all that could be called mine. It was as if I had been born that instant, brand-new, mindless, innocent of all memories. There existed only the Now, that present moment and what was clearly given in it. To look was enough and what I found was khaki trouser legs terminating downwards in a pair of brown shoes, khaki sleeves terminating sideways in a pair of pink hands, and a khaki shirt front terminating upwards in – absolutely nothing whatever! Certainly not in a head.
>
> It took me no time at all to notice that this nothing, this hole where a head should have been was no ordinary vacancy, no mere nothing. On the contrary, it was very much occupied. It

> was a vast emptiness vastly filled, a nothing that found room for everything – room for grass, trees, shadowy distant hills, and far above them snowpeaks like a row of angular clouds riding the blue sky. I had lost a head and gained a world (pages 5–6).

I didn't catch up with Harding's book until the mid-1970s but it had an immediate and extraordinary effect upon me. On reading his introductory account I suddenly felt my awareness swivelling through three hundred and sixty degrees, as if the view from a small television screen had suddenly been stretched out into full Sensurround; my visual perception in particular seemed greatly enhanced. Then, after a while the experience gradually faded. Subsequent attempts to reproduce this experience were not very successful and I only discovered why much later, when I learnt about the dangers of trying too hard or, in fact, of trying at all.

Douglas Harding's story is so arresting because he points to something that is immediately apprehensible: we have no direct perception or knowledge of our own heads! We have an idea of a head resting on our shoulders, but close inspection reveals nothing like a head – only space, a conscious space filled with the world. This insight seems so simple that one wonders why it appears to have largely escaped comment in centuries of spiritual literature. Perhaps, as Ramana Maharshi would have said, it is because headlessness is an "open secret", something so contrary to the common or cultural sense, that it defies detection.

Something else that struck me forcefully about Harding's account was that headlessness involved a radical *change in perception with eyes open* and not some exalted mystical state obtained through hours of grinding meditation. Of course, as a callow youth back then, I was looking for shortcuts, and now forty years later, realise that such things are generally only available at a hairdresser. However, the idea of having no head did set me on the path of looking for other accounts of spontaneous and radical *changes in perception* and the freedom that such transformation promised.

I soon came across Franklin Merrill-Wolff's *Pathways Through to Space*, a unique account of the one hundred days that followed a sudden transition into spaciousness. Besides being a follower of Advaita, Merrill-Wolff trained as a mathematician and philosopher and so provides a detailed philosophical exegesis of his experiences both in *Pathways* and a subsequent volume *The Philosophy of Consciousness Without an Object*. The later work in particular places Space as the central orientating concept through which he was able to make sense of his mystical journey.

His writings might have passed into obscurity had it not been for the fact that John Lilly (of float tank and LSD fame) came across an early draft and was moved to write a laudatory introduction for the 1973 edition of *Pathways*. Such is the depth of Merrill-Wolff's deliberations that I hesitate to say more about him at this stage. I have included an introduction here for the sake of chronology and context, but we will return to his work later in the book when we have built up sufficient stamina for his more rarefied cogitations.

Instead let me turn to another remarkable spiritual autobiography written by Flora Courtois, and published by the Theosophical Society in 1985. Like Douglas Harding's book, *An Experience of Enlightenment* is a refreshingly small volume, a mere ninety pages, yet it is astonishing in every way. Not only did Courtois's spiritual quest start at an early age, but it was characterised by an unusual singleness of purpose and a very early fruition to her search while still a young adult. It is also particularly interesting to me because of the way she emphasises the changes in her visual sense and in her experience of space. Here's how she describes a pivotal experience that occurred when sitting quietly on the edge of her bed gazing at a small desk:

> The small pale green desk at which I had been so thoughtlessly gazing had totally and radically changed. It appeared now with a clarity, a depth of three dimensionality, a freshness I had never imagined possible. At the same time, in a way that is utterly indescribable, all my questions and doubts were gone as effortlessly as chaff in the wind. I knew everything and all at once, yet not in the sense that I had ever known anything before.
>
> All things were the same in my little bedroom yet totally changed. Still sitting in wonder on the edge of my narrow bed, one of the first things I realised was that the focus of my sight seemed to have changed; it had sharpened to an infinitely small point which moved ceaselessly in paths totally free of the old accustomed ones, as if flowing from a new source.
>
> What on earth had happened? So released from all tension, so ecstatically light did I feel, I seemed to float down the hall to the bathroom to look at my face in the mottled mirror above the sink. The pupils of my eyes were dark, dilated and brimming with mirth. With a wondrous relief I began to laugh as I had never laughed before, from the soles of my feet upward (pages 47–48).

Courtois continued to experience unfolding changes and insights over the subsequent weeks and months, but the most obvious revelation was in the new way that her sight seemed to function: her eyes "released from their former tension to reach out and see the world outside, were now as free as if they had been blanked out, eliminated altogether" (page 56). In addition, she particularly notes that any trace of her nose or face had completely disappeared from her field of vision. I found this latter comment particularly amusing but also important, because Douglas Harding singles out the nose for special mention on more than one occasion, when he ridicules the old saying "as plain as the nose on your face". Clearly there is nothing less plain than the nose on my face or yours, and this is especially the case when we practise Courtois's Open Vision, a form of looking that relaxes our habitual narrow, restricted focus.

We return to Flora Courtois in later chapters because her little book is packed with nuggets of wisdom relevant to our discussion of attention and the way in which we use our senses to mould the Great Space around us.

To complete this introduction to spacious perception, I close this chapter with a contemporary and local account of 'seeing'. It was told to me by a friend in a totally matter of fact fashion, which is, of course, the Aussie way.

> I had been attending a conference in Brisbane for two days. It was beautiful spring weather but I'd been cooped up in a soulless hotel concentrating hard on a particularly demanding subject. On the third day I decided to 'cut classes' and go for a walk. It also happened to be Grand Final day with the Brisbane Lions playing Collingwood and so it was very quiet for a Saturday afternoon. I walked along the riverside for a while admiring the tropical flowers and the harmoniously designed recreation areas. Everything was very fresh and light. I eventually found myself in the Botanic Gardens and sat down on a bench beneath a tree with strange dangling fruits. I felt a mixture of pleasant weariness and muted excitement as I looked out over the city. Suddenly everything I was looking at came up to greet me. That is the only way I can describe it. At the same time I noticed that my internal chatter had receded to my voice box and was burbling away down there in a barely audible fashion. And as I looked out, I realised with complete clarity that seeing was all that was happening. There was only seeing. Nothing in particular was seen and no-one doing the seeing. Just seeing. This understanding was completely ordinary and obvious, yet extraordinary at the same time. Yes, of course, there is just seeing, just hearing,

> just doing and so on. After a while the indistinct talking in my voice box moved back up into my head, I got up and went on my way.

I like several things about this account, but most of all the idiosyncratic feature of the voice receding to the larynx. The intruder had left the building and gone back to his rightful spot leaving the owner free to SEE, or rather leaving a free space in which everything could arise naturally.

When we look at these three accounts it is clear that there are many similarities, especially with regard to seeing and spatial awareness. It is also of interest that the individuals involved had all been regularly practising some form of self-enquiry, so that although these unusual experiences seemed to arise spontaneously, they did so against a background of disciplines that involved attentional change. Flora Courtois, for example, had realised that since Reality obviously transcends the mind, then it could not be attained through any conceptual or strategic approach. As a result, she adopted a posture of waiting and letting be. In effect she radically changed the way she attended to her experience. So perhaps a change in attentional style is the key to attaining a new form of perception and understanding. This is the question that will occupy us for the rest of the book.

2

Please Pay Attention

If you endeavour to construct knowledge of what you're trying to seek, you close the door to the actual experience.
Russel Williams

While doing medicine at university I was foolish enough to do an elective year in experimental psychology. I remember we studied attention and perception in some detail, and this involved laboratory work in which we followed dots on screens and listened to weird sounds through headphones. We were assured that there was some relevance for air traffic controllers, but the connection to everyday life or the practice of psychotherapy seemed remote. I don't think that much has changed since then. Students are still not taught that there are different modes of attention, and that attending to the way one is paying attention is the most important skill that any adult can have.

We should not be surprised at this lacuna in our education. As Westerners we tend to be preoccupied with foreground experience and with the isolated objects that appear there. We could say that our attentional style is both narrow and monotonic: we tend to see the trees and not the wood. This style has so pervaded every aspect of our scientific, artistic and intellectual lives, that until recently it has escaped any serious comment or investigation.

Fortunately there are always those who slip through such cultural nets and I want to introduce you to two such individuals who definitely fall 'outside the box': Marion Milner and Les Fehmi. Marion Milner was a British psychologist born in 1900, who like Douglas Harding lived to the ripe old age of 98. As a young adult she decided to investigate what made her happy and how she should manage her life. The genius in her subsequent enquiry resided in the fact that she determined to answer these questions solely by experiment and not by recourse to tradition, external authority or rational theory. Her only method was scrupulous self-observation and keeping a detailed diary of her experiences and reflections. A summary of this process as it unfolded over several years was published in her first book, *A Life of One's Own* in 1934. This was the first of several books devoted to the various approaches that she took to personal development, and it is hard to praise any of them enough. However, in my mind, *A Life of One's Own* stands out as one of the most significant psychological texts of the 20th century and I return to it again and again for inspiration.

Milner's discoveries are too numerous to describe here, but included "blind thinking" and the distortions so beloved of cognitive-behavioural therapy, as well as mindfulness practice which she describes as a "continual readiness… to accept whatever came." Yes, Milner uses the word mindfulness in 1934! However, it is her approach to attention that most interests us here. Her findings were based on very vivid periods of perception, such as the one described below, which was recorded when on holiday and looking out over a valley. This opening of "a door between me and the world" was initially facilitated by naming to herself everything that she was experiencing through the senses.

> I sat motionless, draining sensation to its depths, wave after wave of delight flowing through every cell in my body. My attention flickered from one delight to the next like a butterfly, effortless, but following its pleasure; sometimes it rested on a thought, a verbal comment, but these no longer made a chattering barrier between me and what I saw, they were woven into the texture of my seeing. *I no longer strove to be doing something, I was deeply content with what was.* At

> other times my different senses had often been in conflict, so I could either look or listen but not both at once. *Now hearing and sight and sense of space were all fused into one whole* (italics mine).
> (*A Life of One's Own*, page 79)

This episode of enhanced perception was also accompanied by a radical change in mood from bored and frustrated to pure joy. Little wonder then that she went in search of ways to reproduce such experiences. Eventually her enquiries led her to a simple but profound conclusion: it was largely a matter of changing the way she paid attention to the external world. She noticed that normally attention was narrow and concerned only with its own interests and purposes. She called it a "questing beast", always moving on to the next thing and neither interested in objects themselves nor in the broader context. This was in contrast to wide attention which arose when the questing purposes were held in check and she was free to attend without wanting something from the objects concerned. Such widening of focus could sometimes be achieved by a voluntary gesture or by using a phrase such as "I want nothing".

Over time, however, the question of a broader kind of absorptive consciousness gave rise to an expanding sphere of considerations to do with expectancy, purpose and the everyday ability to feel relaxed and secure. And to find out what Marion Milner discovered about these matters, dear reader, you will have to read her books – you will not regret it. I will say only one thing here: her journey brought her to concepts that we would now recognise as very Eastern in quality, and to the central idea of mindfulness, a term which she used very much as we use it today, but based on a truly profound understanding. Her journey also tells us much about the importance of finding out things for yourself, and that the touchstone to self-knowledge is rigorous self-observation.

Much water has gone under the bridge of attention research since Marion Milner's day, but it has mainly been concerned with narrow focus. A good contemporary example is the invisible gorilla experiment described by its progenitors Christopher Chabris and Daniel Simons in their 2010 book *The Invisible Gorilla*. You may wish to go straight to the video on theinvisiblegorilla.com before I describe it any further.

The essence of the experiment is very simple: subjects watch a video in which two teams are playing with a basketball and are asked to carefully note and count how many passes are made by one of the teams. On the surface this seems to be a simple vigilance task, except that halfway through the short film a man in a gorilla suit walks across camera. About half the subjects in the early experiments did not see the gorilla, indicating that their attention was very narrowly focused by their intentional set (the task which they had been given). Chabris and Simons call the phenomenon of assuming that you have seen more than you actually have *the illusion of attention*.

They also describe *illusions of memory and confidence,* and point to the role of this deadly duo in miscarriages of justice. These important illusions ensure that eyewitness reports are often totally valueless, and human nature being what it is, many of us would rather tolerate gross miscarriages of justice than admit our own fallibility (see *Mistakes Were Made (but not by me)*, Carol Tavris and Elliot Aronson). Another arresting statistic from their book concerns driving while on a mobile phone, which produces as much impairment as being over the legal limit with alcohol. It would be difficult to find a more vivid illustration of the importance of paying attention to how we are paying attention.

For a broader approach to the psychology of attention, however, we must turn to the work of Les Fehmi, not only on account of its clarity, but also because of its applicability to everyday living. This is not to detract from the epidemic of mindfulness literature to which we are currently subjected. It is just that Fehmi provides a fresh perspective on the topic and one that has interesting neurophysiological correlates.

Fehmi was a significant pioneer in the field of biofeedback, and in his book *The Open-Focus Brain* he recounts how, back in the 1960s, he constructed his own machine to provide brainwave feedback. There was particular interest at that time in alpha waves which were thought to potentially hold the key to relaxation and even expanded states of consciousness. Consequently, Fehmi connected himself up to his machine and, over twelve two-hour sessions, tried various strategies to enhance his alpha production. Nothing seemed to work and finally he had to admit failure. Fortunately he was still connected up at that moment, because as soon as he accepted that nothing was going to work, the alpha waves came through in spades.

This unexpected outcome was one of Fehmi's first 'Aha!' moments and a very clear demonstration of the constraining effects of narrow focus and its twin: expectancy. It also illustrates one of the important lessons that most people learn when they are in any sort of biofeedback loop: trying in the conventional sense is usually counterproductive. For example, imagine that I have a small temperature monitor on my finger and that I am looking at a screen which shows me whether my hand is warming or cooling. If the point of the procedure is to warm my hand, then I might easily become too strategic and over-focused on trying to feel my hand getting hotter. The result will be hand cooling, because over-focus stimulates the sympathetic nervous system which in turn constricts peripheral blood vessels. When I see the monitor trace falling I may become even more stressed and so enter the over-focus/anxiety spiral, at which point it is best to break the biofeedback loop, take a deep breath and see the funny side of the whole thing before 'trying' again.

I was first able to do brainwave biofeedback on myself in the 1970s with an early Maxwell Cade machine, but just couldn't get the hang of it. By the time I had gone through the tricky business of connecting electrodes to my skull and getting good contacts, I was usually in a state of high stress. You could have almost seen the high frequency beta waves emanating from my head. Later, with a more modern machine (Neurodata II), I was able to accommodate myself to the technology, but it took at least fifty hour-long sessions to be able to use the biofeedback signals in a spirit of non-expectancy and relative detachment. In this way I gradually learned some of the patterns that seemed to correlate with 'successful' meditation, although from my present perspective I can see that much time would have been saved had I applied the following insights from Les Fehmi:

> Whenever you think of it, carry out your everyday tasks while at the same time being aware of infinite space, silence, and timelessness. Be aware of the three-dimensional space between, around, and through objects. Attend to all your senses: seeing, hearing, feeling, taste, smell, mental activity, and time. Include both objects and space. Imagine an awareness of space that permeates everything. Imagine feeling the background space against which everything is highlighted.
> (*The Open-Focus Brain*, page 136)

This is an eloquent summary of Fehmi's key discovery and the royal road to a more open focus: IMAGINE SPACE! The method is simple yet profound, instantly available, and applicable to any situation or problem. At the same time, it is not an instant or pop remedy against all our ills for the simple reason that our nervous system constantly works against spaciousness. Its "questing beast" is remorselessly drawn to any novelty that might promise either satisfaction of desire or avoidance of pain. This ensures that it is active 24/7 unless we remind ourselves to deliberately work against its narrow, grasping constraints.

Fehmi makes a further distinction between different modes

of attention as follows:

Narrow versus Diffuse

We are familiar with narrow attention, the kind we use to focus on an object, person or task, but the diffuse style requires a little more explanation. If I take in a visual scene or a picture in diffuse focus, my aim is to include everything at once in order to create a general sense or feeling of my perceptual field. We could use the term Broad instead of Diffuse, because in opening to broad attention I exchange any sense of the particular for a diffuse, overall impression of the whole. For example, if we take the analogy of exploring a large room, it is the difference between using a narrow torch beam and the diffuse light of a candle. We can have either great clarity over a small area or less detail over the whole area.

If I include my other senses, as well as the awareness of space and even of the timeless present, then I have moved into full Open Focus. Look again at Marion Milner's account to get a sense of how this might feel.

Objective versus Immersed

These terms are more self-explanatory. With objective attention I am *distanced* from the objects of perception. This is the cold scientific gaze that stands back to measure and evaluate. In the human sphere it is the realm of judgement, calculation and manipulation and is *strongly associated with the sense of being a separate self*. Immersion on the other hand implies a much greater *identification* and merging with the object; for example, deep absorption in a maths problem, a book, a film drama or another human being.

In Narrow versus Diffuse attention the issue is the width of the perceptual beam. In Objective versus Immersed it is the distance at which I am holding this metaphorical torch. Open Focus is the awareness of my current attentional style and the appropriate correction of imbalance. For example, a counsellor listens to a client and moves between:

> Understanding the meaning of the words being spoken and putting together a sequential history (narrow/objective).
>
> Judging the verbal content against the overall backdrop of the client's behaviour and affect (diffuse/objective).
>
> Feeling into the client's overall state and situation (diffuse/immersed) – so-called 'gut feelings', 'felt sense' or intuition.
>
> Empathising and being deeply moved by specific emotional content (narrow/immersed).

At any point the therapist may realise that she is stuck in a particular mode, and as a result, may take a moment to become more attentionally spacious, flexible and balanced. This is, of course, easier said than done, but is the most important part of the therapist's art.

We can add two more qualities to the idea of the attentional beam:

a) how quickly it moves around i.e. its restlessness and
b) its brightness or energised quality.

In Attention Deficit Hyperactivity Disorder we see problems created by a narrow attentional beam being 'hooked' by sensory stimuli in very rapid succession. It's as if the brain is trying to take in the whole world by rapidly scanning with its narrow beam. In situations of fatigue or rest the opposite is true, with the attentional beam becoming diffuse and weak and the nervous system reverting to its so-called default mode of drifting thoughts and imaginings.

In fact, there is a natural rhythm between focused activity and the default mode, which is one of the reasons it is so hard to maintain tightly focused concentration for long periods. When doing such work it can be a good idea to occasionally drift off and allow the brain a brief catch-up in its processing work. Such breaks reduce stress in the nervous system and can enhance the task in hand, especially if your imaginings are positive, future orientated and 'on topic'. (See Caroline Williams, "Daydream Believer".)

Ideally, we aspire to an attentional field that is flexible and appropriate to the moment. Most of the time this means a 'Goldilocks' style that is in a mid-zone and ready for whatever experiences arise. The Open Focus approach ensures such readiness.

Fehmi has found that Open Focus tends to be associated with synchronous alpha, that is, alpha brainwave frequencies that are in lock step with one another across different parts of the brain. This implies a powerful brain state of *relaxed full attention*. It also suggests that the narrow style of the left brain hemisphere, and the more diffuse, broader style of the right side, are in greater harmony than the 'business as usual' mode which privileges left-sided styles of awareness.

There are, of course, precedents in world literature for the different types of focus that are being described here. Most religious traditions have well-trodden paths of attentional training, whether they be in the form of meditation, prayer or other devotional practices. These mostly involve keeping a narrow focus on a single object and bringing awareness back to this single place each time it strays. The focus may be on the breath, a mantra, a murti (image), a movement or anything that can act as a steady reference point to the flickering current of normal consciousness.

These narrow focus methods all depend on stabilising attention by channelling mental 'doing' in one direction. Normally the stability of our perceptual and subjective worlds is maintained, paradoxically, by constant motion. This can be illustrated by reference to our eyes, which are ceaselessly darting to and fro with micro-movements called saccades. These unnoticed movements are necessary because if an image remains static on the retina it simply ceases to be registered – it disappears.

Sounds, tastes, smells and touch all disappear if experienced in a monotonous way. For example, after a short while we cannot smell a perfume that is right under our noses – it has to waft to and fro. We generally do not register the pressure of clothes on skin and a background noise slips out of awareness. And so it is with the mind. It has to be in constant motion to maintain the sense of a discreet 'I'. Content is irrelevant, it just has to keep going. If there were any more constructive purpose to most of our mentation other than self-preservation, then we would be generally thinking in a more salubrious way, but that is clearly not the case.

Focused meditation methods encourage a situation akin to the static image on the retina: the object tends to become less distinct and gives way to the background from which it is arising. The yang of focus taken to its limit evolves into its yin complement. This may leave the practitioner in the 'witness' position observing a blank, empty state or, more hopefully, in the expansiveness, bliss and tranquillity of Conscious Space. The latter outcome, however, tends to be predicated on a great deal of conscientious practice.

Notwithstanding the many benefits of the focused strategy, there are, however, one or two problems with this approach, especially when the focus is on an internal object such as a mantra or the breath. This is illustrated in the following story (which I think comes from Ramana Maharshi):

> A great spiritual teacher was instructing his disciples one day, when he became very thirsty. A chela rushed off for a drink but when he returned found that the guru had sunk into deep samadhi. The chela waited patiently for the teacher

> to wake from his deep immersion in bliss. Time passed and the disciple grew old and eventually died, but the 'vigil of the water', as it came to be known, carried on through the next generation and the next. Then one day, after many, many years, the guru stirred. The disciples gathered round, breathlessly anticipating the great wisdom that would come from this remarkable feat of absorption. The guru opened his eyes and shouted, "Where is my water?"

Focused methods are usually practised within a context of eyes-closed, still body meditation, a situation that lends itself to trance states that are *conditional,* that is, they are attained by *excluding* most sensory input and by inhibiting any spontaneity or reactivity in the system. In contrast, *inclusive,* open or wide focus approaches accept into awareness everything and anything that arises. Nothing is excluded, including perceptions (internal and external), emotions and thoughts. The slowing of attentional motion is secured through non-reactivity to whatever comes into awareness, the 'observer' remaining centred in herself and not going out to grasp or chase whatever is passing through. An analogy that is often used invokes the image of sitting on a riverbank and watching boats drift by. Don't get in the boat! The issue of the location of the riverbank and the identity of the person sitting there are topics to which we shall return later.

We must beware of false dichotomies, however. Both narrow and broad focus approaches share a common base, especially with regard to two features:

1) Both attempt to stabilise attention and wrest it from its normal obeisance to craving and aversion, thought and circumstance.
2) Both emphasise a 'conversion' from doing to sensing (in advanced focused states, concentration becomes effortless, one is 'captured' by sensing). We become open to direct

experience *relatively* unfiltered by preconception.

This latter point cannot be emphasised too much. Our nervous systems are built around doing, and even those circuits that serve 'higher thought' have hijacked brain programmes that originally evolved to plan movement. The mind is a 'doing mind', and sensing is normally subordinate to the purposes of personal action.

Attention ***is*** agenda-based awareness: narrow and directed.

Waiting and letting be without an agenda is OPENNESS TO SEEING.

In emphasising the senses, we make doing subordinate to Reality as it presents through the senses. And in talking of the senses, I am including the experience of emotion and everyday thought, for even the latter, when divested of its spurious sense of doing, appears to us as an internal monologue to which we are listening.

So we can say that both narrow and broad focus approaches move the practitioner in the direction of:

OPEN ATTENTION/SENSATION
which is present-centred awareness in a field of
CONSCIOUNESS/ENERGY/SPACE.

When in open attention/sensation, we are in a position to be 'taken' by and to cohere with this field of BEING, the mystery of GRACE.

The meditator sitting motionless with eyes closed will experience sensation in progressively more refined and special ways, but the question of how well his attainments translate into everyday life is moot. The practitioner of an eyes open approach or everyday mindfulness/self-remembering is, to my mind, more clearly manifesting the reality of 'sahaj samadhi', or easy liberation, the very ordinary 'flowing with' Reality's inherent multidimensional and spontaneous nature. And as we shall see in Chapter 4, awareness of the body is a crucial aspect of such a grounded freedom.

In the final analysis, however, the choice of a path comes down to personal preference and one's inherent constitution. As Alan Wallace points out in his book on shamatha (exclusive) meditation (*The Attention Revolution*), practitioners may, from the start, choose to focus on the breath, or the contents of the mind or even awareness itself. Shamatha involves focused, attentional development and these different objects of concentration would normally be selected in a sequential way as the meditator progresses, each involving greater spaciousness. But individuals must follow their instincts and remember that we need not be too precious about getting things right. The important thing is to practise creatively, try out different approaches and learn by experience. For example, in my personal practice I apply both broad and narrow methods depending on the circumstances, something that I shall discuss further in Chapter 15.

Tim Burkett in his book on Zen practice (*nothing holy about it*) recalls his frustration when first learning to meditate from Suzuki Roshi (of *Zen Mind, Beginner's Mind* fame). Suzuki specified a strict sitting posture but did not direct him to a particular focus of attention. This more open method was obviously a difficult way to start his meditative career, and Burkett advises us in his book to use the anchor of the breath whenever we need to settle down or centre ourselves.

In contrast, Flora Courtois discovered her own open method which involved just waiting without expectation, with all the senses alert. After meeting the Zen Master Hakuin Yasutani Roshi, she seems to have quite naturally taken to the practice of shikantaza or sitting massively like a mountain. This physical and mental posture allows great stillness and a field of attention that "has become maximally open and receptive to Being" (*An Experience of Enlightenment*, page 85).

The reader is probably aware at this point that in making a distinction between narrow and broad approaches, we are faced with the paradox that narrow focus methods can be the best place to establish enough stable concentration to enable the openness of attention/sensation. With inclusive methods, we are in spaciousness from the beginning and there is no repression or self-manipulation. It is very ordinary and in complete continuity with everyday life, but at the same time it is doubly fragile due to the ever-present tendency to identify with and respond to sensory content.

To draw a perfect circle the compass point must be sharp and firmly fixed.

Thus broad and narrow approaches are complementary and as such reflect the cosmic dance of connection and separation. In fact, the relationship between connection and separation can be thought of as a general ground rule of creation, seen in every aspect of the physical and mental world from quantum physics to the functioning of the brain. But to understand some of this idea's ramifications can involve some mental heavy lifting, so I will try to keep things in proportion as I expound some basic points in the next chapter. Feel free to skip ahead if the reading proves too dry. Getting bogged down in the left hemisphere is very far from my wish for you.

Note on terminology: I use the term Open Focus when specifically referring to the work of Les Fehmi. When describing a spacious, open awareness as opposed to a narrow focused one, I tend to use terms such as open attention or open awareness.

3

Systems, Surfaces and Small Worlds

We often think that when we have completed our study of one, we know all about two, because 'two' is 'one and one'. We forget that we still have to make a study of 'and'.
AS Eddington

It is simply not possible to think about objects without simultaneously acknowledging that they both exist in space and also contain space. It is less evident that the obverse is true, until you consider whether it is possible to contemplate pure space without form. Try the experiment right now and see what you think.

You may have found that whether you were contemplating space on a small scale or whether you were conceiving it on a vast universal scale, your mind still imposed a limit or form which contained space. And no matter how endless or empty this space might seem, there, at the centre of it all, was a familiar companion, your imaginary head.

Thus space and form seem to be co-dependent and mutually imply one another.

When we consider that modern myth, the Big Bang Theory, we think of an unimaginably hot primal fireball exploding into space. But that is not how the cosmologists see it. According to them, a swarm of superhot energy exploded into existence *together with space,* all at the same time. Actually, the theorists think that space had a slight lead for the tiniest fraction of time, but *before* the Big Bang, no concept can go – mine, yours or theirs.

It is because space and form (as things, energies and processes) are co-dependent that it is necessary to digress a little into how forms and processes relate to one another in space and time. Such a consideration stands us in good stead for later discussions on the properties of space.

But before we get on to a topic that can get somewhat complex, let me reassure you that the basic message is very simple and is something that you know already:

THE WHOLE IS GREATER THAN THE SUM OF ITS PARTS.

This is a premise upon which we can play many variations, but ultimately the message is always a straightforward one.

A whole can be anything that you care to name: a molecule, a concept, a human body, a tribe, a novel, an organisation and so on. You can place boundaries wherever you like, but enculturation and language generally suggest demarcations upon which we all agree. Let us take a very simple example, water. A water molecule consists of two hydrogen atoms and one oxygen atom bound together, but there is no way that the many surprising properties of water can be predicted from knowing everything about the individual elements hydrogen and oxygen. The whole (a large gathering of H2O molecules) is much more than the sum of its parts, either as molecules or as their constituent atoms. Thus we say that the *emergent* property of water is *surprising, unpredictable* and *transcendent*. In the same way, but at a different level of complexity altogether, a detailed knowledge of the constituents of the brain (eighty billion nerve cells) can in no way predict the emergent qualities of memory, cognition and affect. Please note that I do not include consciousness here. That is a different matter altogether.

A lively argument has been going on for thousands of years between thinkers who privilege investigation of parts (reductionists, materialists) and those who favour a primary consideration of the whole (holists, idealists). The former cling to the idea that the whole *can* be understood by reference to the properties of parts. They believe that if something is unexplained, it means that the examination has not been detailed enough. Holists, on the other hand, stress the organising effect of the whole on the part and see 'top down' processes as equally or more significant than 'bottom up' ones.

Stubborn dichotomies invariably point to a higher truth, and contemporary thinking is more inclined to cut through this division by using the term 'holon' to refer to the whole/part. Now it is very difficult to think of the whole and the parts at the same time; it's just too much for our limited working memory. So the term 'holon' is really a 'process injunction' that tells us to adjust our attentional focus when we notice that we are being too narrow (parts) or too broad (whole), to the exclusion of the other pole. You will recognise a parallel with the practice of Open Focus: being aware of how we are paying attention and when necessary applying a corrective. This broad principle applies whether we are in the realm of perception (narrow/diffuse attention), cognition (abstraction/integration) or affect (minimizing/dramatizing). The Oxford biologist Denis Noble (*The Music of Life*) uses the term 'middle in' to describe the sort of investigation that includes both 'top down' and 'bottom up' modelling.

Any kind of knowing creates a distinction (a boundary or line) between one thing and another. Some boundaries naturally suggest themselves, for example, when something moves, is novel or stands out against a background. Others are more intangible and complex, as in the intricacies of social custom or the subtleties of abstract thought. It is in the latter realms that we get into most trouble when, for example, we begin to believe that the distinctions we make between cat and mat or Mary and John are of the same order as those which we have erected between good and evil or particle and wave.

The important thing about making a distinction (which is to eat from the tree of knowledge of good and evil) is that the boundary which separates is also the boundary that connects.

Try pressing your hands together hard and concentrate on the sensations coming from their point of contact. See if you can distinguish the pressed from the pressing, the separateness of your hands from the connection. It's all a bit of a blur isn't it?

Connection and separation are processes in a unity. Douglas Flemons (*Completing Distinctions*) renders this relationship with the formula:

> CONNECTION/separation
> OR
> THE WAY PARTS ARE CONNECTED/The way they are separate.

Parts are subsumed by a whole, but that whole is necessarily subsumed by a greater whole. The distinctions that we make are simply pragmatic settings imposed by our particular needs – perceptual, affective and cognitive. When a pickpocket meets the Buddha he sees only a pocket. It's Connection/separation all the way up and all the way down to the One. As Lao Tzu said, the One gives rise to two, two gives rise to three and three gives rise to the ten thousand things. One, two and three in esoteric number theory stand for the Whole, the making of a distinction, and the 'holonic' description of that distinction in terms of how the parts are separate and how they are connected.

The dance of CONNECTION/separation is the most fundamental description that we can give to the play of space and form in time, but this simple idea also has considerable explanatory value across innumerable fields. Here are some representative dichotomies:

> Tender/tough-minded, wave/particle, male/female, divergent/convergent thinking, idealist/pragmatist, rational/intuitive, it/bit (i.e. things/information), Keynes/Hayek, matter/space, body/mind, love/power, narrow/broad focus and so on.

(If we observe the formula Connection/separation, which of the above are the wrong way around?)

When we consider something both from the point of view of the parts, as well as how the parts are connected into a whole, then we can say that our view is a more complete one and the equation according to Flemons becomes:

> **COMPLETION**/CONNECTION/separation.

The capitalising of Connection implies that it is the more inclusive term, contextualising the relationship and pointing to a greater whole. For example, men and women are different in many ways, but their differences are better understood by the way they connect and function together. In fact, the differences fuel the actual force of attraction and relationship: all the action and excitement occur at the boundaries.

> CONNECTION points in the direction of greater SPACIOUSNESS and OPENNESS.
>
> When we move toward CONNECTEDNESS, there is more *potential, complexity* and AWARENESS as epitomised in that loom of infinite connection and potential, the brain.
>
> As we move toward SEPARATION there is more *actuality*, definition and boundedness.

When you think about it, everything that you are aware of is a boundary or boundary effect, except the feeling 'I am'. Your visual field at this moment is the result of light reflecting on, or being emitted from, a surface or boundary. Everything of which you are perceptually aware is just one continually changing surface with ripples, colours, sounds and other sensations. You never see the 'thing in itself', only aspects of its boundaries. This surface of sensation, like all surfaces, must be a boundary between two realms, and as such it must *separate and connect them.*

So what could be separated and at the same time connected in your sensory world? I suggest that it is the finite and the infinite, the ponderable and the imponderable. If you could poke your head through that boundary you would probably have to agree with William Blake:

> If the doors of perception were cleansed, then everything would appear as it is, infinite.

On the other hand perhaps it's the head which is the problem in the first place.

There is a parallel situation in the subjective realm, where concepts exist at the contiguous surfaces of other concepts and mental objects. The only difference is that our internal world lacks three-dimensionality; in fact it is mostly a flat, attenuated, washed-out kind of reality that resembles a poorly tuned 1950s television. We would die of boredom in this realm if it were not kept going by the fuel of emotion and drive. These provide contrast, brightness and a sense of solidity derived from our somatic reality of feeling, the solid undeniable sense of the body. One of the aims of meditation is to *see into* the gossamer insubstantiality of this personal world without the supportive effects of reactive emotion. This is true *in-sight*, the understanding that comes from direct seeing/sensing.

So, before our TV pictures get too fuzzy, let us return to the matter of systems and connections. Complex systems are invariably arranged in a hierarchy of holons which exhibit increasing wholeness and integrative capacity. This is most clearly seen in biological and social systems and is the normal state of affairs. Take our Westminster system of government, for example. A member of parliament, like any human, is a holon and as such is nested within countless other holons: work, family, football club etc. In the context of parliament, an MP will usually be a member of a faction, which in turn will be subsumed under the umbrella of a party, which in turn functions within the context of the parliament and the rules of our democratic system. Beyond parliament we find ever-widening circles of context: legal, economic, social and geographical until we arrive at a holon named Australia. This in its turn is part of… well, you get the idea.

Our system of government attempts a balance between the respective needs of the parts and the whole. The conservative side of politics emphasises competition and the rights and responsibilities of the individual. The left stresses cooperation and the duty of society as a whole to create fair and just conditions for everybody.

The comparatively healthy hierarchy to be found in our form of democracy is not to be confused with the pathological variety, however, in which a particular holon assumes undue influence to the detriment of other levels. This dominator holon forgets that it is part of a greater whole with more far-reaching values, and begins to act as if the whole is subservient to its needs and dependent on its organising dictates – "Apres moi le deluge." This is the malignant arrogation of power that is at the root of so much human suffering. For there is nothing worse in this world than finding yourself at the wrong end of a social power structure, whether it is in the home, at school, work or in society as a whole. And there is nothing more destructive to mental and physical health than the abuse that inevitably follows this basic lack of status.

As it is, our capitalist/democratic system seems to strike an uneasy balance between competition/oligarchism and cooperation/democracy. At least in this arrangement we get the impression every few years that we have rearranged the deckchairs of influence, even though the powerful still dine together at the same clubs, send their children to the same private schools and schmooze with the same gravitational centres of money.

Worse still, we need look no further than our own brains to find a usurper who has acquired far too much power and has even had the temerity to admit its own dominance. I am referring, of course, to the left (or so-called dominant) hemisphere of the brain, which according to psychiatrist Iain McGilchrist has got way above its station and needs to be cut down a few sizes. (We shall have reason to return to McGilchrist's wonderful book on this subject in Chapter 13.)

Although we think of being 'well connected' as an aspiration characteristic of the middle and upper classes, the importance of good connections operates at every level of society and life.

And at long last science is beginning to embrace a discipline of connection, although it masquerades under various names such as network theory, or in the case of the brain, the study of the 'connectome'. This turnaround is happening very much through necessity; the success of reductionism, especially in the biological sciences, resulted in such a plethora of 'parts' that there was a pressing need to put Humpty Dumpty together again. It has been very much a case of Blake's fool who persists in his folly and thereby becomes wise.

The science of connection and an understanding of how information flows through networks is still in its infancy. However, you may have heard the term 'small world' network in reference to social structures, the Internet or indeed your own nervous system. The idea originated with Stanley Milgram's experiments in which people were asked to send a package to a distant unknown person via intermediaries, but without the benefit of an address (see Watts, D., *Six Degrees*). So, for example, if you were given a parcel to send to a named individual in Cote d'Ivoire, your best bet might be to send it off to someone you know in Africa, or failing this, to someone whom you surmise might know someone there. They in turn will repeat that process and lo and behold, the item usually gets to the addressee in a surprisingly small number of six to seven steps. It *is* a small world and works as such because people, as we shall see, are connected in a particular way.

Most of our social interchange happens at a local level with family, friends and colleagues; these are our strong connections and can be thought of as a tight, self-reinforcing (and recursive) network that shows only modest change over time. On the other hand, we have many more 'weak' connections with people we know by name and who would recognise us if we rang them up, but with whom we rarely interact. In the case of our parcel experiment, for example, that person in Africa might be an old college friend who has moved to Cape Town and unexpectedly sent you an email recently about a mutual acquaintance. It is such weak connections that create the small world effect and which facilitate speed and ease of communication right the way across a complex network.

It is not unexpected, then, that we tend to see small world networks wherever there are complex integrated systems, irrespective of whether they are found in biology, society, information technology or elsewhere. It may come as a surprise to you, however, that a variety of benefits can accrue from these longer, less used pathways. For example, people are more likely to find new jobs through their 'weak' contacts, and highly creative or inventive individuals tend to have more 'weak' connections.

The relevance of this digression down the path of systems and networks can be illustrated by another story from Flora Courtois. At one point in her journey she began to have visions which were hypnagogic in quality. In one of these she found herself sitting in a cubicle, facing a wall and engaged in manipulating coloured blocks. All around her were others performing similar abstract tasks. At one point she happened to turn around only to find a long window opening out on to a "breathtaking vista." She stepped out into the scene where "everything seemed alive and dancing and the horizons and the firmament extended to infinity in all directions."

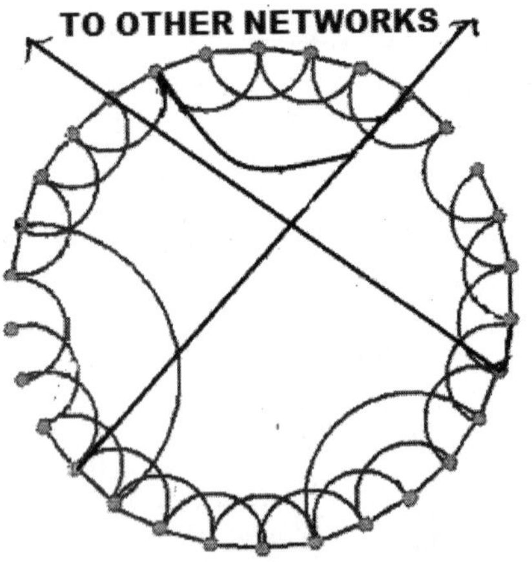

Fig. 1 A Small World Network

The three-dimensional quality of this experience was in contrast to the place from which she had just emerged which was: "squared off in flat two dimensional planes." This experience, so reminiscent of Plato's cave, is a vivid analogy for our normal stuckness in personal local networks – cognitive, affective and social. When you look at Figure 1 it is obvious how tight and self-contained the local connections are. Nothing can change unless an influence comes from outside: the so-called 'shock' to which Gurdjieff refers at critical points on the enneagram of change, something that we will consider later when discussing a philosophy of process.

These 'shocks' are generally mediated through the 'long' connections. It is through the 'long' connections that the whole regulates the part and the part informs the whole; it is through these channels that we receive our "intimations of immortality." In her vision, Courtois just turned around without knowing how or why. Jean Klein might say that he was solicited by reality; the whole wants to inform and nurture the part, but the self-referential nature of the local cluster can make this difficult.

Incidentally, there is nothing wrong with the local nexus wanting to preserve and perpetuate itself; that is its function and a feature of the universal tendency to retroflection. It is just that overzealous self-focus leads only to contraction, stagnation and redundancy.

The question arises as to whether we can deliberately turn outwards. The simple answer is, "No." Everything in my perceptual/conceptual world is conditioned by the closed world of memory and habit and there is no help for that. All I can do is realise that the issue is out of my hands and, in the company of Flora and countless other spiritual aspirants, simply decide to wait and let be. The surfaces that we have constructed to circumscribe our world are porous, and in fact not existent in any real way. Waiting allows the porosity to manifest, thus letting connections from a greater world pop through. These connections are there all the time, but a conscious act of connection and communion completes a feedback loop whereby the part begins to sing from the cosmic song sheet.

Waiting without expectation gradually unravels the knot of 'I', revealing spaciousness, connection and freedom.

Waiting quietly and letting yourself be provides the answer to Da Free John's mantric question: "Avoiding relationship?"

4

Spacious Body

Fools stand on their island of opportunities and look toward land. There is no other land, there is no other life but this.
Thoreau

As soon as a fertilised egg begins to replicate, we see two complementary processes at work. The dividing cells first form a ball, then a sphere and finally a tube which then gets elaborated into the final form of the organism. This movement toward growth and expansion is balanced, however, by the individual's retroflective tendency to turn back on itself, cohere and stay separate.

All multicellular organisms are basically tubes that take in nourishment at one end, expel waste at the other, and at some point manage to reproduce. Humans are no exception to this rule, although we seem to have made something of a major production out of these simple requirements. When we observe the human tube developing in utero, we see that it is bent forward on itself, literally in the foetal position. This dominance of flexion over extension will remain throughout life, with flexor muscles mainly along the front of the body generally stronger than extensors along the back. An infant's developmental thrust promotes a gradual 'uncurling' toward extension and growth upward and outward. At the same time, self-preservation may periodically necessitate flexion, contraction and giving in to gravity. The dynamic interplay of these two tendencies is the hallmark of health, but contraction is the default setting: when sick I lie down, curl up and sleep. This inherent bias is also evident after a stroke, when the flexors emerge as the stronger muscle group and a person is left with a spastic flexed limb.

It will not be lost on the reader that there is a parallel to this situation in the dynamics of consciousness. Our intuitive sense of freedom and connection with the universe is in constant interplay with a contracted, reactive 'I', nebulously but firmly associated with a body. The result is that much of our daily awareness gravitates toward a sense of restriction and separation. At the same time, we expend a good deal of energy in convoluted attempts to distract ourselves from these feelings of unsatisfactoriness.

The terms extraversion and introversion come to mind when thinking about connecting and expanding versus separating and contracting. Both tendencies play their part in the dynamics of the social body and each has its own strengths and weaknesses. Extraverts do tend to be healthier, wealthier and happier than their more miserable introvert contemporaries, but their addictive fascination with objects and people produces its own forms of contraction and enslavement. Introverts, on the other hand, seek to avoid stimulation and novelty because their sensitive nervous systems are easily over-aroused. Their sensitivity can be a great boon, making them very valuable, empathic friends for example, but it may also lead to anxiety and withdrawal.

There is more discussion on the yin and yang of these differences in temperament later in the book. Suffice it to say that for our present purposes, the extraversion/introversion divide is reflected in two very different ways in which the body organises itself in the play of CONNECTION/separation.

In his book *Somatics*, Thomas Hanna, an American Feldenkrais practitioner, has identified two basic trends in musculoskeletal organisation:

The Red Light Reflex

This is the pattern the body follows when suddenly alerted to a potential danger, or when the best option is to freeze in the face of an actual danger. It is what your body does automatically in the event of a sudden loud noise, but it is also continually activated by all the lesser stresses of daily life. It involves tensing the jaw, pulling the neck forward, lifting the shoulders, flexing the elbows, hands, knees and feet, tightening the abdominal, perineal and diaphragmatic muscles and holding the breath (usually on inspiration).

The Green Light Reflex

This is how the body organises itself for action, either in an acute emergency or to simply meet everyday challenges that require us to get actively involved. It involves: extending the spine (arching the back slightly), pulling back the neck, dropping the shoulders, opening the chest and freeing the breathing.

For a more comprehensive description please consult Hanna's book. In practice both reflexes are being continually stimulated, often in an attenuated form, by the exigencies of everyday life, and may also be activated below the threshold of consciousness by mental as well as physical events. This is all well and good as long as we return to a balanced condition through periodic rest and relaxed enjoyment. For continually stressed individuals, however, there comes a point when the tensed muscle patterns may never have a chance to recover and this creates a situation where unremitting musculoskeletal tension gives rise to chronic pain. This is most likely to happen in the lower back and neck/shoulder regions, since these areas are activated in both reflexes.

Pain of all descriptions rapidly sets up a negative feedback loop wherein:

pain → distress → further tension → pain

As we saw in the previous chapter, negative feedback loops separate the part from the whole, and with chronic pain a situation can rapidly develop that sees the painful part become progressively more isolated, eventually assuming the status of an alien, persecuting entity. This is why it is important to get on top of acute pain very quickly with analgesia, sedation (especially if sleep is disturbed) and other soothing influences such as 'hands on' healing. With chronic pain the part has to be gradually reclaimed and reconnected to the whole, a process in which quality of attention plays the central role.

Narrowed, focused attention is, in itself, a cause of stress and fatigue and so adds further fuel to the pain/distress cycle:

pain or stress → narrow focus → stress/tension

For Les Fehmi, the solution is to open one's focus around the painful area. This will lessen tension, improve circulation and the supply of nutrients and generally reclaim the part back into the regulatory environment of the whole. Fehmi's general approach, described in his book *Dissolving Pain*, is to transition from a narrow/objective to an immersed/diffuse style of attention around the pain. This is easier said than done, of course, and first involves learning how to cultivate a more diffuse way of attending. As we saw earlier, Fehmi uses brainwave biofeedback to help people enter the coherent alpha pattern that is the signature of this broader awareness, but admits that it took him a while in his early days of personal practice to generate substantial alpha.

The secret to his success was to give up both trying and attending with narrow focus, the very things we are most likely to do when confronted with a situation we desperately want to control. He also serendipitously discovered that imagining space in the body was a quick route to relaxation and alpha generation. His audio sequences encourage ever clearer feelings of spaciousness in the body as well as the connection between that space and the space outside the body. Once a spacious open focus is well established, Fehmi suggests various approaches toward the pain experience. I think describing them here, however, would be of little value to you. One really needs to get some practice with the spaciousness exercises first and a good place to start is the CD that accompanies *Dissolving Pain*, or one of Fehmi's downloads.

It is also important that everyone develops their own particular approach. Personally, I just aim to cultivate whole-body spaciousness and then allow a painful or tense part to simply be in that space without expectation. Attempts to *do* something with pain simply narrow one's focus. Consequently it is important to experiment in a relaxed way; as with all healing journeys, the little individual discoveries often count for most. And relaxation and spaciousness are both aspects of the same process: allowing contracted energy to unfold and release.

The American psychologist Judith Blackstone takes an approach which is somewhat similar to Fehmi's. Her personal story as told in her book *The Subtle Self* is an intriguing one. Blackstone is, amongst other things, a dancer who in her youth badly damaged her back. She eventually required surgery but found that the operation had left her in a worse state than before: the bone fusion was essentially 'off centre' and had fixed her spine in the injured position. Fortunately, this painful outcome provided the impetus for a journey of self-discovery and healing, one with the many twists and turns so characteristic of real life adventures, where you find out important things for yourself.

Because surgery had left her uncomfortable in any position, Blackstone would lie on the floor for long periods, praying to be healed. Over time she noticed that the more she surrendered to gravity, the more she would experience spontaneous movements toward balance. This corrective process could be encouraged by conscious intervention: for example by attending simultaneously to symmetrical points (e.g. the hip sockets) on either side of her body. Blackstone realised that the gradual healing which resulted from this process rested upon a system of subtle energy that underlay her grosser corporeal reality. This energy system in turn moved within a space filled with consciousness, something (or no thing) that she came to name as "fundamental consciousness". This is what she says about it:

> Fundamental consciousness is experienced as a vast unbroken stillness and spaciousness, pervading our whole body and environment as a unity. It is a profound openness to life, a direct intimate contact with everything that we encounter. (*Belonging Here*, page 4)

As a psychotherapist, Blackstone is often focused on the psychological causes of physical and mental pain, especially the enduring effects of childhood trauma. However, like Fehmi, she first helps individuals to cultivate a sense of consciousness-filled space throughout the body and to feel the continuity of this space across the boundaries of the body into the surroundings. The sense of body consciousness is refined by:

> Identifying the quality of energy in different parts of the body, for example, power in the abdomen, love in the chest.
>
> Aligning and balancing through the body's central axis.
>
> Identifying feelings and memories associated with tensions, pains and blocks.

Students of metaphysics will recognise Blackstone's description of coexistent levels of awareness as having a parallel in esoteric literature:

> Causal – fundamental consciousness
> Astral – emotional awareness
> Etheric – energy awareness
> Gross – normal body sense

This is not to say that Blackstone's work is derivative in any way. It is very clear from the freshness of her insights that these discoveries arose entirely as a result of an *experiential* search, driven by a need for very definite and tangible results.

The reader may legitimately ask whether these space-oriented approaches have any advantage over more traditional relaxation and meditation methods. In fact, as pointed out before, spaciousness and relaxation complement one another well and form a virtuous feedback cycle:

Spaciousness → relaxation → spaciousness etc

I favour an initial emphasis on space because it allows attention to be absorbed into *what is already there*. This tends to defuse trying, focusing or 'end-gaining'. Space awareness also stops us getting stuck on the part in itself, but rather points away from the part to the whole body and beyond, while at the same time including the part. In systems language we might say that space awareness cultivates 'holonic' consciousness.

Space awareness is also supremely simple, something that should be the case in all healing methods. I am reminded in this context of Ainslie Meares, an Australian psychiatrist who was a pioneer in deep relaxation for both physical and psychological problems. Like myself, Meares was deeply dissatisfied with his chosen profession and sought inspiration from yoga and Eastern philosophy. As a result of his studies and experiences in the East, he developed an approach that he named "mental ataraxis". To achieve this state he did not use any special methodology, but rather seemed to work on the assumption that the body/mind had an intrinsic knowledge and memory of profound rest if given the appropriate cues.

I used to see Dr Meares on a regular basis in the early 1980s and would sit with a dozen or so other people in tall-backed leather chairs, while Dr Meares and his assistant walked around ministering to us. He would lay his hands on our shoulders and upper chest while intoning a low-pitched rumbling sound from which one could occasionally detect a word such as "ease" or "giving in". I must say that I was quite poor at relaxing, but was very impressed with Meares himself, who treated me as a colleague and shared with me some of his results. I remember one day he showed me X-rays of a man who had had many large malignant melanoma secondaries in his lungs. After a few months of intense practice (4 hours/day plus) these metastases had shrunk to a quarter of their previous size.

Ataraxis, from the Greek, means impassive or free from mental disturbance. Space by its very nature represents stillness and silence. It is inclusive and omnipresent and as such is a counterpoint to the constant disturbances of everyday life. In our endless doing, the body/mind has to prioritise its activities; some systems are turned up, some are turned down. For example, if you have to run, your muscles will get more blood and your brain will get less – try doing mental arithmetic when walking at a brisk pace. The body/mind is forever reorganising and simplifying in the service of its immediate need. The result is that 'parts' are continually being disconnected from 'the whole' and then reconnected later on when rest or sleep supervenes. When stress is severe or chronic, however, reconnection may not be complete and the 'part' gradually languishes from lack of nurture and exchange.

Deep sleep and all forms of rest and relaxation are reparative states in which reconnection can take place in a more democratic way. The authoritarian hierarchies constructed during the emergency of doing are dismantled and everyone gets to express their needs and hopefully have them met. There is *space for everyone*. The analogy with human groups is a close one. Organisations with rigid hierarchies, tight boundaries and poor 'bottom up' communication do not fare so well in environments characterised by continual change and uncertainty. Authoritarian control *is* essential, however, in a sudden emergency where there is a need for someone to make and implement quick decisions.

In summary, during daily activity the organisation of the body is stereotyped into action and avoidance modes in order to meet the requirements of the mind and its main programmes: craving and aversion (to use the Buddhist terms). During sleep and rest the mind is simplified in order to allow full intercommunication at the somatic level. The body dominates the mind. And… the body and mind are not separate!

During the day our principal mode of being is contractive in the service of the ego and away from subordination to Life. At night, in deep sleep, we expand and allow the natural harmony of Life to supervene. As Nisargadatta said: during the day we suffer and know it, during deep sleep we are happy but don't know it!

It can be legitimately asked whether there is some form of contraction in every dis-ease. There is a long answer and a short answer to this question. The short answer is "almost always". Although the causes of disease are many and varied, there is a simple and traditional naturopathic model that sums up the situation, illustrated in Figure 2.

TOXAEMIA

↑ ↓

ENERVATION

Fig. 2

Toxaemia refers to any environmental challenge, including infectious agents, chemicals, foods, drugs and psychological and social stresses.

Enervation refers to physical and mental states of deficiency, depletion or exhaustion. An enervated organism clearly has less resistance to toxaemia than a fit one, and different constitutions will vary in their ability to withstand insults from the environment. In modern lingo we say that disease arises when an organism's allostatic ability has been exceeded. Allostasis refers to the constant adjustments our bodies make as conditions vary and, as Heraclitus knew, conditions are continually varying.

Any toxic challenge elicits both a specific and a general response. For example, a virus will prompt the production of tailored antibodies to fight the infection, but the body also undergoes a more widespread adjustment, which the physiologist Hans Selye named the General Adaptation Syndrome (GAS). A major part of the GAS involves the production of cortisol, a hormone which has the effect of rearranging many of the body's priorities to meet the new emergency. As we saw before, this process is essentially one of simplification and strengthening of hierarchical control. The result is the somatic equivalent of narrowed attention with its accompanying contractive quality.

Inflammation is a hallmark of the body's defence against challenge. It used to be thought that inflammatory responses were confined to infectious agents, allergens and circumstances of 'mistaken identity' where the body attacks itself (as in rheumatoid arthritis). We now know that this is not the case, and that inflammation accompanies and/or precedes a very wide range of complaints including cardiovascular disease, cancer, diabetes, depression, dementia, and the list goes on. In fact we know that any stressor, including psychological ones, will elicit the release of inflammatory substances.

Thus, wherever there is disease we tend to find inflammation. Inflammation is a sign of the body's defences in action and a manifestation of the contractive quality that inevitably accompanies the defensive response. Contraction is generally *local and general* and so in the face of disease it would seem appropriate to cultivate spaciousness both in the dis-eased part and the body as a whole.

Our subjective experience of somatic disharmony supports this model of restriction and contraction. Dis-eased parts are usually experienced as tight, hard and darker in colour than the surrounds. Here is a vivid passage from the American mystic John Allan:

> I recall some of my more difficult times in dealing with the cancer. Sometimes I could feel a lot of Spirit and still not feel the tumours being touched. Then I began to realise that Spirit was not touching the tumours because there was tension, tightness – a holding on to those areas where the tumours were. So I began consciously to release those areas and as I did, the love would flow into and fill all those places that needed the healing.
>
> There was often extreme resistance to releasing and yielding the body. It was as if those places of disease were wound up so tightly that they refused to let go. So it took a dedicated persistence to get the resistance to diminish. And then the miracle of Spirit dissolving the tumours would take place.
>
> (*The Healing Energy of Love*, pages 83–84)

He then goes on to describe how, with continual yielding of the hurt and painful places, what previously felt hard, opaque and impenetrable began to feel more transparent and less material and therefore more open to Spirit's energy. If we substitute the term fundamental consciousness for Spirit, it would seem likely that Judith Blackstone and John Allan are talking about very similar processes.

Allan makes another important observation: that in naming a part or a disease we tend to give it a self-perpetuating reality which, in fact, it does not possess. So we need to get past the idea of having a complaint with a label and go into the pure sensations and their underlying strata of energy and consciousness. This is just the point made by the Advaita Vedantist Jean Klein who discusses how we usually experience the body, not as a whole, but in a fractional way:

> In these fractions there are contractions, heaviness and reactions. So the moment our body becomes an object of innocent observation – and by innocent I mean that the observer is free from expectations and free from memory – then in this innocent observation there is no place for an 'I', a 'me', which created the reactions and heaviness. There is no longer an accomplice to keeping the contractions in the body and they become free. Then we come to a global, empty feeling of our body. What we call unconditioned observation, innocent looking, has everything to do with a body which is free from any grasping or taking.
> (*Transmission of the Flame*, page 162)

Klein is speaking from a long tradition of Eastern healing practices that apply to both body and mind (which are not separate). Here are two such approaches that particularly exemplify the idea of creating space.

Sat Nam Rasayam is an ancient practice whose principles were embodied and taught by the 16th century Sikh saint Guru Ram Dass. More recently it has been described by Subagh Singh Khalsa in his fine book *Anatomy of Miracles*. One of the meanings of Sat Nam Rasayam is "giving oneself up to the essence of the True Identity". Such a giving up involves creating a 'sensitive space' that allows all sensations and other mental contents to come and go without any reactivity. The neutrality of this space is maintained by an unfocused, unselective alertness that 'equalises' the sensitive space. There is also an emphasis on *feeling*, on the direct experience of oneself uncontaminated by mental evaluation.

This description seems very reminiscent of the contemporary approaches described earlier, but there are differences. In Sat Nam Rasayam, a healer can enter a sensitive space that includes their client. With healing intention and without a personal agenda, the healer allows resistances to disappear. There is an added refinement in that the practitioner can sense and correct imbalances in the five elements: earth, water, fire, air and ether. This has been of particular interest to me because the five elements represent a hierarchy of relationships between the two poles of something (earth) and nothing (ether) and are thus central to the dynamic of CONNECTION/separation. Put simply, they are a vivid way of explaining relationships across a wide variety of phenomena.

There is also a close parallel between Sat Nam Rasayam and the self-development traditions of Taoism. Two volumes on Taoism by BK Frantzis stand out in terms of accessibility and clarity: *Relaxing into Your Being* and *The Great Stillness*. Importantly, Frantzis makes a distinction between Fire and Water methods, one that is not made explicit in many contemporary accounts of Taoism. As their names suggest, these are quite different approaches. The Fire philosophy, for example, privileges the control of energy by the mind, the exertion of the will and the subordination of the body to the dictates of conscious intention. Water methods, on the other hand, follow in the tradition of Lao Tzu and stress moderation, doing what is comfortable for the body and going with the flow of 'what is'. Its 'feminine' emphasis on 'listening' and mutuality between body and mind is a much-needed counterpoint to the masculine fire obsession with control, struggle and domination.

There is an uncanny similarity between water methods and those of Open Focus and subtle body work. Taoist practitioners following this path aim to locate contracted, frozen internal energies and then dissolve them through immersion in a relaxed, steady, *feeling* consciousness. This allows the frozen energy (ice) to melt into water and, as spaciousness increases, to transform into gas which is dissipated outside the body. In more advanced practice, the blocked area is transformed from ice into water which is then imploded into unbound inner space. The vital ingredients here seem to be the cultivation of a sense of internal and external space and a relaxed, immersed mode of attention.

The choice between Fire and Water methods depends on many factors, and every individual must use their intuition for guidance. In general, Fire methods are preferred by the young and those with male and extraverted brains. Water methods tend to appeal to those who are older, female or who are more introverted. But bear in mind that we also need periodic correctives that go against our constitutional grain. Thus as an older person, I may prefer quieter environments and blander diets (Yin), but at the same time I should consider judicious doses of weight training, social excitement and new tastes (Yang). Attaining balance is always a challenge, however, and my experience of various teachers and gurus over the years strongly suggests to me that those who work with a fire approach are more likely to 'go bad' with issues around power and sex.

It is also good to remember that the body/mind spontaneously heals through these same contrasting avenues, phenomena which the Ancient Greeks knew as Crisis and Lysis. Mostly we heal in an unobtrusive way: cuts and bruises go away without drama and a bad back sooner or later fades from our field of attention. On the other hand, the body may need to throw off infections and toxins in an acute way, with a resulting crisis that manifests fever or vomiting or, in the case of psychological shock, shaking and emotional catharsis. Sometimes we can help these processes by the application of external stimuli, for example, heat to stimulate detoxification or water and ice to calm and balance overactive fire.

But whatever path we take into healing there are certain simple principles that need to be borne in mind:

Enervation is addressed by appropriate nurture. Most problems, both psychological and physical, are related to poor nurture and our inability either to listen to what we need or to secure what we know we need. The body knows very well what nutrition it requires, but most of us no longer eat by instinct. If we do care about our diet, we are more likely to follow some expert or fad. Similarly, we generally know what nourishes us psychologically and socially, but may have great difficulty in finding even the minimum requirements for adequate satisfaction (derivation – Latin, to make enough).

The other side of good nurture is the avoidance of toxaemia. Again, we are usually well aware of what poisons us, but addiction and other factors get in the way of our self-regulation. Many of our relationships with other humans are particularly toxic; how many times have you come away from an encounter with a 'friend' feeling drained and dispirited? You have been poisoned as surely as if you had eaten rancid food. Unfortunately your body remembers food poisoning much better than you remember your encounter with an emotional vampire!

Beneficial nurture has the property of conveying pleasure, but pleasure of a particular sort. It is not the high-pitched shot to our dopamine system of a cup of coffee or a flattering stroke to our ego. Rather it has a deep, warm and satisfying quality that is *expansive* in nature. We feel the empty places being filled, the knots being undone and the dry zones replenished. There is a movement away from the heaviness and stasis of Winter toward the lightness and growth of Spring. Genuine organic pleasure shares in all the elements equally. When we feel deeply satisfied there is an unmistakable sense of our organic, earth selves, while at the same time an openness and connection with the world that feel marvellously spacious.

It is very important to remember that these feelings of rightness and satisfaction are conveyed to us through the body. They do not appear as thoughts or even intuitions, but as very real sensations in our immediate experience. They are manifestations of the body's intrinsic knowledge of how to be on this earth, and are based upon countless aeons of evolution and adaptation. As Reginald Ray says in *Touching Enlightenment*:

> This can be a rather surprising discovery for many of us who, as modern people, are so very alienated from the body. We can't imagine the idea that the body might be a living force, a source of intelligence, wisdom, even something we might experience as having intention.
> (*Touching Enlightenment*, page 63)

The body is not the body as we normally conceive it: a dumb machine with no other purpose than to serve our wants and needs. It is more in the nature of a mystery to be explored; a reticent sage to be cultivated, respected and cherished. But when we first stumble into this realm, often prompted by pain and fear, we are liable to find nothing but difficulty. Here is Reginald Ray again:

> The first step in this process is that we move from a state of insentient numbness backward into a state of discomfort. Then, as the work progresses, we move through layer upon layer of discomfort, sometimes feeling great freedom and fulfilment, but often just finding another layer to peel away, as if we were an onion. The discomfort becomes more subtle and transparent as we move deeper and deeper into the body, through each successive layer of emotion, feeling, sensation, mood and felt-sense. Finally we arrive at our core, the empty space at the center, which is open and free but, at the same time, the basis of our entire being. At that point our embodiment is complete, our realisation is actual, and the solid 'ego' has become a distant dream.
> (*Touching Enlightenment*, page 82)

Ray makes the process sound rather awesome, a reminder that we are investigating and freeing a key aspect of our separate egoic identity, an endeavour that can be testing and confronting. As a long-time Buddhist, he proposes disciplines in the Tibetan Vajrayana tradition, but this is just one approach, there being innumerable ways of effecting a rapprochement with our oldest and most intimate friend. Whichever path we take, our basis will be listening: an open spacious attention, in which there is freedom from judgement or any expectation. This allows the body, which was once simply the recipient of endless demands ("a beaten dog" to use Pundit Acharya's words), to finally speak – a truly 'bottom up' process. Initially it may protest at such a long period of neglect, but one should never doubt that it is the most loyal of allies.

In response to this new spaciousness, the body may react in various unpredictable ways: with twitches, spontaneous movements, unusual sensations, emotions, memories and thoughts. Many years ago I took several months off from my regular job and basically hung around doing very little. After a month I noticed occasional twitching in my fingers which gradually spread to my face and a leg. I became so alarmed at the prospect of some nervous system disease that I consulted a neurologist. He reassured me that there was nothing wrong and I was forced to conclude that this was a release phenomenon. But it was only after this episode that I began to feel that I was truly beginning to decompress and slow down. To this day I know that I have relaxed into the 'release zone' because twitching arises, often in an unpredictable part of my body.

I learned from this experience that relaxing and releasing take time, and that the body has its own agenda and timetable. We may need guidance with some of these manifestations, but mostly we simply need them explained. We may also want to create certain conditions or formats that allow the cultivation of spontaneous movements more deliberately. After all, why should the body stay still as part of a healing process when its nature is to move, breathe and vocalise? As Bradford Keeney points out in *Shaking Medicine,* there are many traditions in which allowing the body to move in its own way is the preferred mode of spiritual practice. The Kalahari Bushpeople and the original Quakers are good examples. In fact, a compelling case can be made for balancing the abnormal state of sitting still in meditation with spontaneous dance and singing.

It is all a matter of balance and discrimination. Spaciousness opens us up to all the parts, and discrimination allows the parts to find their right connection to the whole. The dynamic trio of Water (feeling/sensation), Fire (energy/drive) and Air (cognition) manifest their life-enhancing alchemy when they are in a balanced relationship between Earth (the manifest) and Heaven (space, potential). It is only then that energy can flow and *dissolve the stasis that inevitably accompanies dis-ease, both physical and existential.* Orientating ourselves between heaven and earth will be the subject in Chapter 12, where we also encounter that form giving and limit setting force: gravity. But for the moment, our 'one-liner' is:

> A SPACIOUS WHOLE BODY SENSE IS A PRECONDITION FOR EXPERIENCING ALL STABLE FORMS OF SPACIOUSNESS.

Thus the simple message in this chapter is that bringing spacious, non-judgemental awareness to the body and its contracted parts is an essential element in healing our physical ills. But since the body and the mind are not separate, we must conclude that the same principle applies to our psychological and spiritual difficulties. Let us go on to explore that possibility.

5

Spacious Mind

Only the hand that erases can write what is true.
Meister Eckhart

Writing about the mind is a perilous endeavour at the best of times, a hall of mirrors where the slightest reflective error becomes magnified into gross and misleading distortions. Consequently, in this discussion we shall try to keep our feet on the ground by contemplating the common sense of the senses as revealed by the many facets of mindfulness practice.

Readers may therefore wish to 'bite-size' their progress through this chapter, with plenty of digestive and settling time; in the words of the East, to periodically allow the turbidity of the mind to settle and thus return to one's true clear nature. Concepts can then hopefully gestate in the darkness and reappear in a fresh and useful way.

In the West we have been particularly subject to the 'yang' of indiscriminate cerebration without the necessary counterweight of reflection and silence. This is particularly true of our academic institutions where competition and a 'publish or perish' culture have completely obviated any chance of contemplation or measured collegial discourse. The result is that we have made very little progress since the Ancient Greeks in answering the really important questions about Life and Living. We continue to float upon a vast sea of unknowing in our little coracles of individuality, and are saved from complete panic by the reassuring cluster of other boats vaguely travelling in the same direction. The bases of our collective meteorology continue to elude us, however, and it's usually only when a storm blows up, or when separated from the pack, that we remember how deep the ocean actually is.

Science tries to tackle some of our basic questions by looking into the constitution of matter. It has done this in its inimitable reductive style by breaking 'stuff' into smaller and smaller parts. But lo and behold, by the time it has arrived at the quantum level, matter has disappeared into ethereal, dynamic strands that have relationships with one another but very little 'substance' in themselves. Moreover, the ghostly entities in this realm seem to defy our normal ideas of space and time, choosing sometimes to be somewhere (a particle), and at others to be spreading out everywhere (wave-like). Niels Bohr, the quantum pioneer, said it well when he declared that an apparent grasp of quantum physics was a sure sign that you understood nothing about it.

The weirdness of the quantum realm is just one manifestation of the deep paradoxes that we encounter when we press into any realm of knowing. Ultimately we never seem to uncover what anything is in itself, because nothing exists by itself. Instead, we find that the world is a web of relationships arising in something unknowable which we call Being or Consciousness.

The great law that governs the connecting network between apparent 'things' is complementarity: the idea that what appears to be oppositional on one level is, when looked at from a wider perspective, complementary. We have already encountered this idea in a different form as:

CONNECTION/separation

which is a shorthand way of saying that there is unity in diversity and diversity within unity. And with apologies to the well-known story about the world resting on a turtle, we can confidently say that it's CONNECTION/separation all the way down (and up).

As humans we stand between the infinitely great and the infinitely small, as the measure(rs) of all things and the embodiment of that most central of paradoxes, the mind/body mystery. More strictly rendered this is the paradox of a finite perishable body on the one hand, married to elusive, insubstantial and all-pervasive consciousness on the other, just like the particle and the wave. More mysterious still is the fact that our complete unknowability to ourselves seems not to disturb us. Is it not disconcerting, for example, to consider that we cannot account for our own awareness, the most central fact of our lives? Or, put another way, that we have no knowledge of and have no say in the processes that form and live us? Remarkably, these weighty matters have little effect on us, and we live out our circumscribed stories apparently unperturbed by what Gurdjieff called "the terror of the situation".

Various explanations have been put forward to account for the deep trance into which we all fall. It seems reasonable to believe, for example, that Nature has provided us with some built-in protections against ruminating on vulnerability and death. If this were not the case, then we would be unable to function in everyday life. The complementary view is that we constantly intuit our deep connection with the cosmos and are reassured, albeit on a subliminal level, that all is well. There is probably truth to both assertions and, no doubt, many other factors that help to maintain the myths of personal success, security and happiness.

The counterscript, as the Buddha observed, is somewhat different and revolves around unsatisfactoriness, sickness and death. The difference between these two scenarios is that life seems to have ordained the former as arbitrary and the latter as obligatory. This realisation so shocked the young prince Siddhartha that he sat and pondered the situation for several years until he got to the bottom of the matter. He was not alone in this, for as various authors have pointed out, there seems to have been a development in human consciousness around 2,500 years ago that permitted a stepping back from immersion in cultural myth and immediate experience. This new reflective capacity allowed the cognitive mind to evaluate experience in a more detached way. We see this in Socrates' dialectical approach as well as in the dialogue between Confucians and Taoists. But it is from the Buddha that we inherit our modern idea of mindfulness.

The Buddha's genius lay in his willingness to start from scratch and find out for himself the root causes of suffering. As a result, he abandoned methodologies that had been handed down in the Hindu tradition and relied solely on dispassionate self-observation. After much struggle, he came to certain conclusions that had a liberating effect on every aspect of his being. At the same time, he realised the uselessness of his ideas to others if they could not be verified by personal experience and insight. Consequently he stressed that the key to liberation was a particular sort of self-reflective path which was open to all and which could and should be used, without preconception, to come to one's own conclusions. There is an obvious parallel with the path taken by Marion Milner, except that her starting point was the complementary one of discovering what made her happy.

The idea of finding out for oneself is one of the reasons that Buddhism has been embraced in the West. It has a modern, existential ring and at heart is profoundly anti-authoritarian, a fact that has not stopped it from establishing all manner of male-dominated, rigid and doctrinaire structures over the centuries. The simplicity and eclecticism of the Buddha's approach also seem to explain why mindfulness practice has been grafted on to practically every known psychotherapeutic modality. The result is usually a very pale reflection of the core teaching and often contaminated by our naïve modern ideas about happiness and personal fulfilment.

The popularity of mindfulness practice is also why I am labouring this topic, as it is so easy for misconceptions to creep in and obscure what it actually means and how it can be fruitfully applied. For example, mindfulness is often portrayed as 'here and now' awareness, even though the words 'here' and 'now' give little idea about how to practically encompass these two very slippery concepts.

I can remember very clearly my first experiences as a young man with present-centred awareness. I had become involved with Gestalt therapy and was trying hard to remain present in the midst of everyday life. I found it very taxing, not only to remember to be present, but also to stay focused on my present experience. This was my downfall; I was trying too hard and would literally give myself a headache in the process. It was not clear to me then, nor to a great many other people since, I suspect, what mindfulness actually involves.

First some definitions are in order. Mindfulness has many names including present centredness, self-remembering, self-observation, here and now awareness, choiceless awareness, unconditioned mind and others. Each definition conveys something of its meaning, but the essential point is that we are talking about a process, not a thing. This process leads into Natural Spaciousness.

Before launching into further discussion I want to add another point that I hope will simplify your further reading. Mindfulness, letting go and relaxation are all aspects of the same process and each one embodies elements of its siblings. The differences reside in the energy centre most involved. Thus mindfulness begins as an act of recollection at the head level, letting go always has a strong feeling (heart) component and relaxation is usually initiated by a physical gesture. They all represent an opening into spaciousness and as such are also the key elements in meditation. So let us look at these processes in more detail.

Mindfulness is:

Returning to oneself. We return to ourselves through the contemplation of our sensory reality, becoming absorbed in sensation without evaluation. Searching for that which experiences sensation, on the other hand, naturally gives rise to ***the awareness that the subject cannot be an object, and thus the giving up of this kind of goal-directed attention and a letting go and letting be.***

A democratic revolution in awareness. Under normal circumstances our attention is exclusively at the behest of desires and aversions. If we define the ego as that which is tasked with ensuring survival, then we may imagine it at the top of a ruthless hierarchy of self-interest. Mindfulness institutes a regime change in which all the parts get a say; not just all of our exiled parts, but other people and our environment as well. There is a 'flatter' organisation to our lives, but not a total workers' utopia. We don't cut off the heads of our former ruling elite (not initially anyway), but we do introduce better negotiating procedures where everyone gets a say and the ego has fewer voting rights and no performance-linked bonuses. ***Inclusive, NON-JUDGEMENTAL attention is open awareness.***

Centering. Finding our centre is a physical process in which we become fully embodied at the centre of our world. Our relationship to the six directions can make a big difference to how we open focus in a balanced way.

So, let us look at some of the important reminders that can be of use in the actual practice of mindfulness. There are three steps:

Remembering, stopping and centering *and*
Relaxing and attending to attention *and then*
Opening attention and sensing.

Remembering, Stopping and Centering

Our normal everyday trance is a state in which we are totally *identified* with whatever drama (minor or major) is going on around us. This process of becoming one with the objects of attention is the natural way that consciousness operates. The potential subject-object field 'collapses' toward the object pole as its default setting, just as in certain situations the indeterminate nature of a photon always 'collapses' into a particle rather than a wave.

In George Gurdjieff's philosophy, *identification* is the primary error from which all other problems flow. It implies that we are completely and *unconsciously* entangled with whatever is arising, and that our unwitting fascination with the 'reality' of our everyday soap opera is no different from absorption in a book or film. Where are you, for example, when you are totally enthralled with a story you are reading? Paradoxically you can only answer the question when you 'come to' and try to remember your previous state. Your memory may be hazy because no one was at home; you only remember an absence.

The idea of being 'at home' is very ancient, and one whose meaning is brought out in countless stories and myths about getting lost and, after many hardships, eventually finding the way back home.

So, the first step is to STOP, WAKE UP and realise that we are lost. Think of William Blake's angels blowing trumpets in the ears of recumbent and sleeping humans. If only we could rely on such divine help! But sadly, in the absence of a heavenly alarm call, we need something of a more prosaic nature, something astringent enough to counteract the hypnotic effect of everyday events. Before the era of mobile phones, I had a useful wake-up device in the form of a little box attached to my belt which would vibrate at any specified interval. It was used as a reminder to engage whatever sort of behavioural change one was practising. But it faced a formidable enemy in the form of behavioural extinction. This technical term describes a universal process whereby the nervous system no longer reacts to stimuli which have become monotonous. Brains are built to detect difference and novelty: neophilia rules. Keep staring at a dot on the wall, for example, and it will eventually disappear.

So it transpired that after a while I just did not register the vibration from my machine anymore. A temporary solution consisted in moving the device to another part of my body, and I heard of one fellow who had eventually resorted to putting the box in his underpants! I don't know how he fared, but I suspect that, like me, he might have found it all a bit tedious and counterproductive. I imagine that the situation is no different today, even with all the bells and whistles available on modern phones.

Subsequent experience has taught me that pain is the best initial prod to 'self-remembering'. After all, it's the unsatisfactoriness of the dream that is our only reliable stimulus to awaken. Consequently I have found that difficult circumstances provide the best reminder for returning to present awareness. Once the habit is established, however, it tends to generalise out to all manner of situations and becomes an (extra)ordinary part of living. There has to be some sort of gain, of course, and fortunately 'self-remembering' is generally self-reinforcing because it is effective in reducing the distress of difficult situations and enhancing the enjoyment of happy ones. It also feels good to be fully present, and we come to appreciate that we only feel real when we are open to the sensory reality of ourselves and the world. Being present may also enhance our memories because there is conscious attention to the senses. PD Ouspensky, one of Gurdjieff's original disciples, thought that all of our clear memories represented times when we were more or less 'at home' to what was happening around us.

Pausing and waking are more likely if you are not already going too fast. Back in the 1990s I trained in a psychotherapeutic system called Hakomi, which was then one of the first mindfulness-based therapies. It practises a form of body and emotional awareness under the guidance of a very useful dictum, "start slow and then go slower." When we go slower, whether physically, emotionally or cognitively, we begin to open our focus, see a bigger picture, make better decisions, save time and generally feel better. But once we are trapped in the merry-go-round of excessive speed and narrow attention, we believe that there is no other way to get things done. We are stuck in the activity trance of modern life, with few exemplars to help us escape, that is until we begin to suffer too much.

Having 'woken up', however briefly, we have an opportunity to centre ourselves. This is best accomplished by seeking a centre of gravity in the body with respect to the three directions. Traditionally, the heart or the hara (below the navel) are associated with such an orientating point. I devote several chapters later on to this topic and so make only one comment here. When we have a moment of waking, we are called back to *both the body and feeling,* giving us an opportunity to notice our *whole body felt sense* of the present and to move into a truly different mode of knowing.

Relaxing and Attending to Attention

Once you stop or slow down, then you can relax. Making a simple gesture of relaxation is relatively straightforward if you are accustomed to some sort of regular low arousal practice. A deep breath and a bodily letting go on the exhale are all that is required. It is important, however, that attention comes back to the body and that letting go is initially a whole body felt sense. The soma is part of the psyche (and vice versa) and our aim is always to integrate the part with the whole. Visualisation or other mental devices are all very well, but there is a very real danger that they can promote a dissociation in the body/mind. Mentally splitting off from bodily awareness can be useful in painful or traumatic situations, but as a general rule we need to stay grounded in our somatic reality.

Briefly relaxing provides an opportunity to attend to your present mode of attention. Is it narrow or broad, objective or immersed? Generally when we are in the midst of things our attention will be narrow and either immersed (computer work) or objective (driving in unfamiliar territory). In such circumstances, awareness must be reasonably *vivid* and *stable* for us to function. However, when we are tired or low in mood, awareness becomes dull and we may need to correct the situation by taking some deep breaths or becoming more physically active. Alternatively we may just need to rest or take a break.

Coming back to the torch analogy, we have so far looked at the width and intensity of the beam, as well as how 'close' our light is to its object. The other factor to consider is the beam's stability: can it remain steadily poised on an object or is it constantly wavering? There is enormous variation in attentional constancy amongst individuals, from severe attention deficit to the rock-solid concentration of the very experienced meditator. Most of us don't do terribly well on this dimension, and it is likely that the modern world of continuous distraction is making things worse. Practice, as in some form of attention training, is the only remedy, together with starving the mind of unnecessary 'junk food'.

At first sight, paying attention to attention may seem a complicated business, but with regular self-remembering, the process becomes second nature. Thinking of the torch analogy can make it easier to know how to apply a corrective, but in most instances it is just a matter of RELAXING AND BECOMING SPACIOUS.

Opening Attention and Sensing

As I described earlier, my first attempts at 'here and now' awareness were marred by lack of suitably clear instructions. I was narrowing my attention in an attempt to focus serially on the many sensations constantly presenting themselves to consciousness. This is, in fact, what attention normally does, flitting hither and thither, driven both by novelty and the tape loops of our current agenda. To this already narrowed style of awareness I was adding the strain of keeping the 'observer' in view. Given that the 'observer' does not exist as an object, it was no wonder that I gave up the whole enterprise as a bad job.

The idea of simply being aware of space cuts through these complications. When you become conscious of the whole body all at once you have already begun the process of opening focus. The act of whole body sensation necessarily involves defocusing the visual sense and at the same time appreciating the space in which all of your bodily sensations are arising. It is the same with all of your experience: in opening to space you defocus any sensation in particular but open to the multidimensional nature of experience as a whole. As in Sat Nam Rasayam, nothing is favoured, attention does not clamp down around any particular modality or object. Experience flows without the constant interruption of our expectations, the constant mantra of "What if?" and "What next?"

In open attention you can rest back in yourself. Attention still moves, this is its nature and without this movement the world of form ceases to be (as happens in some meditative states). The difference is that you are not pulled around by it like a boisterous dog on a lead. You are RELAXED AND SPACIOUS. You notice the whole body sense and feel its spaciousness. Periodically you reinforce this whole body feeling/attention by relaxing and letting go of tension into spaciousness.

Spacious awareness is no bar to activity, but it is sobering to see how quickly any action interferes with it. This is a simple equation: action requires direction and the arrow of purpose always leads away from the centre. This is especially true if a great deal of deliberation or effort is involved. For example, I can maintain spaciousness while talking, but only if I'm happily going on about something with which I am very familiar. It is amusing to watch myself spouting 'on automatic' and to see that there is no one formulating the words before they come out. I have a taste of the condition to which Jean Klein alluded when asked about his normal state of consciousness: in silence the question is heard and out of silence the answer is given.

As soon as aversion and desire raise their ugly heads, however, we are swept away from the calm and spaciousness at the centre of the cyclone into the swirl of identification. Focused intellectual activity has the same effect and testifies to the brain's limited capacity to process sensory and cognitive channels simultaneously. In fact, you cannot be self-aware while doing focused cognitive work, you have to be resigned to the fact that such activity requires you to be unconscious for a while. The 'isness' of our aliveness expresses itself most strongly in our bodily sensations and the overall sense of being a body. This is why feeling the whole body is so important: I don't think alive, I feel alive. We connect with the world and other humans through the feeling sense and this is somatically based. Thinking, on the other hand, is separative in nature, with a very attenuated sense of 'isness'. Consequently it has a devilish side to it, its power is matched only by its hollowness.

Our individual senses express themselves quite differently in space. Vision has the most expansive quality, but is also the mode in which narrow focus can be most compelling, especially as we have designed an urban world specifically devoted to promoting constricted, stressed consciousness. Vision is also very 'frontal' and as such promotes a pronounced sense of subject-object dichotomy. An important part of opening focus is to soften the gaze and begin to include peripheral vision. One can then proceed to relax into the whole visual field evenly. As a person who feels very much in their head most of the time, I find it easier to start opening focus with the visual space and then allowing in the whole body sense followed by other senses, especially hearing. In fact, if I am sitting quietly and move into more open, diffuse vision, I find that my visual movements naturally settle down, while at the same time the aural and somatic fields become more prominent. The whole body sense is particularly important, as it provides the substantiality and stability of Beingness.

As a preliminary exercise, you might like to try the following: hold out your two index fingers in front of you at arm's length. Slowly move both arms in an arc out to the side while keeping both fingers in view at once. You can only accomplish this if you relax into an open spaciousness and resist going with your natural tendency to track the individual fingers with narrow focus.

Do not forget that open attention is a ***movement into relaxation***. If you are straining, then spaciousness has eluded you.

The intimate connection between the visual sense and identity is brought out in the following account from Fred Wolf's *The Dreaming Universe*.

Wolf describes the experience of a physicist, Saul-Paul Sirag, who closely observed his reactions while taking the anaesthetic ketamine, a drug that also relaxes the muscles, including those responsible for eye movement:

> As he watched the visual field, he noticed that first it flattened out like a Matisse painting. Then it became hyperdimensional, abstract and dynamic – very active. Music was playing and all of the music was in synchronisation with the changes in the visual field. There was no sense of 'I', just awareness. There was affect, a feeling of awe, fear and elation.

Later, when the ketamine began to wear off:

> After forty-five minutes or so, the self began coming back. He found this the most interesting. His eyes could move just enough so that he could begin to see in three dimensions, and a perspective began. When that occurs, a unique point

> in space, the focus of the perspective, appears. Without this focus there is no 'I'. An eye for an 'I' so to speak.
> (*The Dreaming Universe*, page 314)

Clearly, the eyes have an important role in localising us in space and in reinforcing the 'I' sense, but they are only one cog in the whole machinery of identity. We return to Mr Sirag's experiences later and learn how other ingredients gradually 'kicked in' to re-establish his normal self-sense.

The reader may also be aware of an apparent paradox that arises from this account. Doesn't it imply that becoming aware of the three-dimensionality of space only reinforces personal identity, in contrast to some of the experiences recounted earlier in the book? The answer is a qualified yes, but only if one is using a particular sort of narrow attention. In open attention, the spaciousness that may initially seem a visual quality is expanded and blended with other sensory modalities to produce a multidimensional experience of OPENNESS. Openness, or welcoming as Jean Klein puts it, transcends the normal subject-object sense that is reinforced by doing, trying and expecting. You can look at this process in another way: enhanced awareness of space initially locates an apparent observer in space, but then reveals the emptiness that Douglas Harding found on top of his shoulders. In other words, our attention is brought to the obvious fact of our absence.

Before leaving the subject of vision, I must mention Alexandra Horowitz's marvellous book, *On Looking*. Horowitz made repeated trips around her New York block with different companions, including her young son and her dog. She used her companions' observations to reveal what she had previously ignored, a world of infinite freshness and novelty. Along the way she tells us about the science of attention, both human and canine. Her work is a vivid illustration of how surprising the world is when we look at it innocently, and how good it feels to emerge from our everyday perceptual rut.

Unlike vision, hearing is truly omnidirectional, and as such is a window into opening focus in a 3D way that includes awareness of above and behind. Open listening is best done in a natural setting such as a forest, where the aural landscape is evenly distributed around you. Initially you may find that you are 'grabbing onto' prominent, loud or novel sounds. After a while, however, you may be able to relax your attention and simply notice sounds arising and falling away in the expanded space of awareness. You may also notice that hearing still has a frontal bias which is easily entrained by vision. Closing your eyes can partially correct this, although our general sensory bias to the front is strongly hardwired in our nervous systems.

The link between hearing and seeing is especially important in human communication. In listening to another person we are paying attention to a wide range of signals. Not only are we processing the content of speech, but we are also interpreting its rhythm and intonation (prosody) in relation to the accompanying play of facial expressions and gestures. A huge amount of mental machinery goes into both receiving and generating all of this information, and if you are paying close attention the whole process can be quite exhausting. Which reminds me of a story.

Years after graduation two psychologists meet at a university reunion. One looks tired and worn out, but the other is youthful and full of energy. "How come you seem so fit and well after years of listening to so many miserable people?" enquires the exhausted shrink. "Who listens?" came the reply.

There is more than a grain of truth in this story. Freud warned about listening in a highly focused way, and advised therapists to allow attention to float freely. In this way, therapists could be open to their own fantasies and associations as well as those of their clients. Freud was clearly talking about a form of open awareness in which attention could include both therapist and client. The Gurdjieffians, who are the experts on self-remembering, call this 'split attention'. This is something of a misnomer, however; attention cannot be split into two opposing directions, but it can be widened to include them both.

Another feature of hearing is that sounds tend to be intermittent. Whereas most visual objects appear relatively stable in the perceptual field, auditory sensations are constantly coming and going. The seriality of hearing emphasises the passage of time in a way that vision does not, and finds its purest expression in our experience of musical rhythm. Rhythm and tonality are very basic to human consciousness and some argue that we sang before we talked. However that may be, there is no denying that the meanings in speech are strung out on a rhythmic necklace and take much of their emotional power from the speaker's prosodic skills.

We talk a lot. It is estimated that social extraverts produce up to 36,000 words per day as opposed to the introvert's 12,000. For most people it seems, this incontinent overproduction of words is a sort of 'whistling in the dark' that helps stave off silence. Thought is its ghostly partner, carrying on the good work when no one is around or no distractions beckon. Little do we realise the value of silence until it is completely taken away from us. If you want to drive a person crazy, then subject them to constant noise and bright illumination. Even the most robust nervous systems need periodic darkness and quiet.

Our predilection for social engagement has helped to entrain our hearing habits to the frontal ways of vision, and detracts from audition's unique properties. Not the least of these is the ability to detect lies and insincerity by noting stress patterns in speech. Research has repeatedly found that insincerity is best recognised when we listen to the voice alone, so close your eyes the next time a politician comes on the TV. It is interesting to note in this connection that many of our politicians in Australia have developed a slow, mechanical way of talking that makes them sound like automated train announcements or kindergarten teachers speaking to their three-year-old charges. Rather than masking the inevitable lies that they tell, this strategy only confirms our sense that we are being deceived and disrespected.

Correcting the tendency to be over-frontal is a matter of continual practice in opening attention. As I suggested above, a natural aural landscape, away from urban life, is ideal for experiencing true Sensurround. Bird calls are particularly felicitous, as their clear harmonious songs can be likened to stars flashing on and off in the night sky. But don't strain to listen. When I was in such an environment recently, I noticed a developing pain in my neck; I was trying too hard (again) to listen behind me and my neck muscles were registering their version of a frontal headache.

The intermittent quality of natural sounds also tends to highlight the silent spaces between. In the literature of Zen, there are many accounts of satori following an auditory event such as a stone hitting a hollow bamboo or a frog plopping in a pool. The marriage of sound and ensuing silence suddenly cuts through normal attentional focus and allows a freer, expanded perception. A wonderful example is struck by some songbirds, whose solitary recitative in the dusk of a summer's evening enhances the natural tranquillity of the day's ending.

Hearing and vision are the modalities in which we seem to spend most of our time, but we must not ignore the potential of the other senses in creating spaciousness. On the surface, taste and smell seem not to have a spacious dimension. They are, instead, very immediate and hark back to our most primitive ancestors, simple blind and deaf creatures smelling and feeling their way through ancient seas. As then, our relationship with a taste object is very intimate, and grants us a truly immersive experience which blurs the boundaries of subject and object. After all, we are ingesting the object and making it part of ourselves.

It is this immediacy of taste and smell that makes them such potent catalysts of emotional and perceptual change. Robert Svoboda, an authority on Ayurvedic medicine, makes a nice analogy between the 'primitive' parts of our brain that modulate these senses and a city's old quarter. There you will find the timeless soul of a metropolis with sights, smells and crafts that may not have changed for centuries. This is why smells and tastes can halt us in our tracks, literally stop time or transport us to another realm of memory or imagination.

If I am running a seminar for any length of time, I usually hand around some perfumes to help the participants 'clear and reset'. To suddenly experience a classic perfume out of its normal context is to disappear momentarily into the timeless. In fact, it is the evanescent nature of aroma that is its great lesson. We catch a glimpse of another state and then it is quickly gone; no time to emasculate the experience with a story. Blake captures this in his inimitable way:

> He who binds himself a joy
> Does the winged life destroy
> But he who kisses the joy as it flies
> Lives in eternity's sunrise.

Incidentally, the smells that I use most often are: grapefruit and lemon essences and Guerlain's Apres l'Ondee, Nahema and Mitsouko.

Proust did try to capture the moment in his famous *A la recherche du temps perdu* in which he describes how his awareness was magically transformed after tasting a madeleine cake:

> An exquisite pleasure had invaded my senses, something isolated, detached, with no suggestion of its origin. And at once the vicissitudes of life had become indifferent to me, its disasters innocuous, its brevity illusory – this new sensation having had on me the effect which love has of filling me with

> a precious essence, or rather this essence was not in me it was me. I had ceased now to feel mediocre, contingent, mortal.

As Proust discovered, the great virtue of taste and smell resides in their intimate connection with pleasure. Is there anything more reliably pleasurable than food? In the modern world we are privileged with an extraordinary range of eating and drinking experiences, but our endless cooking programmes are not matched with a commensurate effort to educate our gustatory and olfactory sensibilities. A simple remedial practice consists in letting a pleasurable taste spread through and infuse the whole body sense, allowing every part to luxuriate in pleasure.

ENJOYING THE SPACIOUSNESS OF PLEASURE

This is a sure way to come into friendlier relations with our somatic reality, and our bodies will truly respond and thank us for sharing. It is also a way to fully experience the nature of a particular pleasure, and whether it is 'thin' and transient or 'deep' and truly beneficial. Such a discrimination can be a good basis for evaluating many other pursuits, pastimes and predilections (people too).

Unfortunately, the act of eating is usually overlain with so many connotations and complexities that we are seldom able to commune with a meal in a simple and grateful way. Even mindless eating, however, is still a source of great pleasure, and indeed, sociable eating has been found to have a more consistent and reliable effect on mood than any other human activity. In fact our daily meals may be the only source of true enjoyment and relaxation in a stressful or humdrum day. Eating can also be a metaphor for other aspects of one's life:

How do you nurture yourself?
Can you chew through (problems)...?

Can you experience enjoyment slowly and sensuously?
Do you deserve nurture?
Can you take it in?
Can you take time just digesting and absorbing?
Can you eliminate the inessential or poisonous?
Do you like feeding others?

Children tend to have little difficulty with such questions, they simply don't arise. Life is play, play is enjoyment, play is your best friend, play is imagining, play is mastering and learning, play is an ice cream. It's not complicated, it just gets complicated later on, and often unnecessarily so – "Unless ye become as little children."

The pleasure of play in all its forms is expansive. Play continually opens up new physical and imaginative spaces. It is our primary impulse – homo ludens, but gets lost or perverted into obsessive recreational activities that are not intrinsically playful at all, or at best are excuses for controlled aggression and tribal competitiveness. I think that the Steiner educationalists have it just right: facilitate play and creativity for the first seven years. There is plenty of time later for learning the endless and often useless information that passes for an education.

Depending on your perspective then, the 'one liner' from the preceding discussion might be:

If you care to undertake any of the exercises or approaches suggested in this book, make sure that they feel enjoyable and playfully inquisitive.

I am not naively proposing that the pleasure principle should dominate in every circumstance; there are times when we have to work hard 'chewing through' difficulties on our way to a goal. Overall, however, there should be satisfaction, we should feel pleasantly nourished and relaxed. As with cooking, there must be hard work, skill, experimentation, good taste and love, and even then things don't turn out right every time. But none of these facets of an activity need feel onerously effortful. As Moshe Feldenkrais pointed out in *The Potent Self*, a "good action" is always effortless, the presence of effort indicates that actions other than the intended one are also in play.

One of the virtues of self-remembering and the self-observation that it makes possible is that we can become familiar with 'the other actions' that are apparently running interference with our main aim. When we allow them a voice we can learn a lot about our often mixed motives and the other 'I's that populate our psyche.

But before summing up these thoughts on self-remembering, there is one more sensory modality to consider: that of touch, which encompasses more than sensations from the skin and erogenous zones. Every second our brain receives innumerable messages from every part of the body. Most of them are outside or on the periphery of consciousness, although a surprising number can be made conscious with appropriate gestures of attention. Specifically directing awareness toward internal sensations can open up a whole new world of fluidity, energy and insight. I recommend two contemporary authors on this topic: Emilie Conrad (*Life on Land* – more on her work later) and Ged Sumner (*Body Intelligence Meditation*).

Sensations from the skin have a special importance because the nervous system and the skin are derived from the same embryonic tissue. They have a resonance with one another; touching the skin *is* touching the brain. I cannot think of any chronically depressed clients whom I have seen over the years who were touched and hugged appropriately in childhood. Highly sensitive individuals are particularly responsive to the calming or exciting effects of touch, but tend to have considerable 'armouring' against tactile stimulation if they have a history of touch deprivation or abuse. This may even extend to a phobia about people entering their 'space'.

Tactile therapies are an essential adjunct to any healing endeavour and can facilitate a deep relaxation and letting go not possible through other means. Releasing the body from its ingrained tensions is a sure way through to a spaciousness which goes far beyond the purely somatic. The following quote is from a client of Jeffrey Maitland's in his book *Spacious Body*. Maitland is a Rolfer, and consequently does deep muscle and tissue work to reorganise the body in relation to gravity.

> You know, before the session it was like being in this little room. And now, after the session, it's like being in a great big room (page 38).

But whether we are talking about touch or other sensory experiences, the common denominator is that we are coming to our senses. It is no accident that we talk about common sense or 'sense and sensibility'.

The senses are the common ground upon which we establish reality, everything else is a story open to question. The key to mindfulness, then, consists in being able to come to one's senses with a spacious attention that does not grab on to experience, but lets it flow. To do this requires the kind of alert relaxation which strikes an appropriate balance between active and passive poles, between doing (staying alert) and sensing (remaining open).

The particular balance point that you use will depend on the circumstances. Self-remembering while walking in a busy crowd will be different from your stillness while listening to a Chopin nocturne. Both conditions, however, share a common spaciousness, together with a presence within or as that field of awareness. We might say that this commonality of presence manifests with different boundary conditions: I am much more concerned, for example, with my body's boundaries in a crowd than when sitting quietly meditating.

Openness to what is immediately present also allows me to stand on a steady platform from which all manner of further explorations can be made. In conversation with a colleague or friend, I may have more space to observe my reactions and create some space around judgements and resistances. Sitting in formal meditation or having quiet time, I am able to 'wait and let be', acknowledging my incapacity to do or to know anything whatsoever about the present moment; knowing that I can only be open to it. In his book, *Self Remembering,* Red Hawk (Robert Moore) describes how this kind of waiting can be enhanced by a direct invocation of Higher Power. This may not be to everyone's taste, but I believe that such an approach can be a potent reminder of our absolute inability to change anything fundamental about ourselves. Only Grace can secure our freedom since Grace *is* our freedom.

In the next two chapters I explore further the difficulties and paradoxes implicit in the issues of growth and change. This will involve, I expect, an even deeper immersion in ignorance. Hopefully, I may receive some higher assistance in breaking the narrow mindsets that I sense are already forming in my head and competing for this contentious territory. Will it be a fresh minestrone or yesterday's cold pizza?

6

Spacious Mind in Action

Since everything in life is an appearance, perfect in being what it is, having nothing to do with good or bad, acceptance or rejection, one may well burst out laughing.
Longchenpa

Compared to the body, the mind appears a truly enigmatic proposition, made all the more elusive because to study the mind, we must use the mind. In this chapter I explore three simple ways of introducing some clarity and spaciousness into this often crowded and perplexing realm. The three aspects of this work are: allowing the body/mind to speak, creating distance and letting go.

Allowing the Body/Mind to Speak

When we look inside with conscious attention, it seems pretty messy in there. Thoughts come and go by themselves, we get sucked into all sorts of imaginary mental scenarios, and our own feelings often seem obscure and puzzling to us. The view from within is a vast and mysterious landscape which can only be encompassed one small step at a time. I use the word landscape advisedly, because our mental terrain is a space that simulates the three-dimensional everyday world. Thinking is a form of scaled down action, and as such always has a pragmatic aim: memories and rehearsals are attenuated tropes of action scenarios, screened in a fuzzy, dull Cerebroscope. My constant internal monologue, the star feature of this subjective life, is a pale reflection of dialogue with another person, but without the benefit of feedback.

In its higher reaches, as in mathematics and philosophy,

thinking can take on the form of play, where symbols are manipulated just for the sheer pleasure of exploration and creativity. But such activities are a long way from the monotonous plod of the everyday.

Given the very mundane nature of daily cogitation, it is not surprising that the internal and external worlds are closely linked by spatial metaphors. In fact, most aspects of mental life are described in a dimensional way. Here are just a few examples:

> Up and down in mood, on top of the world, depths of despair, spaced out, open or closed mind, point of view, convergent or divergent thinking, thinking outside the square, getting a perspective (or a handle), irrational (from the Latin, 'not in ratio'), out of proportion, mind expanding, beside oneself, not able to stand something… etc.

The various states of water are also invoked as metaphors for mental life. For example, Eastern spiritual literature has used a number of images to describe the uncultivated, everyday mind, but the most compelling is probably that of restless, turbid water. If stilled, the obscuring particles gradually settle and the intrinsic clarity of mind is revealed. The prescribed settling process tends to be a meditative one in which there is generally little concern for the nature of the contaminating materials. In the West, we are more preoccupied with the opacities themselves, their nature and their relationships. Notwithstanding this, however, there is a developing awareness in the psychological sciences that lowering arousal and settling the mind as far as possible are necessary prerequisites for successful in-sight.

'Focusing' is the name of an approach to self-exploration that has elements of both East and West, background and foreground. It was developed by Eugene Gendlin and his colleagues when they were conducting research on the key variables that determined a successful outcome in psychotherapy. Gendlin, a former professor of psychology at the University of Chicago, concluded that the most important factor was the client's ability to tune into themselves in a particular way. This involved paying attention to their whole body feeling state as it manifested in an overall, diffuse, unclear way, the so-called 'felt sense'. He subsequently formalised this process into six steps which are described in his book *Focusing*. I have summarised them as follows:

1. Clearing a Space

Gendlin has emphasised over the years that *this is probably the most important step.*

To follow this first instruction, tune into your whole body sense, a feeling of *the whole body all at once:* a fuzzy, unclear and ill-defined sense felt more prominently in the chest and abdomen area. As soon as you tune into this diffuse feeling you will notice that your eyes become more relaxed because you are *opening your attention.*

Silently ask yourself about present concerns and then wait to see what emerges. There may be several different worries or preoccupations that are just below the threshold of conscious awareness. Each time one arises, acknowledge the concern and place it in an imaginary coloured container in your immediate surroundings (some containers may need to be bigger than others!). Reassure each concern that you will return to it in due course and that you are not going to ignore or forget it. Having filled a number of containers (usually no more than five or six), choose a particular concern to work with.

2. Experiencing the felt sense

To get a general idea of what felt senses are like, tune into your body and bring to mind someone you like. Stay with this whole body feeling for a while. Then bring to mind someone you have been in conflict with and notice the change. Now feel into the whole body sense of the problem under consideration. This is the process of feeling 'all about that problem' in the body.

3. Finding 'the handle'
Try to access a descriptive quality of this unclear felt sense by allowing a word or a phrase, or less commonly an image, to emerge from the felt sense. Do not rush into this.

4. Resonating between feeling and word
Now shift your attention between the word or phrase and the felt sense to check if they resonate or fit together.

5. Asking
Ask yourself, what it is about this whole situation that makes it so... whatever the quality is? This phase is not so much a questioning by the verbal mind, but a continuing sense of openness and curiosity about the relation of the feeling tone to the situation under consideration.

If a clear feeling tone has emerged, it may illuminate the situation in a way that produces a 'shift' (however small) in consciousness. It is the kind of feeling you experience when you have been trying to remember a name and it suddenly comes into awareness; a connection is made and a feeling of release occurs as energy flows.

6. Receiving
Stay with whatever has come up in a "friendly way" (Gendlin's words), pondering for a while what has occurred.

Here is an example of the focusing process which I have taken from my book, *Hawks, Doves and Other Humans*.

Joan is a 45-year-old woman who, although married, has remained for much of her life under the thumb of her tyrannical widowed father. He has a progressive and debilitating neurological disorder and Joan visits him almost daily in the nursing home. Despite this devoted attention, her father is in the habit of ringing her up and demanding that she drop everything and come to visit him immediately. Joan usually complies.

When I saw Joan recently, she was most apologetic because she had cancelled her previous appointment in response to one of these 'emergency' calls. We decided to do some focusing on the situation. First, we cleared a space. This was very necessary, because Joan is a helper and there were many concerns about relatives and friends in various difficult situations.

After a few minutes, we had managed to fill a number of containers with these worries and Joan was in a reasonably calm and relaxed condition. Joan then elected to focus on concerns about her father's health and so tuned into her whole body sense of "all about Dad's health." Immediately she noticed a great deal of tension and disturbance in her chest and abdominal area, which initially just seemed to feel like constriction or "butterflies". However, as Joan relaxed more into this sense, a hot feeling began to emerge. Joan managed to continue observing this hot feeling without sinking into it or becoming identified with it. Gendlin emphasises how important it is not to go too far inside feelings and sensations as they emerge. As he so elegantly puts it, you can't taste the soup with your face in it.

On more than one occasion, Joan wanted to stop the process, but with some calming and reassurance she was able to stay with these quite intense bodily feelings, which after a while she realised were angry in nature. The words anger and resentment seemed to resonate well with the feeling, so she then asked herself what she was so angry about in relation to her father. To the outside observer this would pose no mystery, but we must remember that Joan was a woman who was unaccustomed to prioritising her own feelings or needs.

This time, however, Joan was able to articulate an assertive response to the effect that her father should show her more respect. At that point I noticed a slight shift in the way she looked, and Joan felt this shift as well; a little more confidence and a slight movement toward a straighter posture in her chair. We finished this round of focusing by just sitting with and receiving this sense of justifiable resentment at being taken for granted, and the accompanying shift in the sense of self.

This process of sensing into oneself through body awareness does not have to be formalised into a six-stage process. Many people do it automatically and seem to condense together these stages in quick movements of attention. As Gendlin himself points out, if you have spent a little time sensing and touching the unclear holistic body sense of a life-problem, then you have been focusing. The important thing is not to have too many expectations, but simply to be open to what comes; to be friendly to the inner prompting and to make as few judgements about the process as possible. Spaciousness is the key.

In neurological terms, the process of focusing is one in which 'dialogue' between the left and right hemispheres is improved so that the brain itself becomes more spacious. Initially, the right hemisphere is calmed by differentiating and compartmentalizing current concerns. Attention then focuses on the whole body sense and its affective tone, which are more prominently right hemisphere functions. There follows a facilitation of left/right-brain communication in the 'handle' and resonating stages, and then perhaps a 'shift' which signals the formation of new cognitive/affective connections and a phase of coherent (i.e. synchronised) whole-brain activity.

The same process can be applied to dreams, and Gendlin's book *Let Your Body Interpret Your Dreams* is probably the best practical guide to the subject (apart, of course, from Carl Jung's extensive writings). In fact, Focusing applies to all realms of human experience. There is always a background feeling sense, wherever we are or whatever we are doing. It is constantly and subtly changing as we encounter different people and varied environments. In popular parlance it is our 'gut feeling' and constitutes a hugely valuable source of information if we care to pay attention to it.

Focusing's power is based on the idea that our personal evaluations enfold many layers of previous experience/feeling/interpretation and therefore consist of complex textures and patterns. These are encoded in a feeling, not in verbal form. For example, if you tune in to the idea of your mother, then the resulting felt sense will tap into an incredibly rich vein of feelings and meanings that is practically inexhaustible. Every time you return to this felt sense, you will experience a different facet or nuance in the 'whole' that is your connection to mother. Yet all this complexity is implicit in the felt bodily sense as it first arises, just as a whole oak tree is implicit or enfolded in an acorn. If you plant an acorn in the right spot it will grow with very little fuss; you just have to "wait and let be" to use Flora Courtois's phrase. So it is with Focusing.

John Welwood, the American therapist who writes so eloquently about matters psychological and spiritual, points out that Focusing has a lot in common with other creative processes; all involve a dialogue between a focal, here and now consciousness, and the broader, diffuse 'knowing' of the whole body/mind, *a knowing that is a feeling knowing*. He also discusses the pitfall of treating this approach as a method with specific therapeutic goals. Such an attitude detracts from *being with oneself in a non-judgemental way*. We are so steeped in the idea of not being good enough (a view supported by both psychology and religion), that any self-exploration is prone to take on a remedial flavour. Hence the wisdom of just sitting with oneself without agenda and *waiting and letting be*. In this way I get to know how I am with myself in a friendly and respectful way; I can allow myself to settle; there are no expectations, *there is space to be*. The critic is respectfully asked to take a seat a little further back in the room.

When I become quiet and open and embodied, a new intimacy

develops with myself, a soft yet powerful sense of love and alrightness. I do not have a problem with my own presence; I am free and capable of listening to what the 'other' may say. To use Blake's words, "eternity is in love with the works of time" and wants to commune with us as much as we aspire to be at one with it. Such a relationship may, on the one hand, take the simple form of an answer to a vexing problem. On the other, it may presage a most profound existential transformation. The level at which I explore my own natural depth depends on my intention, the form and sincerity of my practice and above all on Grace, for the Spirit "bloweth where it listeth."

Whether I am looking to solve a problem, gain psychological insight, create a work of art or attain union with the divine, the process that I am describing is essentially the same. It involves accepting, opening, surrendering and receiving i.e. making oneself a vessel free of effort, evaluation or expectation. The part surrenders so that it can be encompassed by the whole. The whole wants to be known and wants to show itself and enfold (but not extinguish) the part. A relationship develops and matures, a process that Jung called individuation.

In his book, *The Natural Depth in Man*, Wilson Van Dusen uses the term autorepresentation to describe the psyche's tendency to show itself in dreams, creative work and inspiration of all kinds. Whatever we call it, this process has been known to humans of all cultures and at all times. The Native American who goes into the wilderness to solve a problem or receive healing knows that she has to be quiet and wait for the promptings of the Great Spirit. The Christian monk humbly waits in his cell for the blessings of the Holy Spirit. In both cases prayer may be used as a calming ritual, but openness and heartfelt surrender are the crucial ingredients.

The genius in Gendlin's discovery is the emphasis on the whole body sense and the opening of awareness that this involves. Dropping attention down into the body, while at the same time expanding awareness of feeling, is a move toward heart- rather than head-centredness. Such a reorientation is a big step for most of us, especially males, but it brings the true gifts of the Spirit: humility, empathy and compassion. The reader may also recognise that, if desired, it is a gate into the core of our being, as described earlier by Judith Blackstone and Reginald Ray.

Traditional self-observation practices that encompass mindfulness of feelings do not generally have a way of dealing with emotions beyond 'letting go' and 'letting be'. Western approaches such as 'Focusing' add a valuable new dimension to self-understanding, one that is more likely to promote wholeness and humanness than the more ascetic dictums of, for example, Zen Buddhism.

Keeping Your Distance

Another simple yet profound aspect of Focusing is that it points directly to the fuzziness and opacity of the interior realm. It's tangled and confusing in there, and our first reaction is to recoil from this mysterious realm over which we seem to have so little control. This is why the Focusing process proceeds gently and non-judgementally; we go outside of our comfort zone, but only in small steps.

Introspection reveals that our mental processes (both thought and feeling) are generally of two kinds: focused and goal orientated or unfocused and wandering. This latter mode, mediated by the brain's so-called default system, usually revolves around self-centred concerns and often has an unhappy emotional tone. It is true that daydreaming sometimes has a creative, expansive quality, but perhaps this is the exception rather than the rule.

Both focused and wandering mentation have a contractive energy from which it is difficult to maintain any distance; we identify completely with the contents of our own minds. And because we are so wedded to these personal dramas, we can only dis-identify from them with persistent self-remembering and self-observation.

Our ability to tolerate reality is tenuous at best and so safety is a fundamental requirement in any self-exploration. At first, safety may come in the form of a trusted therapist or teacher, a community of like-minded people or faith in a particular tradition or method. In due course, however, safety arises from a growing confidence in oneself and the supportive nature of one's real identity, the benign nature of 'unconditioned mind'. The Sufis have a saying about this journey from ignorance to certainty: there are as many ways to God as there are people and there is only one way. That one path is the liberating spiral from contraction/fear to expansion/love, one step at a time.

Creating space in the midst of our mental clutter is something that we tend to do quite naturally when a problem is complicated. In fact, to do complex cognitive work, we usually have to exteriorize our mental processes, using words, pictures, diagrams and symbols. Some people can do complex operations in their heads, but most of us have to plod along using external means. Even preliterate societies create paintings or sand drawings to ritualise and therefore concretise the idea of an impending hunt, or tribal event.

Our increasing reliance on external aids to embody and elaborate mental processes has meant that our private subjective capacities have become sadly diminished. It was not so long ago that quite complex mental arithmetic was routine, or that recitation from memory was part of every schoolroom curriculum. To this list of increasingly redundant cognitive functions, we might also add the capacity to read and follow a map. Such developments are a pity, because the exercise of these abilities seems to improve overall brain function and mood. And how wonderful it is to hear someone recite poetry from memory, or tell a traditional tale with all its intricate details.

It is interesting to me that the impressive feats performed by memory gurus are generally accomplished by using techniques known to the Ancient Greeks. You have probably heard about the idea of constructing a visualised inner landscape with recognisable landmarks where memorised items can be left. One can then retrieve an item in the same way that one would in the actual world. Such a process works so well because it creates an organised 3D space in a realm that was formerly lacking both clear dimensions and order.

Interestingly, boys tend to learn and integrate new material in a physico-spatial way, whereas girls rely more on verbal processing. Boys fidget and move around in space more than girls, and advanced problem solving in males is associated with greater activation of the brain's motor areas. Emotional problem solving is a somewhat different matter and more easily approached through the verbal route, since all such matters are ultimately interpersonal. This is where men usually find a great deal of difficulty; trying to bring linear reasoning into the realm of analogue feeling!

Language is obviously our most important tool to encapsulate and coordinate both concepts and feelings. Like the creation of an internal memory path, it provides a pre-existent framework which has clear internal relationships i.e. it is another sort of map. In hunter-gatherer groups such as the San in Botswana (Bushmen of the Kalahari), much of daily life amongst the typically twenty to thirty tribe members is spent chatting and gossiping. The projection of individual sentiments into the collective realm creates multiple feedback loops and a complex iterating structure that stabilises tribal life as a whole. On the one hand, language is a medium of exchange which has become increasingly interiorised as thinking and self-talk. Yet when we try to solve problems by talking them through with ourselves, we lack the rich mirroring available from the diverse perspectives of others. So if you have a problem which is proving difficult to solve, then ask as many people as possible, not just your best friend or partner. There can be enormous relief in putting your thoughts and feelings 'out there' into the space occupied by other humans. In this way our worst fears can begin to assume *proportion,* a fact that may explain the origin of the word 'shrink' as a nickname for therapists.

The take-home message is simple: *create more space.* When working alone, our best strategy is to open up a cognitive space with pen and paper or tablet. Keeping a diary is the traditional way to review, sift and *map* one's inner life. There are many wonderful examples of profoundly wise diarists in the world literature, but for me, Marion Milner is without compare when it comes to self-exploration and 'listening'. And as well as being of interest to students of the mind, her works are especially appealing to those involved in highly creative endeavours, whether in work or play.

I am also aware that any instinct we may have to record and understand our daily experiences has largely moved on to Facebook. This new medium is a dream come true for social extraverts with their unreflecting and excited capacity for displaying themselves to all and sundry. Diaries, on the other hand, are private things, and it is no accident that most teenagers (girls at least) instinctively turn to a private journal format to cope with the extraordinary complexity of the adolescent transition. Feedback from others is one thing, feedback from one's soul is another.

But whatever form our explorations take, our efforts are ultimately about enhancing spaciousness within the constraints of necessary, as opposed to arbitrary boundaries. Safety is everything and is the sine qua non of all successful relationships, whether with oneself or with others.

Midway between the solitary reflections of the diarist and the multiple feedback loops of the group, we find dyads, the basic building blocks of society. And it is here that we can most easily discern the play of CONNECTION/separation. A close, intimate relationship offers the possibility of deep connection at a number of levels and, provided there is no power imbalance, paradoxically enhances each participant in their process of individuation and increasing uniqueness.

The CONNECTION/separation dynamic is taken to a higher 'octave' of functioning. Jung understood this process when he compared the therapist/client relationship to the reactions in an alchemist's retort or alembic – either all the elements are changed or none are. Therapists who try to remain aloof from relating to their clients in an equal, ordinary and human way are sadly handicapped and do their clients a grave disservice.

In all forms of psychotherapy the relationship is everything, and grows and prospers under the protection of openness and what John Welwood calls unconditional presence, the capacity to be with experience without wanting to control it in any way. He explains:

> When we let experience be as it is, instead of seeking to alter it in any way, the focus of inner work shifts in a powerful and important way. No longer is our experience something apart from us that we need to change or resolve: instead the focus widens to the larger field: how-we-are-with-our-experience. And when we relate to our experience in a more spacious, allowing way, it becomes less problematic, because we no longer exist in an I/it, subject/object tension with it.
> (*Toward a Psychology of Awakening*, page 116)

Such a stance involves staying with "don't know", something that can be very difficult for therapists as well as their clients. It takes practice to refrain from identifying with or rejecting our experience, but it is "don't know" that has faith in the simple power of acknowledgement and the wisdom of waiting upon the inner voice.

Welwood also makes the point that awareness of feelings per se does not necessarily lead to wisdom, "but the process of opening fully to them can." He goes on:

> When the focus of awareness shifts from a feeling – as an object of pleasure or pain, like or dislike, acceptance or rejection – to our state of presence with it, this allows us to discover new resources and wisdom hidden within it, as we move from the realm of personality into the larger space of being.
> (*ibid*, pages 119–120)

In that larger space, the intrinsic qualities of fundamental consciousness are able to manifest: strength from anger (as in the case of Joan), open-heartedness from grief and courage from fear. Part of the challenge for therapists, however, is to refrain from any concept of such outcomes. Life is a surprise, not least when we rein in our obsession with prediction and control.

Since clients usually have a goal-orientated mindset when they enter therapy, there is an onus on the therapist to 'hold' this unconditional space while the therapeutic milieu is becoming safe. Having said this, I don't want to imply that there is no room for specific methods, only that technique must always be subordinate to presence. The two vignettes below, describing quite different approaches, hopefully illustrate that all roads can lead to Rome.

Cognitive-behavioural therapy (CBT) is the prevailing paradigm in mainstream clinical psychology and psychiatry. It is based on the simple (and simplistic) idea that our difficulties arise from aberrant thinking patterns. These include black and white thinking, catastrophising, jumping to conclusions and others. All of these unhelpful distortions are, in fact, immature cognitive habits that we inevitably find in children, and which most of us don't fully grow out of. Learning to identify and correct them can make a big difference to the way people approach life, but with the proviso that dealing with unhelpful thoughts does not necessarily fix the way we feel. This means that CBT, like other therapeutic tools, must always be used in a way that is subordinate to the empathic milieu of the therapeutic relationship. My observation over the years has convinced me that successful CBT practitioners are ones who bring their human selves to the work and are not bound by formulaic 'cookbook' methods. Here is an account from a client early in their therapy:

> After three sessions with my new therapist, he told me to start a diary to record all the times when a 'should' entered my mind. At first this seemed interesting, although I'm sure that I missed many of the little monkeys along the way. By the second week the whole thing was tiresome and I was getting thoroughly fed up. I was having a particularly demanding day and so I took a few minutes from shopping to have a coffee. As I was sitting there all the 'shoulds' for the rest of the day were racing through my mind. Then I realised that I should be recording them all in my diary. With this last 'should' something snapped inside me; I laughed out loud and continued chuckling to myself for minutes. How ridiculous! There I was trying to take a 'break' and then filling it up with worry about making a list of 'shoulds' because I thought I should! I remember taking some deep breaths and feeling completely relaxed. My critic (as I later learned it was called) had also taken a coffee break and was nowhere to be seen. It wasn't the end of the matter, but I really turned a corner that day.

In contrast, Sand Play would seem to be coming from a completely different angle. As its name implies, this approach involves playing with a sand tray, either with the sand itself or with figurines that are selected from a vast array that are set on shelves around the therapy area. There is immense variety and freedom in such a format, and the whole person is able to express themselves at their own pace. Here is an account from a friend:

> A professional development course on play therapy for young children was offered to me at a time when I was working with primary school age children as a counsellor. Part of the course was on Sand Play. It required only a tray and some sand. All the exercises were to do with children, but we tried them on ourselves first. In one example, we were told to draw something in the sand about our lives at that moment.
>
> My life at that time was very busy – a full time job, children at home and work as a local government councillor. I took the sand tray and drew a line down the middle. On one side I drew a complicated pattern; it was enjoyable and fun. I was about to draw on the other side when I felt moved to tears. Filling in the whole area seemed so wrong. I could not do it. Simultaneously I realised that I needed more space in my life: space to do nothing, to sit in the sun, to enjoy what was around me. It was an overpowering moment and it changed what I would work towards for the next few years.

Both of these wake-up calls seemed to arise in sudden moments of spaciousness whose ground had been laid by a distancing effect: either through the diary method or marks in a sand tray. These 'Aha' moments were also accompanied by an emotional abreaction and a 'shift' that involved the whole self.

Emotional catharsis has been considered a cleansing process since the time of Ancient Greece and is thankfully not the exclusive province of psychotherapy. Thomas Scheff in his book, *Catharsis in Healing, Ritual, and Drama,* draws close parallels between distancing methods in drama and therapy. In the theatre, a drama is considered to be underdistanced if the audience gets so drawn into the action that they totally identify with the stage performance and the emotions portrayed by the actors. This increases arousal and tension to a level that may not be resolved, leaving people shaken but not relieved in any way. Overdistancing is the complete opposite, with audience members remaining bored and unmoved in a purely observer role. The reader will recognise the distinction between immersed and objective attention.

For Scheff, the value of drama resides in its ability to promote emotional release and resolution through appropriate distancing. This means that participants can participate vicariously with the actors, but at the same time feel safe because they are occupying the observing role. Catharsis happens in this middle zone: not too hot, not too cold, like Gendlin's proverbial soup. Scheff describes the cathartic release as taking a number of forms:

> Shivering and cold sweat when fear is released,
> Crying when grief is released and
> Laughing or hot sweats for anger.
> The conditions for effective catharsis are:
> An appropriate mix of provoking and reassuring stimuli,
> A balance in the observer between past distress and present safety and
> A release of tension and increased sense of well-being.

According to this view, catharsis is beneficial and healing even though a conscious connection is not made with specific situations in a person's life i.e. there may not be insight as prescribed by the traditional tenets of psychotherapy. The validity of Scheff's model is confirmed, in my opinion, by its parallels with traditional healing rituals the world over.

It is a pity then that as a culture we do not get more emotional value from TV and cinema. The movies, in particular, provide a wonderful opportunity for emotional release as we sit there unobserved in the dark. Unfortunately, few cinematic dramas are pitched at the right distance. As a film enthusiast, I often talk to my clients about the movies and we share our experiences when appropriate. Some movies make a special impact and become old friends that are visited again and again. When I was ten years old, I found myself on Christmas Eve alone in front of our TV watching Jimmy Stewart in *It's a Wonderful Life*. The movie had a profound effect on me, but I was not able to understand until much later how this story embodies potent archetypal themes of meaning and purpose. I have revisited the classic innumerable times, and always have a good cry, something that does me a power of good. Which reminds me of the scene in *Sleepless in Seattle* where two males are guffawing at their womenfolk because they are having a teary over *An Affair to Remember*. How sad that so many males cannot be vulnerable, even to themselves, and have a much-needed catharsis.

There is a strong resonance between the skills of a dramatist and that of a therapist, since they both must cultivate an interpersonal space where emotional energy can flow in a safe way. As we saw earlier, Focusing is one of many methods which allow subtle modulation of the space in which mindstuff is arising. Scheff proposes that, in general, present time events, fiction or fantasy, rapid review and positive emotion are distancing. On the other hand, past events, detailed recollection and negative or unpleasant emotions remove distance. These considerations are especially important when we are trying to moderate arousal during the recall of traumatic events, something that I shall discuss later on.

I was particularly struck by two examples of distancing from Scheff's book. In the first, he describes a young man who is remembering a knife attack by his father. The client becomes increasingly distressed until the therapist asks if there were any good times with his father. The client smiles and begins to describe such a memory, whereupon he bursts into tears and cries for several minutes. He then declares that he feels a lot better and continues with his story about the attack.

The second account is from Tennyson's *The Princess*:

Home they brought her warrior dead;
She nor swooned nor uttered cry.
All her maidens, watching, said
"She must weep or she will die."

Then they praised him soft and low,
Called him worthy to be loved,
Truest friend and noblest foe;
Yet she neither spoke nor moved.

Stole a maiden from her place,
Lightly to the warrior stept
Took the face-cloth from his face;
Yet she neither moved nor wept.

Rose a nurse of ninety years,
Set his child upon her knee –
Like a summer tempest came the tears –
"Sweet my child I live for thee."

The Secret of Letting Go

The old nurse knew instinctively that the Princess was in a state of underdistanced shock and could only be relieved of her state by reconnecting with a more positive emotion. The dramatic scene illustrates the important principle that we can only let go when we feel safe enough to do so, and when our body/mind is neither too tight nor too slack. Safety is always a key issue, and it may take quite a time to trust life enough to even contemplate letting important issues go.

Concepts of letting go or surrendering also have a dissonant ring to our modern ears. We live in an era of self-determination, self-control and self-containment. It's self all the way down. But for those on a path of understanding and genuine freedom, there can be no alternative to putting aside their obsession with grasping and control.

Connection to that which is more encompassing must entail a surrender of that which is more limiting: the pervasive gesture of contraction away from Life that we call the ego. The catch is that we cannot deliberately let go. Instead, it is usually the case that something about our lives has become so unbearable or unsatisfactory that there is no alternative but to give up and allow Life to take its course.

Such was the case with Les Levenson, an American engineer, born in 1909, who managed to find his way through a life-threatening crisis and arrive at a point of healing and equanimity. Like Dante in *The Inferno*, the middle-aged Levenson found himself in a very dark wood of suffering and confusion caused by liver disease, stomach ulcers, kidney stones, migraines and depression. To make things worse, he had just had his second heart attack and his doctors had given him a very poor prognosis. The old saying that execution at dawn tends to sharpen the mind certainly applied to Levenson, and he began to deeply reflect upon his life and the path he had taken to such a parlous situation.

The answers he found were simple yet profound. Firstly, he realised that happiness arose in him when he was giving love and not when he was preoccupied with being loved. And secondly, he saw that he had constantly been trying to control the world to fit in with his own desires and goals, and that the constant stress of this endeavour had been the cause of much of his ill health. As a result of these insights, he immediately set about letting go of his obsessions with being loved and being in control. Within a relatively short space of time, his ailments melted away and he attained an ongoing state of peace and *imperturbability*, the like of which he had never known before.

Levenson subsequently systematised his discovery into an approach that came to be known as the Sedona Method and which is still taught today. I cannot do justice to this process in a brief summary and strongly advise the reader to look into the technique themselves. Suffice it to say, however, that it involves identifying one's emotional state and then systematically asking certain questions about it. When I did the course back in videotape days, I thought at first that the approach seemed too easy, but then I realised that its apparent simplicity was backed up by a thoughtful philosophy that enquires deeply into the causes and cures of suffering.

Levenson's central idea is based on the realisation that *holding on is always painful* and that the body/mind's natural response to this awareness of suffering is a gesture of release. This applies regardless of whether I am holding a hot object, holding a tight muscle or holding a painful feeling. As soon as attention is brought to these contractions, a spontaneous release can occur. In the case of the hot object, such reactions happen automatically, but as we progress into the affective and cognitive realms the process appears to become more complex.

The Sedona Method has a distinct parallel with the Buddhist tenet of impermanence which argues that since phenomena are transient, all chasing after experiences must lead to disappointment and suffering. Understanding this truth is deepened in vipassana (or insight) meditation, in which one views the constantly arising and disappearing contents of consciousness in the light of their impermanence and their relationship to aversion and craving i.e. their intrinsic unsatisfactoriness. By not identifying with the flow of thoughts and feelings, one is naturally letting go into the constantly changing stream of mental life. The observing 'I' is the spaciousness within which the arising and disappearing occur. And in allowing the contents of consciousness to arise dispassionately, the process undermines the egoic tendency to react to all stimuli in terms of its personal agendas and stories.

The ego, as director of the personal soap opera, has lost his script.

These basic tenets of Buddhism were illustrated very nicely in Jack Huber's book, *Psychotherapy and Meditation*, published in 1965 and one of the first post-World War II accounts of Zen meditation training. Huber points out that if we really accept that suffering is inevitable and that all things change, even if we don't attempt to fix them, then what may happen is that *we no longer care whether pains continue or cease*. Some things we can predict and change, but for most of our worries it *may no longer be possible to be concerned*.

The reader may recognise shades of the Serenity Prayer in Huber's comments:

> God grant me the serenity to accept the things I cannot change, the courage to change the things I can, and the wisdom to distinguish the one from the other.
> Reinhold Niebuhr

The Sedona Method and traditional mindfulness practice are also in agreement about not getting involved in positive emotions either; they too are to be understood as forms of holding on and an inevitable obstruction to the free flow of Life. So, for example, if one is in the process of embarking upon a new project, then there will be positive feelings of anticipation as well as more anxious sentiments. The Sedona Method advises us to let go of all associated feelings, and herein lies its virtue: clearing a wide-open space for us to operate effectively without hindrance from any sort of grasping. Holding on just uses energy and locks us into concepts and behaviours from the past. Contrary to our initial expectation, letting go of our likes and dislikes does not turn us into zombies, but instead, permits free rein to our natural intuitions and abilities as they play out in the present moment. Moreover, such a process allows the universe to move through us without having to do battle with our righteous sense of how things should be.

If criticism can be made of the Sedona Method, it is along the same lines as those that we discussed in relation to Focusing. Any 'method' cannot fail to have implicit aims, and any form of goal directedness is in danger of detracting from the rich potential of present experience. Also, although the Sedona Method does not suppress feelings, and indeed works to uncover them, it is not a psychotherapeutic system that is designed to explore the finer nuances of our feeling lives. Nor does it make any such claims. It is, however, a potent aid to self-observation, and for myself, this is its main benefit. This is particularly true when noting Levenson's views on *approval seeking and control.*

In looking at the flow of internal mental traffic, it is positively mind-boggling to see how much of one's mental life is tied to the ego's preoccupation with these two obsessions. Confronted with the sheer oppressiveness of such daily preoccupation, I find it very relieving to 'just let go'. And incidentally, it can be a real help to have a squeeze ball and practise letting go on a purely physical level. The hand has wide representation in the brain, and the physical feeling of release and openness seems to have repercussions in other brain centres.

We find another personal account of letting go in the writings of the psychiatrist and spiritual teacher David Hawkins, who at age fifty found himself in a remarkably similar situation to Les Levenson. In his book, *Letting Go,* he lists two pages of the physical and psychological complaints with which he was continually afflicted, despite two hours of meditation per day, a successful and rewarding career and obsessive dietary practices. Like Levenson, he realised that there was something profoundly wrong with his attitude to life and so he sensibly set to work discovering what it was. Hawkins concluded that (a) he suffered a profound sense of guilt over his various sins of omission and commission, and (b) he had been disdainful of his feelings which were forced to play second fiddle to his dominating rational mind.

Utilizing the way of forgiveness, as laid out in *A Course in Miracles*, helped enormously with his guilt, but Hawkins is not explicit as to how he came upon the idea of acknowledging and then surrendering feelings. Whatever the origins of his final approach, it seems that letting go was very effective in resolving his illnesses, but not before a host of formerly suppressed feelings surfaced that needed processing and surrendering. Here is one of Hawkins' basic principles on how to let go:

> We surrender a feeling by allowing it to be there without condemning, judging or resisting it. We simply look at it, observe it, and allow it to be felt without trying to modify it. With the willingness to relinquish a feeling, it will run out in due time.
> (*Letting Go*, page 296)

There is a clear echo of Jack Huber here.

With both feelings and physical complaints, Hawkins advises us to concentrate solely on sensations and to refrain from labelling. This resonates with themes from Chapter 3 and the idea of allowing sensations to dissipate by holding them in openness. When we truly feel the freedom and energy of our own ever-present spaciousness, then all personal reactivity and associated sensations and feelings are experienced as a painful contraction. Having felt and seen this, there is no sensible course other than release. Why hold on to something that is literally cramping our style?

Understanding the nature of what we are grasping is all important. As Jean Klein comments, things leave us of their own accord when we understand that they cannot keep their promises. Using any sort of discipline or method to let go introduces a subtle, agenda-based violence that detracts from the natural process of surrender that discernment entrains.

Being able to really let go must be based on a profound understanding of one's limitations as a separate entity.

If letting go were easy, however, the human race would be in a very different condition. Just imagine people giving up beliefs that were not working for them, unproductive negative (and positive) emotions, old resentments, toxic relationships, the need to be right etc. But this is not the usual way with us mortals. I would mention Tavris and Aronson again, who point out in their book *Mistakes Were Made (but not by me)* that most humans are intractably stubborn in the face of their own fallibility, even to the point of allowing gross miscarriages of justice rather than admit to an error. No, the simple truth is that it usually takes catastrophic failure in some shape or form before we will let go of our cherished habits and miseries.

Looking at the biographies of great historical figures, I am struck by how often some personal 'rock bottom' experience marked a critical turning point in their maturation. This was particularly true for Dr Bob and Bill W., the founders of Alcoholics Anonymous. Both men had been enthusiastic drinkers from an early age and had arrived at middle age with a trail of drink-related destruction behind them. They had proven to themselves again and again that they were not able to stay sober by either their own volition or with the help of family and friends. They had nowhere to turn except to give themselves over to an intelligence greater than their own. This fundamental transformation in attitude became the basis of the AA philosophy and the Twelve Steps, the first three of which state:

> We admitted we were powerless over alcohol – that our lives had become unmanageable.
>
> Came to believe that a power greater than ourselves could restore us to sanity.
>
> Made a decision to turn our will and our lives over to the

care of God *as we understood Him.*

When I worked in the alcohol and drug field in the 1980s, cognitive behavioural methods were being newly introduced to treat addicts. I remember how contemptuous some of the CBT (cognitive-behavioural therapy) practitioners were of the Twelve Step programme and what they perceived as its semi-mystical approach to psychological change. For the CBT brigade it was all about systematically gaining *more* control of thoughts, feelings and behaviours. One of the gurus in this field of scientifically-based, incremental change was an American professor called Bill Miller. Professor Miller, who incidentally was not an AA detractor, came to Australia in 1989 on sabbatical, and I had the pleasure of meeting him. Imagine my surprise when he told me that he had taken a year off to research sudden, dramatic personal transformations. He subsequently published accounts of such instances, together with his personal conclusions about 'conversion' in the book: *Quantum Change.*

On opening his book I was glad to see that he had introduced his subject with reference to George Bailey's epiphany in *It's a Wonderful Life,* as well as to my favourite Dickens novel, *A Christmas Carol.* Miller rightly points out that both stories are set at the winter solstice, a time when the sun reaches its lowest ebb and is resurrected after the shortest day (in the northern hemisphere). Many of the other stories that he recounts also have the flavour of renewal after a descent to the bottom, while others seem to come about after a prolonged period in which an individual feels an increasing discrepancy between what they are as a person and what they aspire to be. Whatever the circumstances, however, there seemed to be a gesture from a greater or higher reality which embraced, informed and broadened the personality. The recipients of this grace felt accepted, cared for and part of something infinitely benign.

Such experiences are comprehensible when we think back to

systems theory and remember that a problem arising in a part cannot, as a rule, be solved at the level of that part. There has to be a higher or more comprehensive view to change the dynamic relationship of the part to the whole. In the case of human systems, this means that we have to hold a certain openness to that which we cannot yet conceive. This spacious waiting without waiting for something specific puts aside our desires and fears and allows the possibility of the new. We cannot command the Spirit, but we can put ourselves aside as far as possible and humbly wait on the ineffable.

While insight and failure seem to be important precursors of letting go, they by no means fully encompass the many roads that may lead to the same result. One important avenue, for example, simply relies on the natural release processes that continually recur during the normal course of a day. The first of these is the breath cycle and the yang/yin complementarity between inspiration and expiration. On the in-breath we become more alert, there is stimulation of the sympathetic nervous system and the heart speeds up. On the out-breath, the obverse occurs and there is a natural relaxation and letting go. All worthwhile stress management and relaxation routines take advantage of this phenomenon, and bring attention to the fact that one can 'surf' this inherent tendency to let go on the out-breath at any time.

Less commonly appreciated is the ultradian cycle of twenty minute breaks that the body/mind naturally takes every one and a half to two hours. These rest periods are signalled by the desire to snack or have a short rest, and correspond to a slowdown in brain activity and sometimes to a switch in cerebral dominance. During these periods the brain easily lets go and changes to a more diffuse focus that facilitates daydreaming and creative ideas. The ultradian pause used to be enshrined in the morning and afternoon tea breaks, but such sane institutions have long ceased to function in the high-pressure atmosphere of most modern workplaces. This is a pity, because by ignoring Nature's regular prompts to rest, we build up undischarged tension which has to be dealt with during sleep. We also forego opportunities for briefly letting go and allowing our minds to creatively process whatever they see fit.

Even if we ricochet through our day without a pause we finally have to let go in sleep. We seldom give our slumber much thought, but it is sobering to consider that our normal 'I' sense with all its accompanying self-importance is so easily snuffed out. There is no question of us letting it go – it is let go for us! No wonder, then, that spiritual authorities have often recommended the period before sleep as an excellent time for daily review and systematic release. It is likely that such a habit facilitates the natural sorting and elimination that occurs during our nocturnal excursions, and helps clean the slate for the coming day. As Keats has it:

> O magic sleep! O comfortable bird / That broodest o'er the troubled sea of mind / Till it is hushed and smooth.

As with self-remembering and creating mental space, it is likely that most of us have never been educated about our options in such important matters. Rather, we have stumbled upon letting go either through failure or its close relative, hitting our heads against a brick wall. We have all, at some time, felt the enormous relief that comes after a period of strenuous activity, whether it was after an examination, a period of gruelling exercise or any manner of lengthy effort. When exhausted, either during an activity or afterwards, we are temporarily released from extraneous agendas and a natural space opens up. Here is an example of this kind of experience from Joseph Chilton Pearce's *Exploring the Crack in the Cosmic Egg*:

> I was about twelve years old at the time and it happened on a long hike at summer camp. We had been walking for about

> three hours and I was tired and sweaty. I was climbing a path, looking at the ground. The sun was very hot. Suddenly I felt as if scales had fallen from my eyes. The grass became intensely green, the pebbles on the path were shimmering with reality. I felt as if I had never truly seen the world before this moment (pages 207/8).

There is a parallel here with the Jacobson method of relaxation in which one tenses a muscle in order to feel the sensation of relaxation when one releases it. (Interestingly, the approach seems to work well despite the fact that it leaves more residual tension in a muscle than if you had just let go in the first place!) There is also a resonance with Ramana Maharshi's point that the satisfaction that comes from fulfilling a desire actually derives from the brief period of relief it affords us before craving and aversion kick back into action again.

I gained a further insight into this process when discussing Transcendental Meditation with an experienced practitioner. He told me that the best part of his daily practice was the space between finishing meditation and recommencing his daily round. This set me wondering about the effects of the more uncompromising meditation approaches found in traditions such as Zen. Sitting cross-legged for hours, often in continuous discomfort and with no distracting influences apart from one's own mind, seems to fit the brick wall definition pretty well. Although not wanting to detract from the many benefits of Zen practice, I cannot help but think that the completion may be just as enlightening as the participation – the blackbird singing and then the silence.

Exhausting the ego's tendencies certainly plays a part in the more 'muscular' disciplines such as Zen or the Gurdjieff work, and the idea also crops up in many individual accounts of transformation. But sometimes the process is less dramatic and we just get exhausted with ourselves and our continuous efforts to mould the world into our own image. At some point, often from midlife onwards, it increasingly seems not worth the candle. We get fed up with ourselves and a chink opens in our armour. There is the possibility of space.

If, however, insight, failure, biorhythms and brick walls have not opened the door for you, then you may wish to follow Tim Burkett's advice (*nothing holy about it*) and just let be; have faith in the dissolving effects of time. John Welwood's recommendation is similar – be with experience without trying to control it. There is a proviso, however: if letting be allows unwanted guests to start taking over your life, then going into the issue fully, through Focusing or some other psychotherapeutic avenue, may be the best option. There is always fear at the root of our reluctance to be free, especially when we intuit that we will be left with nothing fixed to hang on to.

And there is one final avenue to letting go which plays as a subtle variation on the themes we have already explored – ignorance. Red Hawk explains in the following passage from *Self Remembering* (page 91):

> It is not my business to change what is in me. I cannot do it, even if I desire to. I don't know anything. I am ignorant, driven by habit and lies, and it is this complex of intellect and emotion which desires to change things. Only chaos and sorrow can result. The fact is that it is the job of our Creator to create change within. My business, my real work, is to place myself in the position of receiving help from Above. This help from above is always, always available, but I do not know how to access it. Instead, I constantly believe that I can do it myself – in fact must do it myself. It is a long process of intentional suffering which leads me to the realization that I know nothing and can do nothing about my situation. No matter how hard I try, nothing changes. I am helpless before my habits and my life is out of control.

The work of Byron Katie moves along similar lines, using a careful questioning method to examine whether tightly-held beliefs are true. It is sobering to realise the insubstantial basis of our personal dogmas and that these thoughts usually engender negative feeling states and behaviours.

For me, the crucial step is to consider that I am being harmed by an idea or emotion; why then would I not let go, especially when the harm comes from a thought whose ultimate validity I cannot establish? Continual letting go of thoughts, whether 'good' or 'bad', leaves a person in what Katie describes as her favourite position: "I don't know."

> ***And the affective companion to ignorance is wonder. And its physical companion is stillness.***

This way of ignorance is a hard road to follow though; it goes against our every mental fibre and is an affront to the iron grip of internal controllers and managers. Perhaps it is a way that we can only really follow in the wake of desperate circumstances. In fact, I think that ultimately some form of existential turmoil, either chronic or acute, has to be brewing before we can really let go in a profound way. It is very much a process that is thrust upon us, often as a result of the final giving up that comes from having nowhere else to go and seeing very clearly the emptiness of all our seeking and craving. At last we realise that surrendering to the unknown is in fact safer than trying to manage on our own.

There is also something highly paradoxical about trying to let go; about intending to be non-intentional. Eugen Herrigel came up against this conundrum during his study of Japanese archery after World War II. In his book *Zen in the Art of Archery*, he describes how, after an initial period of study, he began to realise that somehow he was expected to hit the target without trying. This did not compute in his Western mind, and so he asked his teacher how it was possible to deliberately be non-deliberate. The archery master replied that he had never been asked that question before!

The master's very Zen response is a cue for me to cease and desist from further attempts at explanation. There is a point at which words must give way to a noble silence when faced with these mysteries. We can say only that clearing a space for Spirit is all that we can aspire to, and that waiting and letting be is the 'posture' of our discipline. All else is Grace.

I give the final word to Jennifer Kavanagh, from her marvellous volume *A Little Book of Unknowing*:

> Not knowing is at the centre of spiritual life. It is only by creating a space in which anything can happen that we allow God to speak; only by stepping back that we allow space for that unpredictable Spirit that brings us gifts beyond any of our imaginings. Without that space, we are wedded to our expectations and busyness, our ego-enhancing preoccupations (page 48).

In the next chapter I consider something equally mysterious: how spaciousness and boundedness work together in the psychological realm.

7

Mending Fences, Retrieving Souls

Tis sweet to feel with what fine spun threads our affections are drawn together.
Laurence Sterne

Boundaries

When Judith Blackstone began working to help her clients increase their sense of spaciousness, she noticed that simultaneously they experienced an enhanced feeling of solidity. Similarly, she found that the facilitation of grounding, downward movements produced an upward surge of energy. Both observations are elegant expressions of the interdependence of opposites, and the Taoist idea that complementarities constantly give rise to one another.

Nowhere does this play of opposites express itself more dramatically than in the mind, and to help find our way in this shifting realm, we can be guided by that familiar antinomic pair:

CONNECTION / separation

When we consider the brain aspect of mind, this equation underscores the daunting task of integrating the activity of 80 billion separate neurons into coherent correlates of perception and behaviour. As far as our subjective lives go, the challenge is to integrate our personal concerns and priorities with the vast field of psycho-socio-eco-spiritual influences within which we are embedded. Thus, both physiologically and psychologically, the task is to maintain:

UNITY WITHIN DIVERSITY / diversity within unity

As discussed elsewhere, the mind, by definition, is a boundary maker, and its knowledge comes from the circumscription of experience into compartments. It *abstracts* (separates) from the plenum of data to which it is exposed in every moment, and creates a fence around relevant packets of information. These packets then become *integrated* (connected) into broader pre-existing knowledge networks. This is what my brain is doing while writing this book. It has a very big file called Living Space and is constantly on the lookout for data and experiences that may be relevant to it. It also does the trick discussed before, of moulding my perceptions to fit this file's evolving shape.

The Living Space file is quite large and is currently controlling much of my behaviour. Consequently I have to periodically compartmentalize it to keep it from taking over entirely. Large files can do this and need to be kept in their place. As the Australian spiritual teacher Barry Long was fond of saying, the mind assumes that you love whatever you put into it and so wants to give you more of the same!

Whatever the topic, however, cognitive processes follow the same pattern of iterating sequences of abstraction and integration. And it's abstraction/integration (separation/Connection) all the way down.

The boundary issue is so central to our psychological reality that it surprises me that the literature on the subject is quite sparse. An exception is Ernest Hartmann's *Boundaries in the Mind*, in which he suggests that there is a spectrum of boundary characteristics from thin to thick. He proposes that people with 'thin' boundaries tend to be less black and white in their thinking, and are more likely to answer a question by saying "it all depends". They often experience more dream recall, have vivid imaginations and may even be prone to unusual states of consciousness. They are generally more sensitive to the feelings of others, have greater empathy with children and may be less clear about what they think or feel in relation to a particular topic, mainly because the distinction between thinking and feeling is more blurred. Interestingly, such people are also less likely to discriminate on the basis of social group or nationality, and tend to think of themselves in individual rather than group terms i.e. they are less territorial. Thick boundary individuals have opposing features, as the following research shows.

Hartmann investigated 866 people and categorised them according to their total scores on his Boundary Questionnaire. His research then compared the twenty people who scored highest for thin boundaries, with the twenty who scored highest for thick boundaries. The thick boundary group consisted of six women and fourteen men whose occupations tended toward business, law and engineering. This group did not contain any teachers, health or human services workers or artists. All members of this group seemed normal and fairly conventional and reported very little dream recall.

The twenty 'thinnest' scorers within the group were, as we might expect, very different indeed. There were seventeen women and only three men, and the group contained no lawyers, no engineers and no business executives. Four of the group were homemakers, three were teachers, two were artists and the rest were one of a kind (for example, a nurse, a labourer, a counsellor etc). Recall of dreams was very high and none of the individuals seemed to be conventional or perfectionistic.

Hartmann also notes that the two boundary types seem to have a different sensory focus or 'bandwidth' with 'thin' individuals having a less focused, more diffuse style.

When I read Hartmann's findings I looked at the first twenty of my clients who fit the thin boundary description. Their professions were:

3 Teachers, 3 Psychotherapists, 2 Housewives/mothers, 2 Gardeners, 1 Artist, 2 Nurses, 2 Secretaries, 1 Writer, 1 IT Consultant, 1 Carpenter and 1 Clinical Psychologist.

The Importance of Temperament

From my knowledge of these individuals it seemed obvious to me that Hartmann's findings are another perspective on the well-established differences between introverts and extraverts. These terms, which literally mean turned inward and outward, date back to Jung's original descriptions from 1921, and since that time have become embedded in the popular psyche as well as in psychological research. It is difficult to do justice to our current knowledge about this typology in just a few lines, but here are a few distinguishing features:

Introverts tend to be anxious, pessimistic, low in mood and energy, emotionally restrained, quiet, thoughtful, reflective, empathic and creative. They are very sensitive to all forms of stimulation: physical (e.g. coffee, noise), psychological (e.g. interpersonal conflict) and social (e.g. large groups of people). They need plenty of quiet time to digest their impressions and to recover their energy.

Extraverts are entirely different, tending to: low anxiety, good mood, unreasonable optimism, high energy, competitiveness, impulsive action and emotional insensitivity. Extraverts actually come in two varieties: physical and social. The former are more concerned with physical adventurousness and the latter with social contact.

Both introversion and extraversion are modified by a range of other personality factors, the most significant of which is the systematising/empathising distinction that I explore in Chapter 13.

Versions of introversion and extraversion are to be found throughout the animal kingdom, and both constitutions have different evolutionary advantages. For our purposes, however, it is sufficient to know that the overriding feature of introverts is their exquisite sensitivity to stimulation and their constant battle to keep within reasonable arousal levels. For this reason, the American psychologist Elaine Aron has called them Highly Sensitive People or HSPs. Her book, *The Highly Sensitive Person* is a must-read for introverts.

The increased porosity of the HSP boundaries means that more information, both in the form of substances and sensory impressions, can enter their system and then permeate more widely through somatic and psychological space. This explains why HSPs need more 'downtime' to digest, assimilate, compartmentalize and clarify their impressions. In fact, there is quite a close parallel to the HSP eating pattern where we see a lower tolerance for large meals, more food sensitivities and less time for proper digestion, especially when there is 'intestinal hurry' caused by stress. The boundary characteristics of sensitive individuals also means that they need longer to sort 'the wheat from the chaff', and to properly deal with psychological as well as physical toxins.

The increased traffic between thinking and feeling in introverts may indicate better communication between the two sides of the brain, a trait that is associated with greater creativity and which occurs more frequently in mixed-handedness (see Chapter 13). The downside of this characteristic is that thinking is too often coloured by anxiety and that a pessimistic hue can colour all potentially beneficial plans. There may also be difficulty in 'turning down' emotion to leave a clear space for logical thought.

Extraverts, on the other hand, need to seek out stimulation to remain interested and awake. Their thicker boundaries need more penetrating stimuli to keep information flowing at an optimal rate.

Interestingly, traditional Hindu medicine (Ayurveda) sees these temperament distinctions in much the same way. There are three basic constitutions or doshas in Ayurveda:

Vata – thin, anxious types with low energy and poor digestion.

Pitta – robust, athletic, aggressive types with high energy and libido.

Kapha – sedentary, sociable, calm types with a tendency to obesity.

Various combinations of these basic traits are possible, but the ideal is to have a balance of all three doshas. Ayurveda sees temperament and physical constitution as being strongly linked, and this agrees with the findings of WH Sheldon in the 1930s and 40s. He found a moderately strong correlation between psychological and physical traits, so that, for example, thinness and sensitivity often go together, as do muscularity and aggressiveness. Our modern way of viewing these differences is mainly from an evolutionary standpoint: a group of animals such as a baboon colony profits from having individual members with a variety of traits. Sensitive animals can give early warning of danger, more aggressive individuals provide leadership and defence and sociable types help to smooth over the internal group conflicts. The situation is very similar in human society; in fact our daily antics are embarrassingly similar to those seen amongst our primate cousins.

The social dynamic of the three doshas also mirrors the principal survival functions found in an individual: defence, foraging/fighting and social connection. These in turn reflect the universal 'Law of Three', as propounded in various esoteric systems and crystallised by Gurdjieff as the denying, affirming and reconciling forces of creation.

The Hindu explanation for individual differences is cast in terms of the five elements: Vata is a mixture of Ether and Air, Pitta is Fire, and Kapha is a combination of Water and Earth. I find this imagery very useful in remembering the key features of each type and how they will react to different foods, weathers, stresses and to other doshas. The idea of airiness, for example, is more evocative to me than the concept of thin boundaries. And when I think of an extremely airy (Vata) individual, I can immediately intuit their major characteristics:

Excess Air: openness to sensation, expansive imagination, diffuse self-sense and tendency to dissociation, changeability/variability, sensitivity to wind and falling barometric pressure and problems with 'airy' foods, for example fruits.

Deficient Fire: low energy and drive, low self-confidence, lack of digestive fire and difficulty with uncooked food.

Deficient Earth and Water: lack of persistence, ungroundedness and low sociability.

At first glance the use of this imagery may seem naïve and even medieval, but practical use of this method has convinced me of its utility. If parallels between our constitutional make-up and Nature's elements seem odd to the modern mind, this simply suggests to me how alienated we have become from our physical selves and the natural world.

Gender also makes a difference. Women tend to have thinner boundaries and to be better at empathic connection; in Ayurvedic terms they are more Vata/Kapha. Men are just as social as women, but their interpersonal style tends to be less intimate. Testosterone promotes Pitta fire, strengthens boundaries and reduces Vata sensitivity.

In summary, the concept of Connection/separation goes a long way to explain the extraversion/introversion dichotomy, and is also a way of understanding the intricate play of the five elements. As a universal dynamic we should not be surprised that it has explanatory value in both modern and traditional frameworks.

Windows and Shutters in the Brain

Contemporary research has revealed just how modular the brain is, with separate functions located in distinct anatomical sites. Each module has submodules and, yes, there are modules all the way down to the cellular level. If I am going into action with a particular goal in mind, I don't want unnecessary interference or 'noise' from other brain modules that are not immediately required. It is very important therefore that superfluous traffic across boundaries is suppressed. The chemical dopamine accomplishes this feat, as well as being a principal transmitter involved in good mood, working hard for rewards and high energy: lots of the stuff is released when you take stimulants. Not surprisingly, it also works in the eye to suppress diffuse (rod cell) vision and enhance detailed (cone cell) vision. Taken together, these properties of the dopamine system help to explain the behavioural features of extraverts, and also illustrate how elegantly and parsimoniously Nature orders her control systems.

Testosterone (T) has a similar effect in consolidating boundaries i.e. like dopamine it is a *separative influence*. The reason is clear: in their past role as hunters and defenders, men were wont to encounter dangerous situations and did not need excessive fear or sentiment interfering with the task at hand. Similar considerations apply to the rest of the animal kingdom, with male hormones promoting dominance, aggression and sexual success. Testosterone contributes to these traits by facilitating a focused, unsentimental state characterised by superior cognitive function. Interestingly, T's role in boosting motivation and competitiveness is mitigated in social groups where the approval of others is important. The message is clear – you can modify over-dominant behaviour through the consensus feedback of valued peers.

Incredibly, the 'big T' begins its work in the womb, when testosterone from the foetal testes selectively moulds the developing brain to de-emphasise empathy and nurturing circuits and to promote abilities like spatial awareness. No wonder, then, that many men seem somewhat lacking in the finer emotions and are 'project' rather than relationship orientated. At the far end of this spectrum, the cold psychopath is so compartmentalized that his personal agendas are unaffected by fear of consequences or social disapproval. Such individuals are free to pursue their selfish ends with no consideration other than what they can get away with.

The potent combination of dopamine and testosterone produces a physiological state ideal for competitive sport or war. John Coates' book, *The Hour Between Dog and Wolf*, describes the effects of this heady cocktail on stock exchange traders. After a winning trade, both hormones surge, giving rise to greater risk-taking, impulsiveness and grandiosity. It is then a small step to enter a vicious spiral that can end in huge gains or catastrophic losses. Consequently it is no surprise that, as on the battlefield, this particular profession is not known for its longevity.

The situation with female sex hormones is much more complex and nuanced. There is partial validity to the idea that oestrogen is energising and mood enhancing and that progesterone has an overall calming effect; the two hormones often seem to function in a yang/yin way. But research into their actions, from the biochemical to the behavioural, makes it clear that we generalise at our peril. The reason for this is not hard to fathom: the cyclic nature of their actions and the dramatic changes that occur over the life cycle mean that their effects are very firmly embedded within a broader psycho-social context. This is also illustrated in the case of women's testosterone production. Women naturally have much lower levels of testosterone, but still benefit when it surges in anticipation of a challenge. However, they do not experience this effect if playing against another woman with whom they are friendly.

We are on slightly firmer ground with the transmitter serotonin, a brain transmitter with a very different profile from dopamine. Serotonin circuits participate in a wide variety of functions including the regulation of mood, appetite, weight, biorhythms, sleep and reproduction. I tend to sum up its activities as being homeostatic and balancing in nature, with serotonin pathways forming the hub of an organism's self-regulation. As such, serotonin systems have to coordinate and communicate with a number of different modules and thus act as *connectors par excellence.*

There is an ongoing debate as to whether anxious and depressed individuals have too much or too little activity in their serotonin systems. It is customary to tell such individuals, who are often HSPs, that they have a serotonin deficiency which needs to be corrected with antidepressants. It is more likely, however, that they are producing an excess of the neurotransmitter in an attempt to restore balance to their overstimulated brains. The actuality may be more nuanced, with both over- and underactive areas becoming increasingly out of synchrony under the influence of stress. There is an analogy with insufficiently regulated societies where the rich get richer, the poor get poorer and social upheaval is the result.

Serotonin's place as the darling of neuroscience has, however, been usurped by a new star on the block. Oxytocin, or the "moral molecule" as Paul Zak calls it, is associated with a wide variety of social connecting functions from bonding with children to trusting strangers. The brain systems that use this transmitter could be viewed as one of humanity's redeeming features. Without their nurturing and connecting bias, our social lives would resemble the rough and tumble of a monkey colony, only with guns. In some places this frightening picture is all too real and, of course, it's almost always males causing the trouble. There is a qualification to the oxytocin story, however: it can increase wariness and aggression when someone is identified as a potential threat to your home group. With hormones in particular, it is always good to enquire about the 'other side of the coin' and the broader context in which they are operating.

As we might expect, oxytocin circuits are inhibited by testosterone as it tries to free the brain's action modules from interference, but it is not all bad news. As men age and their testosterone levels decline, they become less competitive and more nurturing; even a tyrannical father may turn into a reasonable grandfather. Add the fact that pair bonding and reproducing have a similar T lowering effect, and we begin to understand how our human social world turns out to be a workable proposition and not a never-ending *Mad Max* movie.

Pair bonding civilises men, and trends to later marriage simply create excessive numbers of high T males who have nothing to do but create trouble.

Compartmentalization in the brain is also very dependent on the dominant neural rhythm, with fast frequencies associated with less inter-module communication. The reasons are very much the same as with testosterone: brain rhythms in the faster beta range tend to be associated with focused narrow attention or states of arousal. Both circumstances imply the need to screen out competing requests from areas not germane to the matter in hand. The obverse situation is reminiscent of Les Fehmi's finding that Open Focus is associated with synchronous alpha, a slower brainwave pattern that connects and coheres our experience into a multidimensional whole.

This brings us back to introverts with their thin boundaries and propensity to overstimulation. All highly sensitive people have had to develop strategies from early in their lives to deal with low mood, anxiety and the impact of excessive sensory load. Some of these coping mechanisms include avoidance, bodily tensing, obsessional control rituals (as in eating disorders), perfectionism and drugs. These strategies all aim for one thing: to create a non-threatening, low stimulus safety zone in which they can feel secure, and where 'noise' in the nervous system subsides to a point that allows clear thinking and self-regulation. At the best of times, it can be difficult to pick up the internal promptings that signal a need or a new direction. When the noise/signal ratio is high, it becomes impossible to know our own minds and we tend to completely shut down and withdraw.

Turning Down the Noise

The usual approach to stress overwhelm is to train people to relax and then help them generalise their low arousal skills into everyday life. Such training would be straightforward were it not for the fact that most of our stress comes from other people. HSPs are particularly vulnerable to having their boundaries violated by insensitive types, and so need to learn skills that will allow them to be more assertive with more resilient psychological and relational 'skins'.

Methods which aim to reinforce armouring against the world are fine, but they never become second nature to HSPs. This is why sensitive individuals must also choose a life path which allows them to have adequate time to themselves, and which minimizes exposure to toxic people and circumstances. This is a big ask, of course, but essential if they are to avoid overwhelm. Their particular creative outlet must also be a matter of priority, and this may mean that they have to sacrifice a measure of prosperity for the spiritual and artistic demands of the inner life. How HSPs partner up with their intimates is another issue of crucial importance, and Elaine Aron has dealt with this topic very thoroughly in *The Highly Sensitive Person in Love.*

Many of the approaches that are tried with HSPs could be called 'yang' methods, because they involve active learning and doing. They do not, however, play to the HSP's strong suites of sensitivity and in-sight, and instead emphasise toughening up to meet the challenges of an extraverted world. But given that yang is always in dynamic relationship with yin, we should also look to complementary methods that align with the HSP's more yin nature. Judith Blackstone's work is one such approach that is very aligned to the needs of sensitive individuals. Some of the more important themes that I have garnered from her work are listed below. I present them as 'one liners' because that is the way I remember things, but please read her books or take a course with her to fully understand the richness of this path.

Feeling fundamental consciousness in the body anchors and steadies the mind and provides safety in its ever-present sense of being.

Feeling the spaciousness of one's natural presence and the continuity of that space with one's surroundings allows one to take up space rather than contract under the impact of world overwhelm.

Feeling the basic qualities of fundamental consciousness in the body (e.g. strength, sexuality, compassion), and feeling those qualities as intrinsic to one's nature, provides an effective antidote to the HSP's tendency toward doubt, guilt and shame.

Just as the physical act of sinking down and surrendering to gravity produces a reciprocal upward current of energy, so does sinking into the tenderness of one's own being generate an outward movement of confidence and solidity.

Experiencing how breath and emotions can move through stillness and space without perturbing them provides a foundation for working with difficult and potentially overwhelming feelings. In a preparatory exercise, Blackstone throws a small imaginary ball toward her client. HSPs will tend to react by tensing up, but with practice, can learn to stay in their fundamental and spacious consciousness and let the ball pass right through them. Interestingly, I came across this exercise many years ago, in a book on Tibetan healing; it's always gratifying to find innovation confirmed by ancient wisdom.

Blackstone's methods are especially useful for those who have been victims of trauma, either as a child or an adult. Sensitive individuals easily leave their bodies under the influence of trauma, a process which in Ayurvedic terms is an extension of their normal tendency toward 'airiness' and 'spacing out' (airy/ethereal quality = dissociation). Sensing into fundamental consciousness allows them to ground within the same spaciousness that was their salvation during traumatic episodes, but which later became a trap, cutting them off from life.

Other approaches include Richard Miller's iRest programme which is ideally suited to HSPs and has a practical foundation based on yoga nidra. Skilfully implemented tactile therapies are also particularly appropriate for the Vata constitution, whose sensitive skin is a 'royal road' to calming the nervous system. As I have pointed out before, the skin and nervous tissue share a common embryonic origin and so easily talk to one another.

Both Les Fehmi and Judith Blackstone emphasise the continuity of space across our internal boundaries as well as those with the external world. This reminds us that boundaries *both connect and separate* and thus mark an area of dynamic change. People who live near a cultural border may speak more than one language and consume food that it is an interesting hybrid of different cuisines. Back in the capital, people are sure of their identity and behave accordingly, but at the border things are more complex and fluid. An even more interesting situation evolves when the border trails off into nothingness as it does in the desert or the far North. In this liminal region, literally on the rim, we find the interface between known and unknown, something and nothing, worldly and unworldly.

Understanding that mental landscapes are no different in their topography prompts us to contemplate our own wild places and the strange creatures that live there. Dreams provide an obvious starting point because they defy the easy interpretations that we would like to make from our 'city' view of things. Jung understood this well, and worked by creatively interacting with the dream life rather than applying clever cognitive templates and pat answers. As we develop the habit of spaciousness, waiting and letting be, we begin to notice that our personal topography or 'cosmic egg' is full of holes. Intuitions, premonitions, strange encounters and synchronicities of all kinds can leak through into consensus reality when we drop our ideas of how things are or should be.

Fissures in our cultural and collective dream are also the

stuff of extra-sensory perception, magic, flying saucers and the realms of 'wyrd', the mysterious net from Celtic mythology that connects all things together. As George Hansen points out in his book *The Trickster and the Paranormal*, creative individuals try to live on the margins of conventional society in order to explore both the personal and the collective lacunae that reside there. Traditional healers fall into the same category and are often identified early in life as a little odd or eccentric. Their capacity to connect beyond the well-worn cultural paths is both valued and feared, collective sentiments which may confer honour or vilification.

Liminal zones are points of contact with the long connections that join a local cluster to the greater whole. Artists, mystics and healers hold on to the delicate balance that these connections require, maintaining their sanity while journeying into the realms of non-consensus reality. It is the long connections that make themselves known in everyday life through hunches, intuitions and physical sensations, showing us that the world is essentially magical, fluid and alive. It is we who are stuck in boxes of our own making, unhappy at how cramped the conditions have become.

Separation/connection (again)

One of the most striking things about humans is their incredible variety of bodies and personalities. Nature seems to thrive on diversity, not least because differences fuel the creative dynamic of complex systems, and an evolving, adaptive system is one that survives and grows. Or as Goethe put it: "Individuality seems to be Nature's whole aim – and she cares nothing for individuals." This situation is, however, one of those Goldilocks scenarios where too much individuality leads to chaos and too little ends in stasis. There is a sweet spot in every social grouping where separativeness and community (connection) are in optimum balance. I leave it to the reader to contemplate where our contemporary societies might be on such a spectrum.

Our individual personalities are an admixture of the inherited traits of temperament, such as those that we discussed above, and the individual habits, attitudes and sentiments that are acquired through social conditioning. These sets of behavioural dispositions interact in complex ways to produce what we refer to as the adult personality, most of which seems to have evolved in the service of our desires and fears. The personality is not a static entity, however, and the trend in contemporary thought is to ascribe a great deal of mutability to our adult characteristics, especially in the face of changing social circumstances.

Judith Rich Harris is an American psychologist whose controversial writings mainly address issues around the development of personality. In *No Two Alike,* she has summed up a child's developmental process in a very succinct way, pointing to three major tasks as follows:

> Learning to get on with the various people in your life (with peers in childhood being every bit as important as immediate family). This is the ***relationship system***, which answers the question: "Who are my friends?"
>
> Learning to adapt to the culture as a whole and to behave in acceptable ways: the ***socialisation system***, which answers the question: "How do I fit in?"
>
> Learning to compete with others to find a niche where you can be successful and where your individual attributes give you an edge: the ***status system***, which answers the questions: "Where am I in the pecking order?" and "How do I stand out as an individual?"

Harris astutely points out that it is the conflict between the latter two systems that drives most personal development. People like to conform, but they also usually want to compete. Handling such complexity requires a reasonable amount of brain power and a good deal of self-control. It is hardly surprising, then, that long-term studies of child development show that self-control is a major determinant of life success on a number of parameters. The situation becomes even more interesting when we consider the findings of Amy Chua (*The Triple Package* with J. Rubenfeld) and others, that another key to 'success' is a constant sense of dissatisfaction with oneself. Taken together, these arguments strongly support the idea that what we call the everyday personality is principally separative in nature, or to use John Welwood's words: "... an activity of judgment, control and resistance."

Pecking Orders

Interestingly, the most popular current personality tests do not have a direct measure for competitiveness, despite the fact that it is the most dominant theme in contemporary society, underpinning economics, politics, art, religion, sport and the life of most institutions. Competition between groups seems to be particularly hard-wired into our brains, and it is truly frightening to see the ease with which an invocation of 'us and them' robs most people of any vestige of empathy or critical intelligence.

Thankfully, civilisation is possible because there are countervailing trends in both persons and groups, and we can summarise them as openness to experience, humility and the capacity to empathise, connect and cooperate. Thus we come back to that time-worn dichotomy between power and control and love and cooperation.

Throughout history this dialectic has worked itself out in endless violent conflicts, with societies under threat inevitably adopting the default position of hierarchical power and exploitation. The mindless historical repetition of this pattern has everything to do with the male propensity for competitiveness and domination, and testosterone's unerring capacity to separate purpose from sentiment. Women's natural bias toward dyadic relationships, connection and empathy may yet save us from the collective dislocations that currently beset us, but it will be a close-run thing.

Hierarchies constrict social space and limit freedom. When I 'know my place', I am less likely to know myself. This may suit many who wish to trade freedom for security, a fact borne out by surveys that demonstrate greater insecurity levels on the conservative side of politics. Such social constraint runs counter to what most of us feel in our bones, however: that we are all equal as humans and deserve to be respected accordingly, by others and by ourselves.

The inevitable drift toward hierarchy to which we and our mammalian relatives are subject gives rise to what I jokingly call 'Holman's Law':

> Most psychological distress results from or is exacerbated by finding oneself at the bottom of a social hierarchy, whether this is in the family, school, work, religion or any other human group.

After forty years of clinical practice in psychiatry, I cannot remember any exceptions to this rule. And there don't appear to be any exceptions in the animal world either; it doesn't matter if you are a rat, a meerkat or a chimpanzee, being at the bottom of the pecking order is bad for your health. Not only are you oppressed from above, but it is also likely that you are *excluded* from many of the normalising social influences that would provide welcome and nurture. The classic example of this process in our culture is to be found among the chronically mentally ill, a majority of whom tell us that their biggest problem is loneliness.

To add insult to injury, being on top proves very beneficial for mental and physical well-being, and the active bullying of those below you improves your situation even more. This 'winner effect' has been described in great detail by Ian

Robertson in his book of the same name. For example, when equally matched experimental animals such as rats are forced to fight over territory, the winner is more likely to triumph in his next bout with another rat of similar age and size. The loser – well you guessed it. The situation in humans is just the same, with success breeding further success and confidence, whilst failure easily leads to a negative spiral of reduced expectations and depression, the so-called 'giving up response'. Research also tells us this situation is compounded by the fact that as people climb the greasy pole, they become less empathic toward those lower down in the pecking order, as well as progressively more unrealistic in their self-appraisals. The logical outcome of these trends underpins the standard right wing response to poverty: that the poor only have themselves to blame and that the rich have obtained their fortunes through sheer hard work and ability.

In human societies, hierarchies quickly become very steep unless tough rules are in place to halt the inevitable trends to extreme inequality. But since the formulation of these rules is subject to the dictates of money, there are huge problems in reforming our social systems. In historical terms, it was only yesterday that our forebears lived under the boot of leaders who thought that they were invested with divine rights: Charles I of Britain was a classic example. Yet all that changed very quickly, so the fact that we are slipping backwards at the moment should not discourage us from making every effort to correct the situation.

It is true that hierarchies are more stable over time than 'flatter' human groups and are easier to manage; the evanescence of most attempts at utopian communal life is eloquent testimony to this fact. However, we must not resign ourselves to a society that disenfranchises a minority in order to secure stability for the rest. Naomi Klein, in her book and film, *This Changes Everything*, makes a strong argument that these human rights issues are inextricably linked with action on climate change. Perhaps the 'big picture', spacious style of thinking that climate change necessitates will bring fresh social action from quarters that we cannot even envisage from our current perspectives.

It is likely though, that change, if it does come, will be led by grass roots movements that take back power and resources from those who are so tenaciously hanging on to the status quo. Thus we have to proceed on two fronts: working for greater social justice and equality as well as dealing with the current casualties of hierarchy in the best way we can, using the limited resources of physical and human capital that are available to us.

As the reader will have gathered, I have spent most of my working life in the mental health realm and I have been impressed by how often my patients have experienced victimisation and exclusion from an early age, usually starting with the family of origin, but just as importantly at school. Children are particularly good at spotting potential victims and quickly move to persecute or exclude peers that they perceive as vulnerable. If a child has been badly treated at home, they will often have a depressed look about them that invites this sort of reaction, but it also happens with temperamentally sensitive, anxious children who are perceived as weaker by their peers. These 'orchid' types need greater security during their formative years, in contrast to the majority of 'dandelions' who get through pretty well with 'good enough' parenting and socialisation.

Fortunately, even a small amount of genuine inclusiveness from a friend, teacher or relative can mitigate many of these harmful effects. We have, for example, many testimonies from artists and writers, supporting the idea that just one interested and protective adult can help turn a potentially disastrous course into a highly creative one. This too is the job of a therapist who, as far as (s)he is able, creates a safe space, free of judgement and free of agendas. This space is ideally also one of equality, by which I mean that the therapist does not assume or wear her badges of status, and the client does not project his expectations of authority on to her. The difficulties of these tasks are considerable, however. So imbued are we with the traditions of hierarchy and status, that much work has to be done in trying to unmask the cultural roots of the therapeutic power imbalance. Often the 'transference' is never resolved, a fact that is hardly surprising in view of the basic paradoxes implicit in being helped. A person goes for help because they perceive the helper as having the power to help. Power confers status.

Healing Fractures

Carl Rogers and other humanistic psychologists attempted to lay out minimal conditions for therapy that would 'level the playing field' somewhat. As well as practising deep empathy, therapists are enjoined to be congruent between their internal sentiments and their external behaviour, and to show unconditional positive regard for clients. Such aims are laudable, but there are still problems with this approach, pithily summed up by Fritz Perls, to the effect that we can't all be saints like Carl Rogers!

So, while we stumble through the beginning, the muddle and the end of the therapeutic process, as all too human therapists and clients, what guiding light can we follow? Long ago I gave myself permission as a therapist to just be what I am: nothing special, ordinary and human in my considerable ignorance. I am often not able to do much except listen to someone's story. But I do take the time to really listen. My special, unspecial talent is to offer the sort of unpressured time that *opens a real spaciousness*, a real sigh of relief.

And if I had to nominate some overarching principle of healing, I would point to the following story from Gerald Epstein. In his book *Healing Visualizations*, Epstein describes how his practice of fairly conventional Freudian therapy was totally transformed by meeting the remarkable Madame Aboulker-Muscat. Their initial encounter is the leitmotif of a later chapter, but suffice it to say that Epstein promptly dropped psychoanalysis in favour of studying healing visualisation. Years later he asked Madame Aboulker-Muscat, toward the end of her life, for some last piece of advice. "Become your own authority" was the reply.

It would certainly be a different world if everyone were to become their own best authority; if we were all self-regulating adults unimpressed with the opinion of experts not in accord with our own experience. This is what Jung meant when he used the term individuation, and what Wilhelm Reich admonished people to become in *Listen, Little Man!* The way is not easy, however; our aspiration to freedom is matched only by our desire to be guided by benign and protective parents who will forever relieve us of the responsibility of finding things out for ourselves.

Charles Brooks, in his book on the sensory awareness work of Charlotte Selver, puts the case very well:

> During my life I have often rejected one authority only to accept another. Underneath I was afraid at the thought of living in a world where there was not someone, somewhat like myself, who *knew*. But I have come to feel that, to know what one is doing with life, it is no use to consult authorities. It is precisely through the veils which authorities have spun for us that our own eyes and ears and nerves must begin to penetrate if our hands are going to grasp the world and our hearts to feel it. We must recover our own capacity to taste for ourselves. Then we shall be able to judge also.
> (*Reclaiming Vitality and Presence*, pages 9–10)

A central theme of our discussions concerns *being in the middle of one's experience*. This is not a metaphor, but a literal injunction to find where the centre of one's experience resides and to act from that place. The processes of enculturation and trauma, however, ensure that our responses are largely asymmetric and that we are all eccentric beings, acting outside of any positive sense of a psychophysical centre.

All real authority resides at our centre.

Severe trauma early in life has a particularly pernicious effect on the sense of self as a secure locus from which to act, and the distortions so produced tell us a lot about all the lesser forms of mental suffering to which we are subject. So let us consider some of the contemporary thinking about trauma and its relevance to the idea of CREATING SPACE.

Probably one of the most important advances in trauma research has been the realisation that the effects of trauma are psychophysical in nature. This may seem obvious to the reader, but until the late 20th century the body was pretty much left out of most psychological thinking. Either this was testimony to how few professionals had been badly traumatised, or more likely, to the glacial pace at which the psycho-social sciences progress. Nevertheless, there is now fair consensus that we can learn a lot about how we react to acute or chronic threat by observing our commonalities with animals in the wild. Peter Levine was a pioneer in this kind of research and it was his book *Waking the Tiger* that helped to open my eyes on the subject.

All animals work within an optimal band of wakefulness, or arousal as psychologists put it. Optimal performance is somewhere in the middle of this band, as when an animal is quietly foraging for food. Occasionally there will be a demand for higher arousal levels, for example in stalking or being stalked. These periods are relatively short, however, and afterwards an animal (or human) returns to normal levels or moves to recover through rest or sleep. This is the balanced play of yin and yang, with natural self-regulation ensuring that no stress load is carried over to interfere with subsequent functioning.

In situations where very high stress levels are encountered, either acutely or over long periods, the organism has to carry a large stress burden until the emergency has passed. Then, at the first opportunity, the body attempts to return to the optimal arousal range by 'throwing off' the accumulated stress. Levine, amongst others, has drawn attention to animals in the wild who, after a shock of some kind, begin to shake and tremble until the burden of stress is discharged. Something similar can be seen when birds, stunned by flying into a window, recover consciousness and twitch all over before flying off.

These reactions occur whether the animal has reacted to danger by flight/fight on the one hand, or freezing on the other. In the former case the arousal level becomes very high, in the latter the organism goes into a temporary but deep hypo-arousal, like a mini-hibernation. In humans, these extreme states are usually accompanied by some measure of protective dissociation, meaning that individuals have entered a state of awareness in which they no longer feel firmly associated with their bodies or securely grounded in reality.

One can clearly see these reactions in someone who has just been severely traumatised. They look pale, frozen and dazed, their movements are slow and they say little. Given a safe environment and appropriate care they may, sooner or later, begin to shake and perhaps cry. The first impulse of those around may be to encourage suppression of these symptoms of shock, but this is very unwise, and they are best left to run their self-regulatory course.

Trouble begins when there is no safe opportunity to abreact in this way, such as in a war zone or in the case of a child in an abusive family. Then the organism has to adapt in a different way by splitting here and now consciousness away from the painful and frightening emotions. This leads to a situation in which distressing feelings and memories are encapsulated in dissociated 'subpersonalities' that remain frozen in time. Richard Schwartz (in *Internal Family Systems Therapy*) calls these split-off parts 'exiles', and characterises them as traumatised children who are no longer an integrated part of the internal family.

The adult personality goes on functioning with the help of 'managers' who take care of the everyday business of living and who may be surprisingly competent in the personas that they present to the world. Some managers are dedicated to keeping exiles at bay, whereas others may focus on a person's career or social life. If an exile's emotions begin to intrude too forcefully, then 'firefighter' parts act to hose things down by some form of distractive behaviour such as drug taking, gambling or compulsive sex.

The managers and firefighters are never completely successful at controlling the situation and as a result symptoms of hyperarousal (anxiety, insomnia, nightmares) and hypo-arousal (fatigue, low blood pressure, stomach problems) constantly intrude. In addition, the relationship system has been badly damaged, and individuals find themselves unable to form or maintain close bonds with others. As a result there is loneliness and a pervasive sense of emptiness and disconnection.

The picture of a family in which unhappy, traumatised children of various ages are ignored or unlovingly controlled by self-centred parents is not a pretty one. Yet this is the internal situation of countless victims of abuse and one which poses a challenge to any therapeutic process. Schwartz's model, however, gives a clear map of the territory and a way of proceeding that mirrors the approach that family therapists might take when confronted with the same sorts of situation. Thus, exiles need to be brought back into a safe and protective environment where they can be unburdened of their trauma, and managers need to develop understanding and compassion for the plight of their wards. Readers may be reminded of Fritz Perls' dictum that the underdogs of the personality need rights and the top dogs need to develop understanding.

Some managers will be left without useful employment and

will need guidance in 'getting a new job', while exiles will require ongoing help in making up for the developmental stages that they missed out on. During this work that aims to reharmonise the internal family dynamic, something very interesting happens: the emergence of the self. Schwartz's view of the self is an unusual one, because if I interpret him correctly, he sees it as always present and fully formed, even in the most distorted personalities. When, however, the internal family dynamics are chaotic, the self is obscured and its natural qualities get overlain by the struggle to contain the exiles' pain and confusion. For Schwartz, the self is naturally open and benign, complete, calm, creative and cooperative. It is a truly spacious awareness that is cramped and obscured by negative, contractive emotion. This means that we do not have to cultivate confidence, for example, but rather clear the disharmony that overlays our intrinsic nature. Such a concept is not far from Eastern ideas concerning the basic health of our natural or unconditioned mind.

The methodology of Internal Family Systems Therapy (IFS) has an elegance about it that reminds me of Taoism or Aikido. All the parts are respected and there is no imposition of an agenda. Through listening, dialogue and negotiation, the parts come into harmony and connection with one another because they follow their own best interests and tendencies. The obviation of unnecessary conflict abolishes the old toxic hierarchy and allows the natural self to function unimpeded. Moreover, the assigning of parts to imagined sub-personalities who exist in an internal landscape, just as would real people, allows appropriate distancing and management of highly charged emotional situations.

From this therapy's point of view, the practice of 'waiting and letting be' is one in which the reality of the self is tacitly established from the start. A safe space is created that allows the emergence of whatever needs to emerge without judgement or preconception. When fear is contained, lost parts can peep out and begin to find their place. Such a posture on the part of a meditator is referred to in Zen as 'practising Buddha Mind'. When you sit in zazen, you *are* the Buddha because you have already assumed an open stance toward reality.

The severe contractive and separative results of trauma can also be addressed directly through the body. Many of the physical symptoms seen in trauma victims represent uncompleted defensive reactions which were either not able to be fully expressed or were used to poor effect. Thus tension in an arm or twitching movements in a shoulder may represent aspects of the 'red light reflex' which have persisted because the cycle of trauma and recovery (abreaction) has not been completed. Therapists such as Pat Ogden (*Trauma and the Body*) track these symptoms very carefully and create a safe space for the full motoric response to emerge as part of the healing process.

The Rolfer, Jeffrey Maitland, whom we have met before, is another somatic therapist who writes insightfully about the body/mind in traumatised individuals. He also has the advantage of having been a philosophy academic and Zen practitioner. From his perspective our personal realities are psycho-spatial in nature and the encoding of experience is an act of orientation in space. He finds that many of his more severely affected patients have soft, overly hypotonic surface layers and a very tight inaccessible core. This no doubt reflects a retreat from life-threatening danger into an inner defensive 'citadel' where there may be a semblance of safety. Physically releasing this deep frozen tension is one way to get life energy flowing back into the organism, where it can then be used to mobilise normal and appropriate psycho-physical protection.

These considerations make it clear that movement is an important part of the therapeutic process. Those individuals who are active during a crisis fare much better than those who freeze. Such copers are in a minority, however, and are usually men with some previous experience in emergency management.

Men fare better than women because their nervous systems are less sensitive to shock and consequently they are more able to follow through with any critical incident training they have received. Being able to act means that a person has been able to orientate in space and that they know where they are. Knowing where you are is a precondition of both the sense of self and of self-efficacy.

Contrast this situation with the individual who has learned to freeze under challenge. Their physical reaction is paralleled by a dissociative movement away from the body. When asked to locate themselves, such people will often nominate a spot above and/or to the side of their heads. There is a measure of safety from such a vantage, but the self is greatly diminished. Later in the book I discuss identity and spatial orientation in greater detail, but the general message is that the healthy self is always at the centre of its experience. That centre is to be found at the intersection of the three dimensions in the body. Traumatised individuals are literally beside themselves, and a major part of their journey must involve relearning intentional orientation in and through the body.

Whatever form bodywork takes, it needs to run pari-passu with integrating the family of split-off parts. Therapies such as the Family Systems approach may be able to accomplish this goal, but the process is never easy. This is why I find Sandra Ingerman's approach (in *Soul Retrieval*) so intriguing, because as a shaman she is able to undertake a psychic journey to retrieve lost parts on behalf of her client. Ingerman's counselling background also means that she is able to contextualise her work within a broader psychotherapeutic framework.

In the world of shamanism, soul loss may take many forms, both physical and psychological, but the cause is conceived in the same way: a part of one's vital essence has been split off under the influence of aversive life events. The shaman travels through the upper, middle or lower worlds to locate and return with these lost parts, which can then be breathed back into the 'patient'. In traditional practice the shaman may have to trick the lost part(s) into returning, but Ingerman's approach is very much along the lines of Internal Family Systems, with negotiation and reassurance being the most important steps. As with all psychotherapies, safety is the key, and the 'exiles' have to be convinced that the situation 'at home' has changed and that they will now be welcomed and protected. The idea of being welcomed reminds me of something one of my Hakomi teachers said: being welcomed is the precondition of all other desirable mental states. If I am welcomed then I will feel worthy, and if I feel worthy I will be confident, and if I have self-confidence then I can act on my own behalf.

We do not necessarily have to believe in the metaphysical realities described in shamanistic practice to be impressed by the metaphors it embodies. The theme of leaving home, being lost and eventually returning to the warm embrace of the family is a universal archetype found in all cultures. As such, its enactment has healing properties quite apart from any specific content relating to personal history. The prodigal son is probably the best-known example in Christian culture, and a vivid illustration of the idea that we *have* to get lost, in order to eventually know ourselves and know too that we are unconditionally welcome back home.

Moreover, the spatial nature of such parables gives them added potency, since so much of our brain's circuitry is devoted to answering the simple question, "Where am I?" It is often easier to make sense of life when it is seen in terms of a physical journey, and it is not surprising that many religious customs make use of this analogy in the form of the pilgrimage or ritual circumambulation of religious sites. In Appendix 1 we shall see how walking a labyrinth is a particularly potent way of embodying some of these themes, and one which unites the physical and the transcendental.

On a broad level, stories of loss and return address universal concerns about identity and purpose. All major faiths speak in terms of our having become alienated from a spiritual source through incarnation in a realm that is both gross and illusory. Consequently our spiritual search involves returning whence we came by overcoming the fears and desires that keep us entranced in this restricted world.

In the last three chapters we have considered some aspects of this journey by looking at ways to release constriction in our bodies and minds to enhance spaciousness and freedom. These approaches have not necessarily seemed spiritual in nature, but it would be a mistake to make a false distinction between the somatic, the psychological and the spiritual. The Zen teacher Tim Burkett makes this point in his tellingly named book: *nothing holy about it* (the lower case is, I think, deliberate):

> The more we open up to our entire being without denying or repressing, the more we realize we can shine our light of compassion and wisdom anywhere (page 107).

Burkett's teacher Shunryu Suzuki Roshi was, like Burkett himself, at pains to draw attention to his own ordinariness and to cut through mistaken ideas of what was holy and what was not. Life becomes simpler and more comprehensible if we just keep shining the light of attention openly and non-judgementally.

In the next chapter my approach to spaciousness may seem to have a more traditional spiritual flavour to it, but don't be seduced by some of the rarefied concepts therein. Space is not complicated, it is basic to our nature: space that illuminates itself.

8

Waking to Space

As vast as infinite space
It is perfect and lacks nothing
But because you pick and choose
You cannot see its true nature.
Seng Tsan

The above quote, from the Fifth Zen Patriarch's classic "The Mind of Absolute Trust", reminds us that the spiritual odyssey, whatever its form, is deeply paradoxical in nature. We are propelled along the path by a need to *do something* to escape a constant undercurrent of unsatisfactoriness in our lives. But given that we can have no real understanding of the release that we seek, the 'doing' part becomes very problematical. And perhaps the need to 'do' is the whole mistake anyway.

We can, of course, take it on faith that a particular approach – moral, psychological or spiritual, will get us 'there' in the end, but sadly, it is apparent that whatever the path, many of us are called but few are chosen. And when the 'chosen' report back, they often tell us that there is nothing to attain and nothing we can do to get 'there' anyway! No wonder that many seekers have concluded, with Flora Courtois, that there is no recourse but to just wait and let be.

However, the idea of doing nothing, as far as that is possible, strikes the mind as highly offensive and sooner or later it tends to create all sorts of 'good' reasons to try something new and different. When this happens to me, I find that an effective calming remedy is to read from one of my favourite spiritual authors. For this purpose I now rely upon a small number of individuals whose 'fruits' have remained impervious to decay.

Finding such beings involves a certain discrimination borne of hard experience, just as you have to get sick a few times before you know what foods disagree with you.

In this chapter I quote largely from modern mystics who, in my opinion, have something important to say about reality. I tend to be biased toward those who can contextualise their experiences within a broader framework of human knowledge, but this simply reflects my tendency toward thinking rather than feeling. Others may prefer literature that has a more devotional or ritualistic feel. *There is no right way.* There are as many ways to God as there are people, and there is only one way.

As a beginning, let me introduce a longstanding favourite writer whom I mentioned in Chapter 1: Franklin Merrell-Wolff (1887–1985) and his two books, *Pathways Through to Space* and *The Philosophy of Consciousness Without an Object*, both published in 1973 and available as a single volume. I like Merrell-Wolff because he is thoroughly grounded in Western philosophy and mathematics, having had an academic background in both of these disciplines. Consequently, he 'speaks' to us in terms that are familiar to the Western mind and at the same time free of religious connotation. He is also a meticulous biographer of his own journey and *Pathways*, documenting the one hundred days after his awakening, is one of the twentieth century's most lucid and illuminating accounts of 'enlightenment'.

Always of an enquiring mind, Merrell-Wolff came upon Shankara's system of non-duality at an early stage in his search, and seems to have used the method of enquiry ('Who or What am I?') with an unusual degree of intellectual rigour. He describes this approach as "a discriminative isolation of the subjective pole of consciousness" i.e. the focus of attention is placed on the personal sense of beingness. The final key which led to a full 'Recognition', however, was the realisation that the Self is not a subtle object of experience or a 'place' or state. He understood that genuine 'Recognition' is:

> … simply a realization of Nothing, but a Nothing that is absolutely substantial and identical with the Self.
> (*Philosophy*, pages 36–37)

He goes on:

> I found myself at once identical with the Voidness, Darkness, and Silence, but realised them as utter, though ineffable, Fullness, in the sense of Substantiality, Light, in the sense of Illumination, and Sound, in the sense of pure formless Meaning and Value.
> (*Philosophy*, page 37)

In *Pathways*, and the more demanding exegesis found in *Philosophy*, Merrell-Wolff tries to describe the infinite vistas of understanding that opened to him as a result of his in-sight, but cautioning us from the start that language is largely defeated in such an endeavour. This did not deter him from trying, however, and his efforts culminated in fifty-six "Aphorisms on Consciousness Without an Object", which are contained in *Philosophy*, each aphorism being accompanied by a detailed explanation. My particular interest in bringing these to your attention is Merrell-Wolff's use of Space as an important descriptor both of his direct perception of Truth, but also of the philosophical explanation that could in some pale way do justice to his experience.

Thus the term SPACE is central to the final six Aphorisms. Number 51 states, for example, that:

> Consciousness-without-an-object may be symbolised by a SPACE that is unaffected by the presence or absence of objects… (page 115).

And later in Aphorism 54:

> The GREAT SPACE, or Consciousness-without-an-object, is the Sole Reality upon which all objects and all selves depend and derive their existence (page 116).

Merrell-Wolff's emphasis on Space seems to derive directly from his experience at the moment of success:

> The critical stage in the transformation is the realisation of the 'I' as zero. But, at once, that 'I' spreads out into an unlimited 'thickness'. It is as though the 'I' becomes the whole of space. (*Philosophy*, page 39)

He also describes this change as being from a "Point-I" to a "Space-I", with the caution, however, that Space is not to be thought of as merely identical to either three-dimensional or conceptual space, but is rather a symbol of the root of all possible spaces. Higher (Spiritual) Evolution may then be thought of as a progressive Spatial Integration, with each step transcending the previous stage, in the same way that we can conceive of a hierarchy of nested spaces in mathematics or systems theory. If we think of Connection as the direction of spaciousness i.e. the crossing of a limiting boundary, then in considering such nested spaces we are in the same territory as the principle of Connection/separation, whose iterating sequences go all the way up and all the way down.

In summing up his use of Space as a symbol, Merrell-Wolff quotes from the much-maligned Madame Blavatsky:

> Space is the *one eternal thing* that we can most easily imagine, immovable in its abstraction and uninfluenced by either the presence or absence of an objective universe.
> (*The Secret Doctrine*, 3rd Ed., page 67)

Ultimately, of course, there can be no proper summing up of these great truths, only a pointing in the general direction. The genius of someone like Merrell-Wolff is that when he circumambulates 'Recognition' with such elegance and rigor, we cannot fail to experience an aroma of THAT.

Published only a few years later in 1977, Tarthang Tulku's book *Time, Space and Knowledge* has an uncanny homology with *Pathways*, and *Philosophy*, although I doubt very much that there was ever any cross-fertilisation between the two men. Tarthang Tulku talks about Great Space in very much the same terms as Merrell-Wolff, including a discussion on the hierarchy of nested spaces within Great Space. He is much more explicit, however, in pointing to the fact that the various spaces that we occupy: cognitive, affective and perceptual are dependent on our 'focal setting'. In this sense he is a more contemporary thinker, emphasising that spaciousness arises out of openness and accommodation. He is using 'process language' to describe space as a dynamic phenomenon rather than a thing:

> The accommodating quality – which is represented at its peak by Great Space – is complete at precisely the point where the notion of a space, which to a greater or lesser degree allows or accommodates a 'thing', collapses. The openness and allowing qualities of Great Space are greatest when not filtered through a 'thing which allows' (page 15).

As an illustration of these principles, Tarthang Tulku prescribes an exercise in which we imagine ourselves as tiny observers moving through and exploring a giant human body. As we observe the various interdependent organs and tissues, we realise that there are no completely solid or opaque structures, just boundaries between interacting processes that are arising in Space. On moving down to cellular and atomic levels, there appears to be ever-increasing spaciousness and proportionately decreasing substance. Thus at the atomic level, space is the overwhelming impression (we are told by contemporary physicists, for example, that if a basketball represented the proton at the heart of a hydrogen atom, then the electron would be like a pea whizzing around over three kilometres away!). Further, we can talk about the *comparative* masses and locations of subatomic particles, but not their absolute dimensions *because they are not discrete things*.

This kind of investigation transforms our view of 'fixed reality' into one of dynamic, ever-shifting relationships; a dance of Connection/separation in a web of interlocking and hierarchical systems. Close examination of the boundaries that define these processes, however, reveals that they too give way to Space, leaving us, as the Tulku says, with:

SPACE PROJECTING SPACE INTO SPACE.

Thus we must live with paradox. On the one hand 'things' appear to have a separate and solid existence and in our everyday experience we seem to be solid to ourselves. Similarly, we must acknowledge that existence seems coherent only because there are higher and lower spaces, calibrated by their level of openness and inclusiveness. At the same time, however, Great Space is no different from any space or form because it contains and accommodates all. AH Almaas expresses this very well:

> Space is the inherent natural openness of experience, which has no bounds, no limitations. It is open through and through, in infinite ways and in all dimensions. Being is not only open in three dimensions, it is open in all possible dimensions, to all possible experiences, which include the usual time and space. What we see as physical space is only the most obvious manifestation of this openness. This is the dimension of space that allows physical objects to be.
>
> This understanding leads us to the unity of Being, in

which all manifestations are displays of Being, expressing and manifesting the same indivisible reality. Space is the openness of this nondual reality, acting to expose and dissolve the representations that normally occlude our awareness and prevent us from objectively perceiving it.
(*The Void*, page 157)

Although it is clear from what has been said so far that the concept Great Space is more encompassing than just the three-dimensional variety, it is hard to escape the notion that the awareness of physical space, *as space*, can be a door to higher understanding. And it would seem to follow from this premise that awakening experiences should be more common 'en plein air', i.e. in circumstances where we are more likely to open our focus in an encompassing way.

When I surveyed modern accounts of expanded awareness, it did indeed appear that being outside has a facilitating effect in opening awareness. Some examples are:

Tony Parsons crossing a park and finding that the doing of walking had simply transformed into the presence of walking (*Invitation to Awaken*).

Jeff Foster trudging along an Oxford street in the rain, when suddenly all sense of separation and loneliness disappears (*The Wonder of Being*).

Suzanne Segal waiting at a bus stop and suddenly losing her sense of self (*Collision with the Infinite*).

Jean Klein seeing a flight of birds and finding that rather than being lost in seeing them, they became lost in him, in his openness (*Transmission of the Flame*).

David Carse staring out into the Amazonian jungle when, for no apparent reason, his intense fear of death gives way to a series of extraordinary experiences that culminate in the permanent loss of any sense of a personal self (*Perfect Brilliant Stillness*).

These and other twentieth century descriptions of personal

transformation find a parallel in other times. The Zen literature is particularly rich in stories of awakening through *some arresting perceptual event*, such as the plop of a frog, a stone ricocheting on bamboo or the sight of a flock of birds. In the outdoors there is the possibility of being taken out of ourselves, or rather out of the thinking mind and into direct seeing unaccompanied by any sense of a seer or of any particular thing that is 'seen'. In Open Attention we are more likely to be "solicited" by reality to use Jean Klein's expression.

Alan Watts was fond of contrasting the salubriousness of natural settings with the very 'indoorsy' nature of Western religions. It is only very recently that Christianity has acknowledged the importance of the natural world, and as usual, has simply tagged along behind secular and scientific thought on this subject. Some would argue that this lack of vision relates to the missing feminine in the Abrahamic religions, an outcome that is inevitable in faiths that have their origin in desert 'sky-god' cults.

When we think of the Christian contemplative tradition we almost inevitably imagine monks or nuns in their cells. All the more interesting, then, to consider the journey of Carmelite nun Bernadette Roberts, whose spiritual vocation took her into territory that had no precedent in Christian spiritual literature, even in her beloved St John of the Cross.

Roberts is one of those rare individuals who, like Ramana Maharshi, seemed destined for a spiritual life from childhood. In early adulthood she spent ten years in monastic retreat, and as a result attained what, in Christian esoteric traditions, would be called an abiding unitive state with God. She subsequently re-entered the world of the 'marketplace' and brought up a family. Her interior sense of union with the divine was not to last, however, and she went on to experience a path of transformation which is described and explained in her trilogy: *The Experience of No-Self, The Path to No-Self* and *What is Self?*.

The Experience of No-Self stands, in my mind, as the great contemporary classic of Christian mysticism. It contains many marvels, not the least of which is its being written with a lucidity and intellectual grasp that is rare in works of this genre. Moreover, its concepts are familiar to those with some knowledge of Buddhism or Advaita Vedanta, although these systems were apparently unknown to the author during her journey of discovery.

I have read Roberts's books many times and continue to be fascinated by a story which culminates in the complete loss of an interior life or sense of personal self. It has also seemed significant to me that the key turning points in her 'liberation' occurred while outdoors, and usually involved changes in perception that were largely visual in nature. I detail some of these critical junctures below, but ask the reader to digest the first eighty pages of *The Experience of No-Self* before looking at my comments. You may well have a different view of her story.

Some key turning points in the journey:

> While walking home she is confronted with a panorama of valleys and hills. Turning inward she realises that her 'self' is missing. She later realises that where there is no personal self within, there can be no personal God.
>
> On a hillside at Big Sur she is mesmerized by the sight of a flying seagull and finds that the usual division between observer and observed has dispersed, to be replaced by a seeing of Oneness everywhere – what she calls her "3D glasses".
>
> While at a camp overlooking the sea, she finds that the seeing of Oneness has turned into an horrendous emptiness, a void that is strangling the life out of everything. The experience of nothingness continues and she enters a 'passageway' of several months in which a pressure in her head pushes her to SEE.

> Eventually, while sitting by a river, a smile arises and she knows that the smile, that which smiled and that at which it smiled were one – which she describes as "the grin of recognition".

These few vignettes can in no way do justice to the trials and tribulations inherent in completely losing the sense of any personal autonomy or do-ership. Add to this, the difficulty in acclimatising to a way of being in which there is just seeing and doing in the moment with no recourse to an interior self.

Many contemporary writers on matters mystical have tried to bring Roberts into the fold of 21st century non-dual thought, but she is a reluctant recruit, stressing that many claims of so-called 'enlightenment' do not represent the radical transformation that involves the loss of any last vestige of personal self. Nevertheless, and with some trepidation, I would venture that there are striking parallels between many aspects of her story and some of the accounts that I have discussed earlier in the book. The acquisition of the 3D spectacles is especially notable in its parallel with Flora Courtois's radical shift in vision, while the disappearance of interiority reminds me of Douglas Harding losing his head and SEEING.

It is this SEEING which is the crucial element, not in the narrow agenda-driven way of the ego, but in a mode that is free of everything but the SEEING itself. The impediment of ego consists in the unrelenting agendas it imposes on SENSING through the "questing beast" of DOING. To use Roberts's words, besides the SEEING, everything else is a gigantic "head trip". Or as Rumi would have us do: dissolve our whole body into Vision.

So please go back to the source and read her books, because this brief introduction necessarily underplays the heroic nature of Roberts's struggle to SEE. As with Suzanne Segal, some of the more harrowing aspects of her voyage may, with hindsight, have been mitigated by a teacher or companion who knew something of the path of non-duality, but we shall never know. Perhaps much of the value of her account lies in its total originality and freshness, aspects that would be lacking if she had been able to fall back on a well-defined tradition with all its preconceptions and obfuscations.

The apparent facilitating effect of the outdoors and the emphasis on seeing remind me of an account in Philip Kapleau's *Three Pillars of Zen*, in which a middle-aged Japanese businessman writes to his spiritual teacher Nakagawa-roshi. In the letter he describes a wonderful experience of satori after reading a quote by the 17th century Soto Zen Master Son-O to the effect that Mind is none other than mountains, trees, the great wide earth and the sun and moon and stars.

The businessman's experience and the words that precipitated it are a vivid illustration of the Zen adage that before the spiritual quest, mountains are mountains and trees are trees, but during the journey, mountains are not mountains and trees are not trees. After attainment, however, mountains are mountains and trees are trees, but with the difference that the senses have been cleansed of the mind and see what is to be seen. There is pure SEEING.

The simplicity of this statement is an eloquent summing up, I think, of the observations and experiences in this chapter; that the themes of Space, Openness/Connectedness and Direct Perception (especially vision) are closely linked, and that their relationship gives us helpful clues in our quest for abiding freedom. But as to saying any more about the liberated state, I am guided by David Carse: "Does exist. Cannot be expressed." With this in mind, you may wish to skip the next chapter, a very cerebral account of esoteric number theory and the principles of sacred geometry. Such accounts can be enlightening, but they may equally be very frustrating, and anything but spacious.

9

Something About Nothing

Constantly regard the universe as one living being, one substance and one soul; and observe how all things have reference to one perception, and perception of this one living being: and how all things act with one movement; and how all things are the cooperating cause of all things which exist; observe too the continuous spinning of the thread and the contexture of the web.
Marcus Aurelius

This quote from the great Roman emperor and philosopher is a wonderfully elegant summation of non-duality. If we add Meister Eckhart's "Isness is God" then we might say: there is One-ly Isness. Beyond that – a noble silence.

Since there is no vantage point outside the Oneness from which to describe it, then we must be content with immersion in the Mystery rather than its dissection. Such a view is, of course, highly disconcerting to the cognitive mind, which has not been discouraged over the millennia from concocting all manner of tales, myths, doctrines and equations to explain the 'big questions'.

In this chapter I pay homage to what I consider some of the more satisfying descriptions of the Mystery In Action. However, if you wish to skip over this section you will not miss anything relevant to the practical application of spacious attention. Alternatively, you may, like me, just enjoy the fun of playing with ideas. As addictions go it is a fairly harmless pursuit, especially if you can avoid becoming obsessed and overly serious about the whole matter. And there is always the element of surprise; an elegant concept may really inspire you or produce a click of recognition in some way.

So here are some interesting tales about how things came to be the way they are in this mystifying world. You may notice that the theme of Connection/separation plays happily through all of them and is the law that spins the thread.

Alan Watts, as usual, has the best line in cosmogenesis (see *Cosmic Drama*). He asks us to imagine that we are God: omniscient, omnipresent and omnipotent. Not unlike we mortals, God gets bored with his own company, especially as everywhere She looks, there He is! The only solution seems to lie in a little reverie, and so God dreams of indulging all sorts of pleasures, which over time become more and more extreme. After aeons of time and after all sensual possibilities have been exhausted, boredom sets in again. So God has to spice up the adventures with danger and uncertainty, but S(he) can still stop the show at any time if things get too frightening. It takes longer to get bored this time, but when ennui finally takes over there is only one possibility left: to get lost in the dream and have no control over what happens, or even when S(he) may wake up.

This, Watts says, is the position we are all in: our divine Self is lost in the dream of individuality and totally identifies with the soap opera of separative life. However, because it is extremely exciting to get lost, and equally exhilarating to find oneself again, such a cosmic game of hide and seek seems to be worth it, even though there is no simple way of calling time on the whole drama. And incidentally, it's the only game in town.

Watts has reworked a number of traditional myths, and brought out the essential storyline of tales such as the prodigal son or Krishna's homily to Arjuna in the Bhagavad Gita. There are a number of corollaries, not the least of which offers a way of approaching the problem of suffering: that after all is said and done, it is God causing pain to Himself. This may initially sound pretty facile, but in my experience all 'explanations' of the nature of pain and suffering have an unconvincing quality that never seems to do justice to the horrors of this world. But the idea of waking from a dream does tap into that familiar experience of relief when we suddenly find that we are not actually in a car hurtling off a cliff, or wandering the streets without clothes. And usually we quickly compose ourselves without significant sequelae.

It is also the case that pain becomes much more bearable when we know it will come to an end at some point, and even better, when we have a measure of control that determines when that might be. In experiments with human subjects, it is a constant finding that someone can endure a painful stimulus for longer if they have an escape button that they can press if need be. We do have an escape button, and the perennial philosophy attempts to show us how it works.

The other major corollary is that there is ONLY GOD, and that the apparent diversity and complexity of the universe is GOD CONTEMPLATING GOD through the medium of manifestation. The way in which the ONE hides from ITSELF in the many is, of course, a profound mystery, but we can analogise again and use some traditional images to help us.

The Uroboros is a snake swallowing its own tale and forming a circle or zero in the process. This eloquently expresses the idea that the Uni-verse, or one turn, is a process in which the One Substance retroflects upon itself in a coincidence of beginning and end i.e. it is doing so in an eternal and timeless realm. The image also implies that the apparent substance of the manifest world (the snake) is, at its core, space or no-thingness.

Retroflection happens at all levels, from spiral galaxies right down to self-reflecting quantum waves (see Arnold Mindell in *Earth-Based Psychology*). On a more immediate level, the Uroboros symbol is an elegant expression of the biosphere, in which everything is eaten and recycled, with nothing left over and nothing left out. The Anthroposhere, on the other hand, clearly does not operate in this way and so is a violation of this most basic law.

Indra's Net, an ancient Hindu image, captures a similar meaning but with an added element that conveys diversity within unity. Named after the Hindu king of heaven and god of thunder, the net is imagined to be an infinite lattice of threads held together at each junction with a jewel or mirror. Every crystal reflects every other jewel in the net, but from its own unique position in the matrix. All appearance, then, becomes but a reflection of all other reflections or appearances ad infinitum. The image is somewhat easier to visualise if one places a central source of light, say a candle, at the centre of a spherical net. One can then imagine the endlessly receding candles, all slightly different, reflected from an infinite number of angles.

Thus do we see the ONE, the analogy states, taking on the appearance of infinite forms but forever remaining the same. Our modern version is the hologram, a picture captured through the interaction of two beams of coherent light. Because the resulting 'picture' takes the form of a wave pattern of interfering ripples of light, the photographic plate can be broken up and still produce a faithful image of the original in each shard. The smaller the fragment, however, the fainter the image, just like human beings, made in the image of God, but often very badly faded.

We also see this idea enshrined in the old Hermetic law: 'As above, so below', a dictum that implies self-similarity at all manifest scales, a phenomenon that we know today as fractality. This kind of patterning can be seen throughout nature and is epitomised by the branching of a tree, where we see that the structure of a bough resembles the general pattern of the whole tree, and similarly for a branch on that bough and a twig on that branch. Fractality can be seen in diverse structures, from the anatomy of the circulatory system to the form of coastlines and river systems. The jury is still out as to whether the overall structure of the universe is fractal, but I am confident that the Hermetic law will be seen to apply on the largest as well as the smallest scales. This may not be in strictly fractal terms, but in the way that both macro- and micro- manifest certain basic laws of relationship and proportionality.

Asking how the ONE hides from itself and reflects back on itself leads us deep into wiseacre territory. However, as long as we keep David Carse looking over our shoulder: "Does exist, can't be described", we need not go too far astray. For the following speculations I am particularly indebted to the work of Stan Tenen, Drunvalo Melchizedek, Arthur Young, John Michell and Matila Ghyka, as well as Marshall Lefferts' excellent Cosmometry site.

If there is just ONE, then that same ONE must be the same everywhere, just as jellies or great bodies of water are the same throughout. We might call this uniform ONE, the Unified Field. The only way that some differentiation can appear within this uniform something that is no-thing is through an internal motion or vibration. Think of a static body of water: it can ripple or swirl, these are its only two options. Of course, the One has no surface to ripple on, and so it must vibrate within itself, an idea not totally foreign to modern physics. In string theory, for example, all the different subatomic particles are represented by little vibrating strings, creating, as Michio Kaku describes it: "... cosmic music resonating through 10 and 11-dimensional space" ("The Power of Staring").

Contemporary sacred geometrists propose that the universe has only one ripple shape: the sine wave, the shape that ocean waves, sound waves and light waves all share in common. It is the shape that the valve on a tyre traces out in space as a wheel rotates and moves forward. As a universal building block its form is particularly felicitous, because according to the Fourier Principle, any conceivable wave shape can be constructed by combining the right sine waves together.

The only trouble with waves, however, is that they don't tend to stand still, and for a universe to have tangibility we need

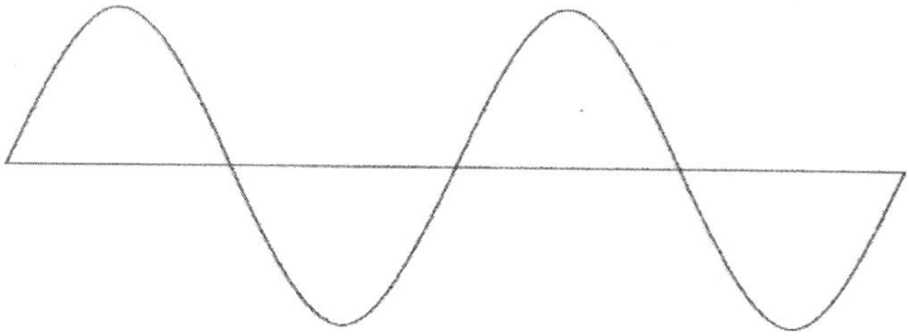

Fig. 3 The Sine Wave

three-dimensional objects that stay in place. Fortunately, there is a way that a medium can swirl in 3D that creates a stable shape, one that 'remembers' itself and stays relatively still. That shape is the torus or donut. There are many Internet sites where you can watch animations of the torus rotating on itself to get some idea of how this dynamic works (my favourite is Torus Fun by ieoie on YouTube) or watch the many clips of people blowing smoke rings.

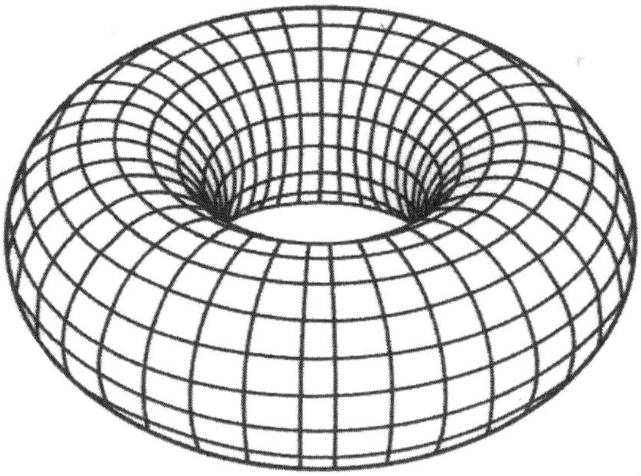

Fig. 4 A Torus or Donut

Arthur Young was a principal pioneer in pointing to the many cosmological implications of the torus dynamic. Some of these intriguing properties are:

It is reflexive, constantly turning back on itself, with the inside and outside in a continuous loop of exchange. As we see later on, Young's idea that the universe is reflexive at all levels could imply that the donut dynamic is basic to this process.

It can be thought of as a three-dimensional sine wave.

A flow of energy through the centre of the donut creates a double vortex, one entering the torus and one leaving. This energy dynamic creates a shape like the field we see around a magnet. These kinds of fields are seen at all scales from the galactic to the atomic.

The torus flow of energy creates POLARITY, the essential heart of all interactive processes.

The Mind of Light

When we consider these characteristics of the torus, it is not unreasonable to believe that this fundamental shape is a way of persuading light to turn back (retroflect) on itself and become matter. Thus, the fundamental 'substance' of the ONE either ripples as waves or swirls as matter. No wonder then that contemporary physics acknowledges that all phenomena can have both wave-like and particle-like properties. This is apparent to observation, however, only at an atomic scale.

The idea that there are waves and donuts made of the same ONE THING also accords with the processes of Connection/separation. In fact, it is the primordial division between 'matter things' (energy separating itself), which at the subatomic level physics calls fermions, and 'force things' (connecting energy) that are known as bosons.

The next step is to simply recognise that all motion of the ONE SUBSTANCE IS LIGHT. This is tantamount to saying that the universe is made of light, or more strictly of photons. Samuel Avery gives a good account of why this is so in his book, *Buddha and the Quantum*. Now I normally run a mile when the word quantum is mentioned in a spiritual context for the following reason: since there is *no agreement at all* among physicists as to how the quantum world works, it ill behoves the rest of us to start bandying the term around in other ill-defined contexts such as consciousness. However, Avery's book is eminently level-headed and he assembles some relevant points about light, as follows:

> The speed of light is constant, whatever the speed of the observer – this fact gave rise to the Special Theory of Relativity.
>
> The velocity of light defines the upper limit of speed for anything.
>
> Time slows, Space shrinks and Mass increases as they approach the speed of light.
>
> Light can be a wave but has no medium in which to wave. It can also be a particle, but not both at the same time.
>
> For a photon time does not exist; its passage from a distant star to my eye is instantaneous (from its 'point of view').
>
> Light defines the relationship between energy (E) and mass (M): $E=MC^2$ where C is the speed of light.
>
> Taken together, these properties of light strongly suggest that it is the prime vehicle through which the ONE manifests, and that far from being in space and time, it CONTAINS SPACE AND TIME.

As Arthur Young has stated, light is not objective in any way, the detection of a photon in the eye is its annihilation; it is not seen, *it is seeing*. Photons, electromagnetic energy, are the way that atoms and molecules exchange energy, but in the process light leaves no trace. It is, Young says, like the smile without the cat, and as such, light can be thought of as *pure action*.

I am reminded at this point of the smile that arose in Bernadette Roberts as she sat by the river, a smile without a subject or an object. Roberts goes on to tell us in *The Experience of No-Self* about the choiceless state of doing that eventually became her norm after the loss of self. Knowing, seeing and doing simply became a single act, since there was no self with its choices and judgements to get in the way. Doing became identical with its content i.e. *pure action*. Perhaps we could speculate, then, that there is an homology between the characteristics of light and the enlightened state. This is not too far-fetched, since there is ONLY ONE SUBSTANCE, and *the movement of that substance is what light is*.

Roberts tells us that consciousness is a product of (little) self (not Self), and as such disappears with the loss of self, to be replaced by the uninterrupted doing of God. Small self simply interposes a delay, a knot of retroflection into what would otherwise be pure action. This accords with our knowledge of the nervous system in which sensation (information) flows up the spinal cord, is filtered and processed at various levels in the brain, and then flows back down as motor impulses. During this journey, information travels through a 360-degree (retroflective) arc, with the frontal lobes at its apogee.

Much of the intermediate processing is at an unconscious level, and it should not be surprising that we often function quite well without the deliberation of the conscious self as, for example, when driving a car. This implies that the ego or self is mainly concerned with checking that all action accords with the 'me' story and its interests. This takes quite a lot of computing time, which in turn shows up as the delay that we experience as the personal 'I' sense. When we are in the 'flow', which is generally when well-learned unconscious programmes are in action, there is a greatly diminished sense of self, and often an enhanced sense of being 'lived'.

Avery also points out that there is something very special about light and its relation to sense-awareness. Because light contains space (and time), it is through the visual sense that we arrange and differentiate other sensory modalities, especially hearing and smelling. For example, when walking in Nature and surrounded by discrete sounds of birds, we instinctively locate them in space before orientating toward them. Similarly, ideas and images in the mind have to occupy different positions in subjective space or else they would blend into a 'massa confusa'.

Thus our very highly developed three-dimensional visual sense can be seen as an evolutionary development that subsumes the other senses; it is the whole that is greater than the parts. In turn, our visual consciousness of objects is but an aspect of the Brilliance that is Pure Unmodified Light which we call awareness. After losing his sense of personal self, David Carse found he was constantly bathed in this Brilliance, and that with his eyes closed, it filled his head, receding to the background, but always present when he viewed the everyday world. He describes It as Presence, Light beyond light, and Sat Chit Ananda.

The idea that the universe is constituted of light is also not far from current cosmological and quantum theories on the subject. Fred Alan Wolf gives a contemporary physicist's version of where matter comes from in *Time Loops and Space Twists*, but be warned, it is not easy-going and you may wish to go to his summary toward the end of the book before attending to the details. Wolf tells us that there are two kinds of light: spin ½ light which forms matter (fermions such as quarks, electrons and neutrinos), and spin 1 light, which forms energy-carrying bosons such as the photon or gluon. The one and the half refer to phase changes in the spin-quantum wave function, but don't ask me what that actually means. Wolf tells us that the spin of particles is a reflection of twists in space, an idea which is obviously very close to the model that we have already described.

Quantum theory has to fudge things to some extent, because it has no answer as to how spin ½ light actually acquires mass. Consequently it invokes the mysterious Higgs field with which spin ½ light interacts, but spin 1 light does not. Wolf chooses to characterise the Higgs field as the mind of God, which I think is the same as saying that light arises as a primal act of awareness, moving within itself as waves and vortices, intelligent, purposeful and evolutionary.

Form and Process

Form and process can be thought of as the two hands of Creation: everything created has form in **space**, and interacts and changes over **time**. We could say that space manifests through form, and time manifests through process, although in the world of direct experience, space and time cannot be distinguished in any meaningful way. For the purposes of discussion, however, it is much easier to treat them separately, and so I defer the topic of time and process to the next chapter.

Our current secular creation myth is the BIG BANG, a story that started over thirteen billion years ago, when the total mass/energy of the universe popped out of nothing in the form of an infinitely small, dense and hot 'singularity'. It is hard, even for theoretical cosmologists, to come up with an explanation as to how something can come from nothing, but the current crop of theories posits an intriguing idea: that something is more stable than nothing.

It has been known for a while that there is no such thing as true emptiness; quantum uncertainty ensures that in a vacuum particles are popping in and out of existence all the time. In more metaphysical terms, we could say that emptiness has a huge potential to BE and therefore WANTS TO BE, and because it is nothing in particular, it has an infinite potential to be everything in general.

We can state this in another way: infinite potential is no-thing because no particular potentiality has been actualized. Thus the no-thing of the ground state or zero point energy, as the physicists call it, is highly unstable and takes only a little prompting (a tickle) to collapse into a some-thing. This prompting might be a thought in the mind of God, like Alan Watts' "Get lost!". The ALL then takes a direction and instantaneously light pushes outward, creating an ever-expanding sphere of space/time.

We can imagine the radiating straight lines of space, but we also talk of the one-way arrow of time. Physicists have a problem with things that go one way and don't observe some sort of symmetry, so the arrow of time is only acceptable to them if there were a very high state of order (low entropy) at the very beginning. This concept does not accord with the idea of a universe arising from nothing in an apparently random way. From an esoteric viewpoint, however, there is no problem at all with this, since we assume that the mind of God was, by its very nature, totally coherent with the nascent form of a universe waiting to be born.

The cosmic tension between nothing and something is also apparent to us in everyday life. It is hard to quiet the mind and just rest in awareness, just being; the mind constantly craves the certainty of the next thought or experience. The natural spaciousness of awareness 'collapses' like a quantum wave function into a focus. The some-thing that then arises inevitably takes the form of a movement, however subtle. As Bernadette Roberts points out, consciousness IS the awareness of energy (which is movement), whether this be within the organism or without. The seer and the seen do not exist separately, there is only seeing. Form is emptiness, emptiness is form, or as Blake eloquently put it: "Eternity is in love with the works of time."

The movement of energy, awareness of which IS consciousness, is ultimately the movement of light, so let us go a little further with our myth of how light builds itself into the world as we know it. We have already seen how the complementary duality of waves and particles might come into being, so now let us consider how these can be built into higher levels of complexity.

In a world of waves or vortices, there can only be stability if these building blocks agree with one another i.e. their frequencies or circular motions do not tend to cancel one another out. This means that **there must be the correct proportion** for these ingredients to agree. We can find a good analogy in music: a frequency of 128cps (C below middle C) can agree with one of 256cps (middle C) because the higher frequency can 'nest' within the lower one and create stability. There will be two waves of the higher frequency nesting within each wave of the lower frequency.

Similarly, vortices can coexist and build complex configurations if they are in the right angular relationship with one another. Amazingly, the optimal nesting of donut vortices is provided by the shape of the Platonic solids: one pair of donut vortices in a tetrahedron, three pairs in a cube, five in a dodecahedron and seven in an icosahedron. These configurations give us the crucial number of electrons in the shells surrounding an atomic nucleus: 2, 6, 10 and 14. The 10 and 14 shells are closer to the nucleus and play no part in the combining of atoms to form molecules; it is the 2 and 6 shells which determine chemical reactions and give us the general rule that 8 electrons create a stable union between two different elements. Thus oxygen with a shell of 6 electrons, and hydrogen with one electron can combine to their mutual satisfaction to form water, H2O, a compound more stable than either of its two constituents. The discovery linking electron shells with Platonic solids was made by Professor Roger Moon and subsequent work has extended the theory to include the atom's nucleus.

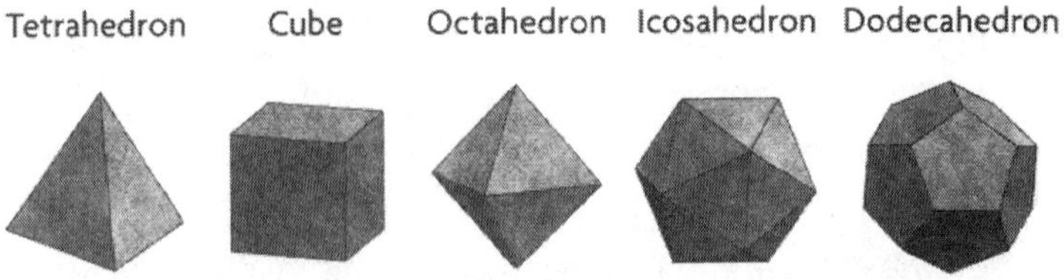

Fig. 5 The Platonic Solids (reproduced with permission from J. Michell's *How the World Is Made: The Story of Creation According to Sacred Geometry*)

This rule of atomic combination is the basis of all chemistry, and therefore of all organic life, and can also be derived in other ways, including a mathematical treatment of the harmonic scale (see Russell Smith's *Cosmic Secrets*). The idea, however, that all chemistry can be derived from Platonic solids is too beautiful to ignore. Truth and beauty go hand in hand, and an aesthetic appreciation of theory is close to the heart of many physicists. Michio Kaku, for example, waxing lyrical about string theory again, says that it is "gorgeous". In my opinion, the idea of a vibrating world in which order is maintained by a universal harmony of proportion is also gorgeous, and it is rather remarkable that Pythagoras and Professor Kaku could sit down to dinner and have a coherent conversation which would probably be illuminating for them both.

Spiralling donut vortices can nest within the geometry of Platonic solids because the latter are symmetrical. All their faces are identical, as are the edges and internal angles between faces. They also fit perfectly inside a sphere with all points touching its internal surface. This means, for example, that you can spin a cube ninety degrees around any of its three principal axes of rotation and it will appear just the same. A dodecahedron has sixty different rotational symmetries i.e. there are sixty different ways you can spin this shape and still get the pentagonal faces to line up as they were before (Marcus du Sautoy, *Grand Designs*). For mathematical reasons that are beyond me, this makes it very special, and the first of a series of so-called indivisible symmetric structures.

The dodecahedron has lots of other surprises for us. Pythagoras thought that the universe was shaped like a dodecahedron because this shape, together with the icosahedron, can nest other Platonic solids. Evidence from the cosmic microwave background now tends to support this view (Zeeya Merali, "Our Finite, Wrap-around Universe"). At the other end of the spectrum, dodecahedrons can be seen in the structure of DNA.

Other Platonic solids are not without their special

characteristics. For example, in simulations to discover what shapes pack best into a given space, the tetrahedron comes out best. But according to Buckminster Fuller, the 'daddy' of these basic shapes (although not a Platonic solid itself) is the cuboctahedron, a shape which can collapse and expand in both left and right hand spirals, in a motion he called jitterbugging. Along the way it gives rise to the icosahedron, octahedron and tetrahedron. Consequently, Fuller viewed it as the core of all energetic phenomena (for more information see www.cosmometry.com).

However, there is a way of deriving the structure of the Platonic solids from an even simpler structure, the details of which you can find in material from Drunvalo Melchizedek, including his two-volume treatise on the Flower of Life. A start can be made by simply taking seven identical coins and placing six of them around the seventh – yes, they fit perfectly; a beautiful manifestation of the Law of Seven which we shall discuss later. Adding more outer circles creates a figure called the Flower of Life, which in its turn can be transformed with straight lines into Metatron's Cube. All the Platonic Solids can be found in this cube, although Melchizedek says that it took him twenty years to find the dodecahedron.

The Foundation of Number

We can go a stage further by considering that all forms are capable of expression in terms of number, an idea at the heart of contemporary mathematics, but also implicit in traditional numerology and sacred geometry. From an esoteric point of view, two particular numbers take on special significance: three and seven. The importance of their relationship has been elaborated most explicitly by Gurdjieff and his commentators, so let us start with his ideas about the Law of Three or Triamazikamno as he calls it in *Beelzebub's Tales to His Grandson*.

The idea of triality is very ancient. For example Lao Tzu (5th century BC) tells us that the One gives rise to Two, Two gives rise to Three and Three gives rise to the Ten Thousand Things. It was Gurdjieff, however, who gave us a contemporary interpretation of triality in which the three components are:

> An Affirming Force that appears to be the active energy,
> A Denying Force that appears to be the passive pole and
> A Reconciling Force that balances the interaction of the above two.

To understand how the Law of Three works, we can invoke systems theory. Thus, the Reconciling force is the proximate effect of the overall system in which the Affirming/Denying dynamic is evident. Everything in the world is constrained by the Whole, which exerts its effect both in top/down and bottom/up processes. A simple example in the human realm might be in the case of a plaintiff (active force) and defendant (passive force) being reconciled through the offices of a mediator or the court system (reconciling force). The mediator or court are aspects of overarching systems that have evolved to help maintain balance in the social environment. Without such a process we see feuds and vendettas continuing over generations without any resolution. The potentially endless shuttling between thesis and antithesis is brought to a conclusion through the reconciling, synthetic effects of outside influences. Those influences may take many forms and may appear to arise from unexpected sources, but it is always a case of the harmonising effects of the Whole.

Another example is the endless conflict between the forces of conservatism and liberalism, which is only kept in check through the overarching structures of a democratic society. In this way slow evolutionary progress is made. We may see sudden movements for a while in one direction or the other (e.g. in the 1960s or 1980s in Western societies), but the pendulum always swings back through the stabilising effect of the Whole:

the Law of Regression to the Mean.

The situation is not different in Nature or the physical world. The Geosphere and Biosphere are intrinsically conservative and maintain a critical balance that allows everything to Be in Form, but not in a way that allows stasis or fossilisation (unless that is, you are meant to be a fossil).

Katya Walter, in her book *Tao of Chaos*, draws the parallel between the law of three and the Taoist idea of yang, yin and Tao, the latter being the very real, but indescribable flow that regulates everything and with which we seek oneness. She also makes the important point that the Taoist view is all about processes that are analogue (both/and) as opposed to digital (either/or). The Western tradition of thought is still stuck in either/or (is it a wave or is it a particle?), but has had to come to terms, at least at the quantum level, with the idea that opposites are implicit within one another.

Analogue modelling is also more consistent with a universe which is waving, rather than being a giant game of billiard balls. Music buffs tend to believe that the analogue signal on vinyl discs has a different and better quality than digital recordings, because the latter are made by chopping up the continuous sound wave signal into little bits which are then assigned numbers. Worse still, to compress data, some of the bits are left out and the brain is left to fill in the gaps. Such recordings have been shown to create nervous system stress because the brain has to work harder to 'connect the dots'. There is a moral here for all perceptual and cognitive activity: try to appreciate the big picture first and work your way down as necessary, rather than starting with the parts and then trying to connect them up into a meaningful whole. START WITH BEING SPACIOUS. It is in our nature to apprehend the essence of situations directly without the interposition of thought. That is, unless there is some special area of problem solving that needs a digital left-brained approach.

Examples of triality are ubiquitous and can be found in every realm of experience. The world of physics tends to come to mind first because physical dynamics are relatively simple to understand. This fact is often forgotten when confronted with the exotic world of quantum mathematics, but in essence, when we look at the subatomic world we see existence at its most basic and uncomplicated, with only a very modest assortment of entities interacting with one another. It is a world uncontaminated by the messy complexity of everyday reality and the mysterious incomprehensibility of biological existence. As a subject of study it is only for those who are looking for certainties and neatness in a chaotic world i.e. male type brains. Ironically, they find only uncertainty, paradox and mystery.

Within the simplicity of the quantum world, the law of three should show up very clearly, if indeed it is basic to the form of things. And we are not disappointed: if we start with the gross structure of an atom for example, we find the proton, the neutron and the electron. Going deeper we find three generations of quarks and even deeper, shadowy hypothetical entities called preons – three to a quark. It's three all the way down.

We can also take another approach to the atomic realm and look at overarching theories that attempt to explain how particles and waves interact with one another. The maths of the standard model certainly makes very accurate predictions about subatomic behaviour, but it is not elegant or aesthetic in any way and cannot take account of gravity. In contrast, an exciting innovation proposed by Garrett Lisi (Zeeya Merali, "Is This a Theory of Everything?") uses a beautiful model called E8, an eight-dimensional pattern with 248 points. By rotating this complex shape and projecting down into two dimensions we are able to see how various forces and particles interact. In one simple simulation on quark behaviour, I was delighted to see a hexagon enclosing a Star of David, that ancient symbol of interacting trialities. As Lisi says: "I think the universe is pure geometry – basically a beautiful shape twisting around and dancing over space-time." The model has been well received by the physics community, but has yet to stand the test of making verifiable predictions.

For the time being, however, it is another confirmation that 'it's geometry all the way down'. Incidentally, the number 248 is very interesting as it is the only three digit number apart from 124 that can express the idea of two successive octaves. Put the two numbers together and we get three octaves 1-2-4-8! Moreover, from a numerological point of view it reduces to 14 = 7+7 and is 8 times the prime 31. It is also a very stable number, with the square 4 and its octave holding the dynamic polarity of 2 within bounds. Further significant aspects of these numbers become apparent when we go on to consider the Law of Seven.

Before we leave three, however, I should mention another theory which is one of several that are turning their attention to the structure of space-time itself. Causal dynamical triangulations (CDT) proposes that space-time is made up of minute building blocks that are higher dimensional analogues of triangles, called 4-simplices. CDT has gone further than most theories in explaining why we have a three-dimensional universe, and is part of a trend to look deeper at the background matrix of existence, rather than being solely fascinated with the foreground 'zoo' of subatomic particles (Rachel Courtland, "Dimensions Vanish in Quantum Gravity").

Complementary to the Law of Three is Gurdjieff's Law of Seven, or Heptaparaparshinokh as he calls it in *Beelzebub's Tales*. Like the number three, seven is ubiquitous in physical law, daily life, mythology and religion, and I am sure I do not need to convince the reader of this by giving endless examples. The essential and key feature of the number seven is that it **defines an octave**, and as such is the basis of harmony and the way that waves interact with one another.

Before considering the octave in further detail, however, I

will say a word about the relationship between seven and eight. We think of a completed scale as having eight notes: Do Re Me Fa So La Ti Do. The second Do is recognisably similar to the first and gives the feeling of returning to a home base. This is related to the fact that a tone one octave above another is vibrating at exactly twice the rate, for example, middle C's frequency is 256 cycles per second and that of the C below is 128cps. Thus the eight note scale gives a feeling of completion, but only contains seven notes that sound distinctly different and which want to move in relation to one another. By this I mean that once you set the home note (the tonic), all other notes in the scale, except the eighth note, feel as if they want to move in relation to it. As a consequence, we only feel complete resolution in a musical piece when all the delightful movements up and down have finally come to rest back at the tonic. Seven is where the action is; the restless play of Shakti dancing, combining, recombining and destroying.

Put another way, the eight note scale is a completed one and as such can stand as a separate entity unto itself. From this point of view there is also a connotation of stasis, since a sequence has been finished and a new one not commenced. For example, in the Crowley Tarot we have the eight of cups as Indolence and the eight of swords as Interference. I have singled out the assignment of these qualities because contemporary research on group dynamics suggests that eight is a very unfavourable number if you want to get anything done in a committee or team; indolence and interference rule!

On the other hand, the second Do in an octave can be the beginning of a new sequence of 'higher' vibration, and thus the beginning of something new. Hence we see the eight of wands as Swiftness, while the eight of discs signals Prudence – things are going well but be careful, advice mirrored in the eighth major arcanum, Adjustment, whose indications are centering and balance. Thus the second Do can be a stop point or a transition which **connects and balances** with the next level. We generally assume that the next level is a 'higher' one in the sense that it represents a broader and more comprehensive system. The Ancient Greeks tended to sing their scales from higher notes to lower in recognition of this fact, and in so doing they hoped that mundane life could be infused with divine inspiration from above. Our current habit is, of course, quite different.

So, in labouring this point, my aim has been to explain how the Law of Seven has two faces: one dynamic and creative, the other stable and balancing. Thus Nirmal and Derek Pugh's fine book *Unveiling Creation: Eight is the Key* is essentially about the Law of Seven as it appears in both modern science and traditional thought, especially Hindu philosophy.

If we take the value of a beginning Do as 1, then the vibrational ratio of the succeeding notes will be: Re 9/8, Mi 5/4, Fa 4/3, So 3/2, La 5/3, Ti 15/8 and Do 2. The fact that these perfect ratios are harmonious to the ear was known to Pythagoras, and indeed, to the Chaldeans before him. The phenomenon is a vivid testament to the marriage of the rational and the aesthetic. Interestingly, however, the above ratios do not produce equal frequency changes at each interval. The actual change from Mi to Fa and from Ti to Do shows a slowing of frequency change, a fact that has particular significance when we consider process and the enneagram in the next chapter.

The evolution of the musical scale from the modes of ancient Greece is a complex story which is beyond our present scope, but one extraordinary fact stands out: that middle C's frequency at 256cps is 2 to the power of eight. Orchestras tune to a pitch slightly higher, around 261cps, but the scientific reference point is 256cps. Similarly, in the real world a perfect fifth on a fixed pitch instrument such as the piano is a fraction below 1.5 (1.498), to allow it to play harmoniously in all keys: so-called equal temperament.

The other obvious seven in our world is the rainbow, whose

sequence of colours follows the mnemonic known to every British schoolkid of my generation: Richard Of York Gave Battle In Vain. The colours do not neatly fall into harmonic ratios like pitch, however, because unlike musical notes, hues blend in to one another and there are no distinct transition boundaries.

There does seem to be a light octave though, with red beginning to appear at 400THz and violet disappearing into ultraviolet at around 800THz. It is also noteworthy that scientific texts do not recognise indigo as a distinct colour, because its frequency band at the commencement of violet is quite narrow. This should not detract from the clear subjective sense of seven colours, however, a fact which was also obvious to Isaac Newton when he originally described the splitting of white light through a prism.

Our experience of light is also remarkable, because the eye and brain between them can appreciate thousands of different hues with information coming from just three (yes, there it is again) colour receptors in the eye. These have sensitivities in the blue, green and yellow ranges. This feat is mirrored by the equally remarkable inkjet printer that can produce any hue, by a process called colour subtraction, with just three inks: yellow, cyan and magenta.

Like sound, the higher frequency bands at the blue end carry more energy and can be focused better than frequencies at the red end. Hence a blue laser like the one found in a Blu-ray player can read more densely packed information on a DVD. In parallel with this, blue is the best colour to activate you in the morning and set your circadian clock, so whenever possible get out first thing and do a few minutes of sky watching on a clear day (but no looking at the sun please). At night, avoid interior lighting that has a strong blue component, and instead use warm lighting that will be more sedative.

When it comes to the third physical manifestation of the Law of Seven, we are on very secure scientific ground indeed. The way that atoms combine with one another is now well understood and the laws in this realm form the basis of chemistry, both inorganic and organic. We have already seen how the electron shells surrounding an atom's nucleus can be calculated from the way vortices nest in platonic solids. The next step, and of course this is the simplified version, is to appreciate that atoms 'seek' stability by having eight electrons in their outer shell. Earlier we looked at the example of water, so let us take another common substance like rock salt, in which a sodium atom with one free electron easily combines with chlorine which has seven.

If, on the other hand, an atom already has the requisite eight electrons, like the gas argon, then it is non-reactive. Argon is like an already completed scale and does not have the dynamic striving toward a completing Do. The fact that chemical properties are partly dependent on the electron configuration also means that elements with the same number of potentially interactive electrons have somewhat similar chemical properties, even though their atomic weights are different. Thus sodium, potassium and lithium are similar, as are bromine, chlorine and fluorine. They are like the same note, only an octave removed from one another.

As we see later, the Law of Seven manifests in many other ways and various explanations have been forthcoming as to why this should be. The model of the octave seems to make perfect sense, but there may be related and even more basic explanations. Theorists such as Arthur Young point to the seven domains of the torus as being fundamental. I could try to explain what this means, but you are better off searching for a visual animation on Arthur Young's site. Similarly, the tetrahedron's seven axes of rotational symmetry could be invoked, or perhaps the sevenfold pattern at the heart of the Flower of Life is the real key.

Psychologists also have their say and quote, for example, George Miller's famous 1956 paper, "The Magic Number Seven, Plus or Minus Two". Miller pointed out that most humans can only classify a broad spectrum of possibilities into approximately seven distinct categories. For example, let's imagine that you are faced with a hundred swatches of cloth graded from jet black to brilliant white. They are then removed and you are presented with individual shades and asked where in the sequence you would place them. Most people can only do this with an accuracy that suggests a mental landscape of seven categories or less. And although Miller's findings have been disputed over the years, seven is still probably a fair rule of thumb for our everyday capacity to position things on a spectrum.

The argument for the ubiquity of seven as a product of our own cerebral limitations should not be discounted, especially when we consider the frequency with which seven turns up in traditional stories and religious myths. There is less traction, however, when it comes to the hard facts of chemistry or the mathematical realities of the octave. We must also be wary of false dichotomies. If seven is built into the universe at a very basic level, then we, as observing subjects, have seven-ness in our very nature, and are bound to have a bias in our perceptions toward this number; the snake eating its tail again. Similarly, it is probably futile to nominate any one form such as the torus as the key to seven's ubiquity. Numbers are supernal, they precede form and constitute the first inkling of manifestation. As such they are all very close to One and should be thought of as manifestations of One, reflecting and complexifying one another like the jewels in Indra's net.

With these weighty arguments in mind, now may be a good time to review the story so far. We have said that the ONE manifests as CONSCIOUSNESS/ENERGY and moves within ITSELF by waving and swirling, and that waves and vortices are thus the basic shapes of everything and at all scales. Vortices (matter) and waves (energy) can remain stable by relating to one another in harmonious proportions and orientations. The universe can manifest only through harmonic proportion, like a well composed piece of music. However, as in music, a vital dynamic is introduced by occasionally breaking the rules to create a measure of unpredictability and excitement, but not to a degree that ruins the whole show. This is the story of music in the 20th century, in which a progressive pushing of the boundaries eventually led to the madness of atonality and serialism. The pendulum is now swinging back; the excitement of novelty for its own sake has worn off, and musicians have realised that people do not pay good money for music that jars the natural harmoniousness of the human psyche (at least, not too much).

To complete our numerical story, however, we need to introduce the number five. Traditionally five is associated with growth, expansion and fecundity in the natural world. This association is not surprising, since so many phenomena in nature have an obvious five-based structure, including many wildflowers and fruit. Cut open an apple around its equator, for example, and you will find a pentagram formed by the seed compartment.

Five's closest association with the natural world is through the famous Golden Ratio, shown in Figure 6.

Fig. 6 The Golden Ratio

In Figure 6 we see how the Golden Ratio is calculated: the ratio of the overall length (A+B) to the larger segment (B) is the same as the ratio of (B) to (A). If we give a value of 1 to (B), then (A+B) becomes 1.618033989... an example of that strange class of numbers like pi that go on forever and which are there to remind us that infinity lurks in the heart of numbers themselves. The value of segment (A) is 0.618033989... These two numbers are known as the larger and lesser versions of phi (pronounced fy), and they are related to the number five through the geometry of pentagons, as shown below in Figure 7. They are also derived from five in the simple equations:

$(\sqrt{5} + 1)/2 = 1.618...$ $(\sqrt{5} - 1)/2 = 0.618...$

These two numbers have an interesting property, for if we add as follows, then we get:

$0.618 + 1.0 = 1.618$; $1.0 + 1.618 = 2.618$; $1.618 + 2.618 = 4.236...$ etc

And if we multiply as follows we get:

$0.618 \times 1.618 = 1.0$; $1.618 \times 1.168 = 2.618$; $2.618 \times 1.618 = 4.236...$ etc

This resonant relationship between adding and multiplying means that the Golden Ratio is ideal for harmoniously nesting waves, as well as basic shapes like triangles and pentagrams. It could be called a universal archetype of form, which is why it seems to turn up everywhere. Commonly quoted examples include the spiral growth of plants, sunflower seeds, pine cones and seashells. It is also found in many of the key proportions of

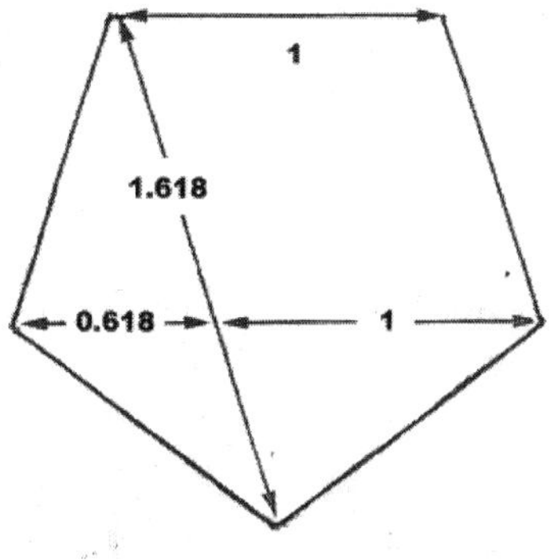

Fig. 7 Ratios in a Pentagon

the human body, and in the segmental growth of organisms in general. The Phi ratio is pleasing to the eye, so it is an important basis of aesthetics in art and architecture, as laid out in my favourite book on the subject (because there are lots of pictures), Gyorgy Doczi's *The Power of Limits*.

Phi is also related to those two very important numbers pi and e, the base of natural logarithms. Phi = 7/5 pi/e. Very elegant, very beautiful, very harmonious.

Finally, Phi can be derived from the Fibonacci sequence: 0,1,1,2,3,5,8,13,21,34… where each new number is the sum of the previous two. As the sequence progresses, the result of dividing any number by its predecessor comes closer and closer to 1.618… The Fibonacci numbers tell us something about how things progress, as if saying: "Add the present to the past and you get the future." There is also an interesting relationship between the Fibonacci series and space. Miranda Lundy, in her book *Quadrivium*, points out that space places some basic constraints on number such that, allowing for only perfect polygons, there are:

> 3 regular grids (think triangles, squares and hexagons), 5 regular solids (Platonic), 8 semi-regular grids and 13 semi-regular solids.

Unfortunately Ms. Lundy remains silent about why this spooky Fibonacci relationship should exist, but the implication is clear: space, number and form are intimately related. Space is not nothing, it is pregnant with the rules of manifestation.

Having added five to our small coterie of numbers, we can now step back and look at 3, 5 and 7, both in overall context and in relation to one another. The most striking thing about this sequence is that it consists solely of primes: numbers that can be divided only by themselves or one. Primes have fascinated mathematicians since ancient times; Euclid, for example, derived a clever proof as to why there were an infinite number of them. Their importance derives from the fact that all integers can be factored into primes, and so they constitute the building blocks of mathematics. They also have an elusive quality in that it has proven impossible to predict where primes will crop up in the infinite number series. This has assumed particular importance in our current world because primes are a central plank in the science of cryptography.

Most writings and presentations on primes tend to be opaque at best, a fact largely attributable to their authorship by experts in the field. I learned most from Peter Plichta's 1997 book, *God's Secret Formula*. His fresh approach derived from the fact that he was coming to the field from a background of chemistry and had few a priori assumptions about the subject. Plichta roams widely, but arrives at the simple conclusion that number is basic to the structuring of reality, and that triality is of particular importance. He sees all numbers as deriving from either 1, 2 or 3, and thus all number-based phenomena have triality at their heart. The sequences are as follows:

1 – 5, 7, 11, 13, 17, 19, 23, 29 etc i.e. primes
2 – 4, 8, 10, 14, 16, 20, 22, 26 etc
3 – 6, 9, 12, 15, 18, 21, 24, 27 etc

His particular attention, however, is on the primes, and we are left with the impression that their presence has an organising effect on other integers. They are the dynamic, unpredictable, but 'intelligent' manifestation of ONE (and hence can only be divided by ONE). Additionally, the number six and multiples thereof recur in the prime sequence, for example, 11,**12**,13 or 29,**30**,31. This is interesting, not only because it is inexplicable, but because six is a special representative of 1, 2 and 3, as it is both sum and product of these three numbers. Traditionally it has therefore been regarded as a harmonious and balancing influence. Thus in the Crowley Tarot, six appears as The Lovers, Pleasure (Cups), Success (Discs), Science (Swords) and Victory (Wands). Such a coincidence suggests that throughout the number sequence, the dynamic and idiosyncratic action of the primes is continually modified and balanced by the influence of 2 and 3. We are not far away, I think, from the Law of Three and the interplay of Affirming (1), Denying (2) and Reconciling (3) Forces.

In the light of these theories, we should also not be surprised that 5 and 7 play such an important part as the foundational two primes after one (conventionally 2 and 3 are regarded as primes, but not in the Plichta scheme). Particularly satisfying, however, is the fact that the basic primes play an important role in process as well as in form, and it is to this topic that we now turn. But first, a word about emergence.

In surveying both conventional and esoteric theories of the universe, one is struck by the fact that they are all highly reductionistic in nature, the product of left-brained, linear, 'tinker toy' thinking. The sad fact about Grand Unified Theories is that even if an elegant and final GUT were to emerge, it would explain nothing about the complex world in which we live. It would be like explaining how individual bits of Lego fit together and saying nothing about how you build a house with them. In this respect, physicists are way behind biologists who, after centuries of being second class citizens in the scientific world, can now to tell their colleagues a thing or two about complexity.

For it is in the life sciences that systems approaches, and the idea of the whole being greater than the sum of its parts, has had most effect. It is now taken for granted that in any living system, a new level of complexity is accompanied by the appearance of unexpected properties that could not have been predicted by reductionistic reasoning. This is the phenomenon of *emergence*. Physicists are beginning to get the message, and Nobel laureate Robert Laughlin is an example of someone at the forefront of this new kind of thinking. In his book *A Different Universe*, he proposes that physical law is an emergent property of aggregates of matter, not an immutable set of nebulous invariants that determine how matter behaves. This is why the lawfulness of matter is so elusive, because scientists insist that the same laws should operate at all scales i.e. that they should remain invariant no matter how much matter is present or how it is organised. Laughlin's view is heresy, of course, but it is the sort of theorising that is long overdue, and will be an avenue to clear the impasse at which particle physics and cosmology now find themselves.

Before moving on to the next chapter, I leave you with a comment from Alan Watts, on whom we can always rely for the last word on a subject, as well as for throwing a spanner in the works at the appropriate moment. His words are apposite for sacred geometrists, as well as for those of us who would seek to corral the Mystery into the confines of our own back yards. In his book *Tao: The Watercourse Way* he points out that geometrization, because of its rigidity and simplification, always reduces natural forms to something less than their living reality, their natural curvaceousness.

The world is always more than we can encompass with thought. We can discern regularities in the way the world works and appreciate that certain laws provide building blocks or notes for its construction, but they don't compose the tune. Instead, the universe seems to be a constantly changing creative act of emergence whose evolutionary path is always surprising.

10

Row, Row, Row Your Boat

Row, Row, Row Your Boat
Gently down the stream,
Merrily, merrily, merrily, merrily,
Life is but a dream.

We tend to think about the form of anything as if it were frozen immutably in time. This is the effect of memory: pale, static images filed, labelled and stuck in a drawer of kindred impressions. The living present, when actually attended without the dead hand of the past, is entirely different. Everything is in a state of flux, even the simplest object offers infinite points of view, and asks for the kind of absorbed interest usually only obtained under the influence of drugs.

The idea of the constant and changing flow of experience is an ancient one, and we find obvious parallels between the roughly contemporaneous Heraclitus and Lao Tzu. The former tells us that we never step into the same river twice and the latter concurs, taking the imagery of water as the signatory metaphor for the ways of Tao.

Thus in the Tao Te Ching we have:

> Nothing in the world is weaker than water, but it has no equal in overcoming the hard.

For a Taoist, the wise person flows within a natural order that manifests in non-linear and multidimensional ways, rowing their boat merrily down the stream and not fighting the whirls and swirls along the way. Inevitably, Alan Watts is our best guide to these mysterious depths of Tao through his many fine books, but especially in the previously mentioned *Tao: The Watercourse Way*. Especially important is the Chinese concept of Li, or organic order which, in contradistinction to mechanical order, is asymmetrical and non-repetitive; the sort of order that we see in natural forms such as moving water, clouds and trees.

We cannot grasp Reality's pattern in any finally objective way because we ourselves are also in the pattern. And just as the eye cannot see itself, so it is that we cannot take ourselves out of the picture to some stationary viewing platform outside the flow, even though this is our everyday conception of ourselves.

Everything is IN PROCESS and Process is to Form as Connection is to separation. In knowing this, we see the danger of using a word like consciousness as if it were a noun. It would be more correct to say consciousnessing for the awarenessing that follows the movement of energying. Being is a word nearer the mark, but cannot always do duty for these other terms. The important thing is to know that when we nominate a form with a noun, it is merely the reflection of how we have calibrated our Process/form (Connection/separation) setting. A good example of Process/form in action is our old friend water.

The ancient Chinese sages would have approved the efforts of Theodor Schwenk, a twentieth century anthroposophist and hydrologist who spent a lifetime studying the behaviour of water. His book *Sensitive Chaos* is an indispensable classic for anyone interested in the dynamics of flow and the relationship between water, ecology and the myriad forms taken by living creatures.

Schwenk was an acute observer of whole systems and realised that water is an organising principle throughout Nature because:

(1) It is the foundation of the planet's **metabolism**, transferring minerals, heat and organic materials in an endless process of recycling and renewal. Its planetary role is mirrored in the metabolism of individual organisms; it is the substance

of life par excellence.

(2) Water always has a **rhythm** as it moves, from the rippling surface of a stream, with its hypnotic tinkling and gurgling, to the daily tides which link us so tangibly to the cosmos. It is the great balancer, connecting and regulating heaven and earth in a round dance of rhythm and movement.

(3) Water is extremely **sensitive**, and its complex inner dynamics can change dramatically when subjected to minute shifts in the environment. In noting this, Schwenk was ahead of his time, anticipating our modern concept of sensitivity to initial conditions in complex systems (the 'butterfly effect').

His description of vortices and intersecting wave patterns is also very reminiscent of our earlier discussion about cosmic origins. In fact, he sees water as a universal giver of form, and illustrates his argument with countless beautiful examples of flow patterns in the anatomy of both organs and organisms. Water's capacity for in-formation exists as an interplay between its archetypal desire to form a sphere and its pragmatic and elegant capacity to flow with gravity.

Many of water's protean attributes still remain opaque to scientific investigation, not least its 'Goldilocks' ability to be solid, liquid or gaseous within just the right range to support and regulate the ecosphere. Viktor Schauberger, a fellow aquaphile with Schwenk, notes in this connection that water accomplishes its myriad roles by sacrificing itself to whatever it encounters, good or bad. Yet it can always regenerate and purify itself back to its pristine condition if allowed to keep in motion. No wonder it is such a potent symbol for the Tao or the Spirit. Moreover, like space, it has no intrinsic energy or motility of its own, taking all of its dynamism from heat and gravity. Yet as an intermediary between air, fire and earth, it moulds the landscape, circulates energy and provides the innumerable templates upon which life rests. Readers will recognise the parallel with human emotion and its role in providing coherence between the body, energy and cognition.

Water is LIVING WATER, just as our planet is a living being and not a great soulless machine set in motion by a blind watchmaker. Water's living quality is best regenerated by getting it to swirl and whirl in vortices. This happens naturally throughout the ecosphere, but there is also much current interest in developing technologies to accomplish the same thing. The general point, however, is that water must be allowed to follow its true nature, which is to be spacious: flowing, percolating, infiltrating, evaporating, precipitating, lapping, waving and exploring every possibility of movement and freedom. Any attempt to capture the spirit of water demeans its nature; bottled water is not LIVING WATER.

In their book *Design in Nature*, Bejan and Zane show how the fractal patterns we see in river deltas, trees or capillary beds are all examples of flow manifesting itself in the most efficient way possible, both in the moment and over time. They also apply the concept to other areas; some are obvious like transport or money, but others are not so immediately apparent: a university, for example, as a flow regulator of knowledge. Although there is danger of overreach in such theories, it is also a timely reminder that everything is in process, and that in its totality, a process is bigger than the sum of its parts. Heraclitus would have been very happy with such ideas – order in flux.

Flow in Psychology

Flow is also a familiar concept in psychology, although not necessarily acknowledged as such. Freud's free association method is, under ideal conditions, an uncensored flow of ideas and feelings, some of which have not previously found free expression. The activation of childlike, neurotic patterns in response to a life stress was likened to the backup of dammed water into old, normally dry channels. The analogy with water is not an accidental one, since emotion has traditionally been associated with the watery element. For example, the water-dominated Kapha constitution which we have met before is traditionally soft-hearted, nurturing and sentimental. Such individuals are easily moved to empathic tears and are a 'soft touch' for any hard luck story.

The flow of water is also the outward manifestation of our most profound emotions: sadness and grief. You may take issue with such a black and white statement, but I think that it is in line with the experience of most psychotherapists who find that beneath the passing parade of other feelings, it is usually tears that deeply cleanse and relax the psyche. The idea of energy flow, or 'streamings' that permeate the body after this kind of emotional release, is also implicit in most somatic therapies from Wilhelm Reich onwards. I remember my Bioenergetics teacher, Gerda Boyesen, repeatedly making the point that in the body, energy follows water and water follows energy. Reports of major fluid release (in one form or another) were legion after one of Gerda's treatments.

Today there is much emphasis on the dynamics of trauma and its effects on both body and mind. As I have intimated earlier, a traumatised individual may go through cycles of over- and under-arousal, both of which lead to unprocessed emotions; water has either turned to steam or solidified into icy hibernation. To re-establish the free flow of water, we have to cool steam by providing a safe therapeutic space and teaching relaxation, and we melt ice through the warm, nurturing presence of the therapist. Once water begins to flow, it finds its own level in its own time i.e. a person can begin to self-regulate. But these processes do need their own time, and must be respected with the same spirit of allowing that we accord any natural unfolding.

No aspect of contemporary science, technology or administration would be possible without flow charts, and ideas about flow have inevitably infiltrated their way into performance psychology, not least as a result of Mihaly Csikszentmihalyi's (C's) book, *Flow: The Psychology of Optimal Experience*. Before going further, however, I extend to the reader a courtesy not usually provided by commentators on C's work, and that is to illuminate the pronunciation of his name, a time-consuming conundrum with which you no longer have to be concerned. According to Jeff Warren in his book *Head Trip*, it goes something like this: Me-high Chick-sent-me-high. So there you have it.

Professor C. began his investigations with the study of visual artists, whom, he found, often entered a state of absorption characterised by present moment focus, altered time perception, loss of self-awareness, a fusion of sensing and doing, and a positive feeling of reward. Professor C. described this state as "flow", an evocative term, and seemingly quite appropriate to the subjective evaluation of those experiencing it. He went on to find the same sort of experience in diverse activities, from sports to surgery.

The concept is not new, of course, and describes a state that has been known and described since time immemorial. The Taoists can claim precedence again, in their concept of 'wei wu wei', the doing that is not doing i.e. effortless action. They would also be suitably appalled at the modern idea that this can be taught as a skill rather than arising from broad-based cultivation over a lifetime. An example of the Eastern approach can be seen in the art of Aikido, a name that derives from the roots ai (harmony), ki (energy) and do (the way). According to this philosophy, the best way to encounter your opponent (or your life) is through a process of allowing rather than doing. This involves using universal energies that are already in operation, which in the case of an opponent is the combined effect of their kinetic energy and gravity. Such is the elegant way of dealing with opposition, the way of least action as Arnold Mindell (*Earth-Based Psychology*) calls it, and a way that accords with the 'desire' of the universe for the easiest way to balance yin and yang. Mindell also draws our attention to the parallel between this concept, and the way a light beam always finds the quickest route between two locations, its least action.

Using an even broader perspective, we might see the ideas of effortless action and flow as being facets of the general notion of play. Our modern discourse on this concept probably owes most to Johan Huizinga's 1955 classic *Homo Ludens*, in which he characterises play as having a number of characteristics, including: lack of seriousness, total absorption, no profit motive and a complete separation from ordinary life. I like Huizinga's approach because he does not fall into the sterile reductionism that has interpreted play in terms of learning, problem solving, social bonding and miscellaneous other psycho-social constructs. Certainly play encompasses all of these ideas, but it is always more than the sum of its parts.

Most of all, there is a freedom in play which escapes easy definition, and which is certainly different from any of our ideas about competitive sport. Because it does not involve "end gaining", to use Jean Klein's term, and has no immediate meaning or purpose, it is the ultimate theatre of creativity. Who can doubt that the artist is the luckiest person in the world, and most envied, because their work is play – absorbing, rewarding, kaleidoscopic? Although the artist's lot is not without difficulties, it is nonetheless Blake's world of eternal delight. It is also a fractal of the divine play, Leela, out of which the world is made and sustained, just for the cosmic buzz of it.

The Enigma of Time

The radically different sense of time that we experience when absorbed in play inevitably brings us to consider the relationship between time and awareness. Just as space implicitly supports form, so does the passage of time act as the backdrop to process. Time is, however, even more mysterious than space, in that we only experience it through the motion of forms, whether they be mental or physical in nature. Time is also paradoxical in that we perceive it as moving remorselessly onward and yet we measure it as cyclical. Process shares this dual nature: things change and evolve, but they also go in cycles; we might say that process is essentially spiral in nature, moving in a particular direction but often appearing to regress to an earlier stage. The stock market is an obvious example of this, one of the reasons for its enduring fascination to investors and theorists alike.

Ideas about time highlight a key difference between traditional Eastern and Western thought. The occidental religions have always viewed human progress as a brief interlude between a creation time and a final moment of resolution, whether this be an apocalypse or the arrival of the messiah. Eastern thought emphasises the eternal nature of creation and destruction, which follow one another like day and night over vast aeons of time. Even then, the life of a universe is but one breath of God. Not surprisingly, science still apes the Western cultural view and sees a straight line from the 'big bang' to a burnt out, cold and lifeless infinity. What nonsense! Everything cycles, rotates, returns and dances around a centre. We feel this in our bones and see it every day in our lives.

The measurement of time is an ancient preoccupation of humans, and we have evidence of a moon calendar from Neolithic Scotland as far back as the eighth millennium BC. Our practical conception of time has probably not changed much since those distant ancestors, with the major benchmarks of day and year fixed by the relationship of the Earth to the Sun. And although we no longer pay much attention to the moon, many people, especially women, will confidently testify to its cyclic powers on both their physical and mental states. Heavenly time has been supplemented in the modern age with atomic time: the unbelievably rapid agitation of caesium atoms keeping a beat in the heart of atomic clocks. But at whatever scale we observe and try to capture time, it is always through rhythmic oscillation. Time is a round dance at all scales.

Those Numbers Again

In the last chapter, when we looked at certain basic ideas about creation, we had a preliminary foray into the number laws that seem built into the nature of things. These laws, together with other mathematical relationships, also seem to be inextricably bound up with process, something that we can begin to examine through the work of Arthur Young, an American engineer who, after helping to develop the Bell Helicopter, turned his mind to more esoteric matters.

In his book, *The Reflexive Universe,* Young explores, in modern terms, the ancient idea that creation manifests as a progressive entrapment or condensation of spirit in matter. The classic Western myth on this theme is the rebirth story of Isis and Osiris, which starts when the latter is entrapped in a coffin by the 'evil' Set. Subsequently, the coffin is further enclosed by a tamarisk tree, but later Set dismembers the body of Osiris and scatters the various parts in a marsh. Eventually Isis collects all the pieces except the genitals, and having put Osiris back together, manages to conceive with him (sans reproductive apparatus). The product of this immaculate conception is the infant Horus, who grows up and finally defeats Set.

Young has taken our contemporary knowledge about evolution, cosmogony and atomic physics to create a seven-stage scheme of entrapment and release which looks like this:

1. Light — 7. Humans
2. Particles — 6. Animals
3. Atoms — 5. Plants
4. Molecules

Fig. 8 Arthur Young's Evolutionary Trajectory

In stages 1–3 we see the involution of light into matter and the restriction of light's infinite potential into the immutable definition of an element. The molecular realm marks a turning point, with progressively greater complexity leading eventually to organic life and an inexorable movement away from fixity and stasis. Within each of the stages 3–7, there are seven substages of development, evidence for which Young gathers from a wide range of data. As a possible explanation for the role of seven, Young invokes the torus, and (as far as I know) was the first writer to do so.

On a much smaller time scale, seven obviously crops up in connection with the universal seven-day week, whose origins, however, seem to be lost in the fog of prehistory. We do know that the Babylonians were using a seven-day week in the 6th century BC, as were the Israelites during their Babylonian captivity. But for a more credible explanation we should probably look back to ancient moon calendars and their tracking of the roughly 28-day moon cycle with its four quarters. The sun tells us about the progress of the day and the seasons, but the moon is the best yardstick for timekeeping between these two markers, especially as it is so closely linked to both oceanic and emotional tides. There is also the intriguing fact that we all have a weekly biological rhythm, with mood being lowest at the beginning of the week and then picking up and peaking on Saturday. It is possible that our seven-day week is a product of this physiological cycle rather than the reverse being the case, but the question remains wide open.

Seven also seems to be an important number in biological development. The brain reaches it full size at age seven, puberty is traditionally around fourteen years and the nervous system reaches maturity at around twenty-one years (at least in girls, with boys lagging somewhat). After this, the seven periodicity becomes less definite, although we can make a case that few athletes reach their peak after twenty-eight years, and few endurance specialists shine after thirty-five years (see Tour de France data). Forty-two marks a definite end to reproductive activity in women, and forty-nine marks the beginning of menopause and andropause. There is, of course, great variability in humans with regard to these transition points and many will think that I am stretching the facts, as I may well be. But it has certainly been my personal experience that life tends to progress in septenary 'chunks' quite independently of my conscious intentions.

Process Maps

If we look to the esoteric literature for further guidance on number and process, our most informative source in relation to the numbers seven and three is the enneagram, a diagram introduced by Gurdjieff to his pupils in the early twentieth century. 'G' claimed that it is a map applicable to all phenomena, but one that requires dedication and practice before it will reveal its secrets. As conceived by the master, the enneagram is dynamic, mutable and multidimensional, and not to be confused with the popular personality test spawned much later by Oscar Ichazo. Those wishing to further their study of the enneagram should start with JG Bennett's *The Enneagram*.

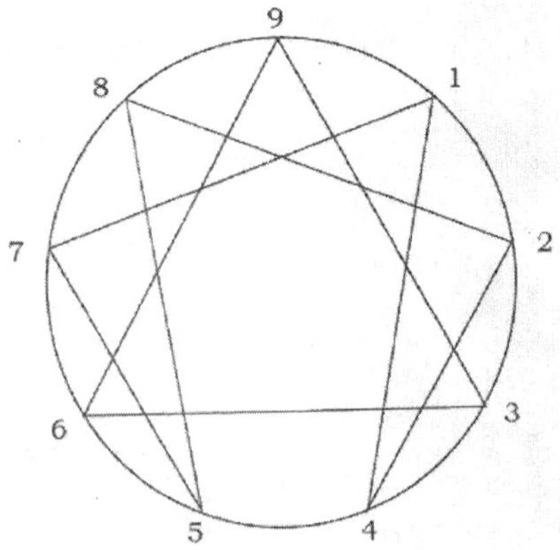

Fig. 9 The Enneagram

Figure 9 shows the basic enneagram structure with the octave of points 1–8 mapping the progress of, say, a particular human endeavour. Klausbernd Vollmar (*The Secret of Enneagrams*) tells us that we should think of these points as being arranged three dimensionally on a spiral. Three, six and nine represent the affirming, negating and reconciling forces respectively, and the progress from one to eight has something of the following stages:

1. Conditions are right and an impulse to undertake something new arises.
2. We begin to gather resources and make preliminary moves, but the process may lose steam unless there is a new impetus at point 3.
3. This is a 'shock' from outside, a new quality in the form of help, or even just new information.
4. The work progresses with all its inevitable difficulties and obstructions.
5. Things are going slower than anticipated, there is a danger of discouragement setting in, even though the project has gone too far to abandon.
6. A second 'shock' in the form of help from outside arises. The striving and the work done so far have made it more likely that we can make conscious use of this assistance.
7. The goal can now be seen clearly and work gathers pace to reach the final destination at:
8. Success.
9. This point is essentially outside the processes described so far. As the reconciling force it symbolises the action of the whole universe in the dynamic of our project. In systems language, it represents the hierarchy of systems within which our project is nested. It can also stand for the creative seed that will germinate as the next (higher) development.

These stages are also linked by pathways which demonstrate how they are related to one another. For example, in looking from 2 toward 8, I am getting a better idea of the goal because I have started to work in a practical way. In looking back from 8 to 5, I am learning about the nature of creative struggle, something that will stand me in good stead for my next endeavour.

The relationship of the stages also reveals the number 7, for if you follow the paths from 1 through 4, and 4 through 2 etc, you will get a number which is the reciprocal of 7: 1.1428571... Reciprocals are especially important in esoteric number theory because they indicate the number's mirror image reflected in unity. The geometric 7 is to be found in the heptagon at the centre of the figure.

The account that I have given so far is, of necessity, highly superficial and I can but remind the reader that the enneagram, like other cosmological systems such as the Tarot, can only reveal its true riches with continuing and patient study. Before I leave the topic, however, I would direct your attention to the strange overlap between the enneagram and Marko Rodin's Vortex Based Mathematics. You can learn more at RodinAerodynamics.org, while at The Enneagram Institute Discussion Board there is an animation which shows how the Rodin scheme transforms into the enneagram by simply transposing points 1 and 8. I suspect that the enneagram and the Rodin scheme are mirror images joined by the centrality of the 3/6/9 dynamic.

There is also a link back to primes. The most important numbers in the enneagram are 3, 7 and 9. All prime numbers end with 1, 3, 7 or 9.

As Rodin has demonstrated, triality is a key dynamic in number-based cosmometry, and so we would also expect to find 'three-ness' as an important theme in the traditional cosmic maps, Tarot and I Ching. With respect to the former, it is surprising, given the glut of books on the subject, how few authors comment on the number relations so clearly evident throughout its structure. The first systematic analysis with which I am familiar is that of Papus (Dr Gerard Encausse, 1865–1916), a French occultist who trained in the Hermetic and Kabbalistic knowledge that was enjoying a renaissance in 19th century Europe.

In his *The Tarot of the Bohemians*, he makes a case for interpreting the Tarot using a 3 and 7 based system. He derives this approach from the four letter name of God in the Old Testament, a word that I do not reproduce here out of respect for the tradition of silence around the Holy Name. He also introduces, well before Gurdjieff, a scheme which is based on the dynamic interaction between active, passive and neutralising forces. Paul Foster Case, another occultist in the Western tradition and founder of "Builders of the Adytum", is another proponent of a septenary arrangement and recommends interpretation of the Major Arcana using the following layout:

1	2	3	4	5	6	7	
8	9	10	11	12	13	14	The zero card is 'outside' the realm
15	16	17	18	19	20	21	of integers.

The first row represents powers or potencies, the second row laws or agencies and the third row conditions or effects. Thus the Magician (I, Will) works through Strength (VIII, dominion over the instinctual nature) to overcome the Devil (XV, entrapment in delusion). The Minor Arcana also have a seven theme, with 8×7 cards in toto, but an even more intriguing pattern arises when we look at the geometrical arrangements that are possible with the various components of the deck. Appendix 2 contains an article on this topic which I wrote for *The Magician* in 2000. I hope that, like me, you will marvel at these patterns that seem so far from being coincidental.

The Chinese Book of Changes, the I Ching, reveals a similar vista of complex internal arrangements as follows:

It is binary in nature with the complementary pair, yin and yang.

Its basic unit is the triplet which has three lines and bears a similarity to the basic code letters in DNA. The trigrams are named after natural phenomena, for example, Thunder or Lake, and each is associated with one of the eight directions.

There are eight basic trigrams which can be combined into 64 hexagrams, each with six lines. In the process, we move from images to multifaceted concepts with names such as Returning or Small Accumulating.

The I Ching, as its name implies, is a process manual par excellence, and comments on the flow of events and their continuously mutating nature. It is quite different from the Tarot, in which forms tend to take precedence over flux.

On the surface, the number structure of the I Ching, as defined so far, could be construed as basically binary in nature with 64 hexagrams, the product of 2 to the power of 6. Things get more interesting, however, when we consider the *process* of divination. Traditionally, a bundle of 50 yarrow sticks is manipulated to ascertain the value of each line of the hexagram, whether it is yin or yang or a changing line (one that is transforming into its opposite). The yarrow method uses only 49 sticks because one is put aside, a parallel to the Fool being set apart from the other Major Arcana in the Tarot. The method whereby the sticks are then sorted results in the following probabilities for any particular type of line:

> Changing yin – 1/16, Changing yang – 3/16, Yang – 5/16, Yin – 7/16

These probabilities are not reproduced by the coin method and practitioners wanting to be faithful to the spirit of the oracle should either use the stick method or, as recommended by Katya Walter (in *Tao of Chaos*), use a bag of different coloured stones that reflect the above ratios i.e. 7 black stones for yin, 5 white stones for yang, 3 red stones for changing yang and 1 blue stone for changing yin.

One may be a regular I Ching user, but still not realise how innately conservative are its comments and prognostications. The bias toward stable yin is clearly a comment on the innate conservatism of the cosmos. Things change, of course, but only against the backdrop of an intrinsic inertia that ensures a minimum chance of irrevocable chaos.

It is also obvious that the I Ching's harmonic structure 'riffs' with all the numbers from 1–8 inclusive. To further the musical analogy, the number series, 2–4–8, provides the form or keyboard upon which the music of the primes 1–3–5–7 works its evanescent magic.

This tension between process and form is most clearly symbolised by the 7/8 relationship, examples of which we have seen in the Enneagram, Tarot and I Ching. Seven represents dynamic energy and transformation i.e. process, while eight stands for conservative, self-contained energy and therefore form. And although this may sound neat and almost convincing, it is also a way of saying rather little about a world that is **very mysterious indeed**.

Keeping a Beat

The two series of numbers discussed above reminds us to look back at our basic principles of world creation and the fact that "it's all about waves and spinning vortices." Standing and nesting waves create forms, travelling waves convey energy, and the movement of energy is the measure of time. Waves have a bipolar pulse form: at one moment rising above the baseline, at the next falling back below the baseline and so on. This basic two-step is the foundation of all rhythm, and one familiar to us all from our own first baby steps – one two, one two etc. The easiest rhythms for moving, singing and dancing have even time signatures because they play to our bilateral symmetry: we go a little bit one way, then we go the other. We like to wave to and fro. When we introduce three into the equation, things are immediately trickier, but at the same time potentially more interesting; waltzing is fun when you arrange yourself opposite a complementary (and complimentary) partner. And you naturally want to start spinning.

The passage of time appears to be substantial and predictable because we rely on the unfailing pulses of Nature. The sun rises and sets, the moon waxes and wanes, and in our ancestral home there is a dry season and a wet season. These become elaborated into a 4-beat with the addition of dawn and dusk, the four phases of the moon and the four seasons etc.

The closer we look at how things progress in life, both on a personal and a collective level, we see how everything is cyclic in nature. *Systems maintain their stability through cycling.* This is comprehensible when we consider how a task becomes easier and more pleasurable when we are in a rhythm, whistling while we work. Without dynamic cycling, it is impossible to maintain long-term homeostasis, things either become ossified or chaotic. Incidentally, the word 'chaos', as it is used in 'chaos theory', is a complete misnomer when applied to complex systems such as the weather, the flow of water or brainwaves. Weather is never chaotic, it just can't be predicted very well using linear mathematics. The planetary weather self-regulates with multiple subsystems all cycling and balancing one another. Another misleading term, the 'strange attractor', is simply a way of saying that complex systems oscillate within certain bounds.

It is not just natural systems that cycle: social mood, the stock exchange, collective violence, population, political leanings, innovation, fashion and much else, all show rhythmic structures over time. In fact, many lives have been spent, and some would say misspent, seeking out cycles of one sort or another, often in search of an easy dollar.

Robert Prechter is one such modern student of the stock exchange whose efforts in this area have definitely not been wasted. For many years he has used a method of analysis discovered by the American financial consultant RN Elliott (1871–1948). In his retirement, Elliott studied the daily vagaries of the market and noticed a recurrent pattern: prices tended to go up in three steps and then come down in two. The accompanying figure shows one such cycle, with the upward trend driven by *motive waves* 1, 3 and 5, and *corrective waves* 2 and 4. The downward trend shows two waves A and C with an intervening countertrend at B. This 5-3 step dance has a fractal quality, so for example, one could put the waveform 1-2 under the microscope to reveal another 5-3 pattern. In the real world of stock forecasting, considerable complication arises, but despite this, the method has shown a good deal of practical utility.

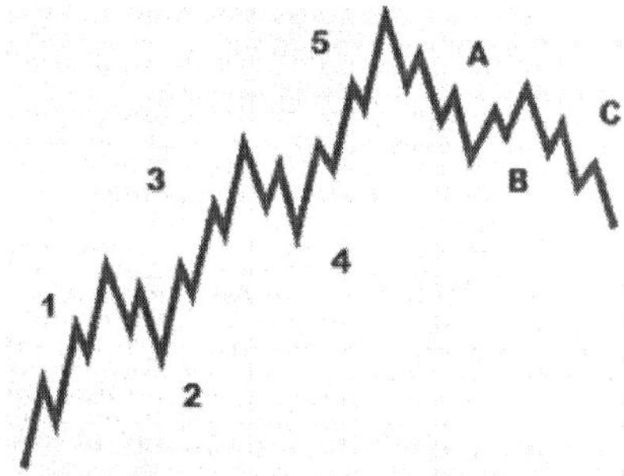

Fig. 10 An Elliott Wave Sequence with Subwaves

In Prechter's book, *The Wave Principle of Human Social Behavior,* you will find a detailed account of Elliott wave analysis and its relationship to the Fibonacci sequence. It should not surprise us that principles which we have already encountered should continue to apply in the dance of form/process. We can also see clearly in the Elliott wave sequence how the general motive trend comes from prime number waves, whilst corrective impulses derive from even numbers whose binary nature tends to cycle the process back toward a mean. The asymmetricality of the process results in growth i.e. it is evolutionary in nature and only found in living systems.

Prechter's most significant finding, however, is that financial, social and political trends follow a cycle that depends on waves of alternating collective optimism and pessimism. Since his original contributions to this new field of socionomics, there has been increasing research interest in how social mood affects economic cycles. As a result, the academic world is finally beginning to relinquish the rigid mathematical models that have viewed the market as merely a collection of rational, self-interested entities. What a discovery, that human beings are affected by tides of emotional fancy that are far from sensible! What would we do without professors?

The idea of cycles of mood is very dear to my heart, because I see mood and its modulation as central to our personalities, something that I elaborate in Chapter 13. Suffice it to say here that a constant shift of dominance between our two cerebral hemispheres, the so-called ultradian rhythm, is the basic beat of our daily lives. When we can feel and flow with this beat, then body and mind are in accord and all is well. If we ignore our basic rhythm, then stress and pain are the inevitable outcome. The most important health imperative is: FOLLOW THE BEAT.

The ultradian cycle, which has a wave of about 2 hours, stands at the midpoint of a hierarchy of beats that extend from the molecular to the cosmic. Here is a small selection of rhythms relevant to humans, from lower to higher frequency: yearly, seasonal, monthly (lunar), weekly, daily (circadian), ultradian, peristaltic (digestive), respiratory, cardiac and cerebral. All of the body's organs have their own clocks, as do individual cells, with the brain acting as a central conductor of our personal orchestra, as well as acting as modulator between the body and the rhythms of the environment.

Like any complex system, we can only maintain our integrity

through *coordinated rhythm*: if an individual part loses the beat, then it either atrophies or goes rogue, like cancer. Thus the best plan to heal from any dis-ease is to live a simple life in nature for a while. This is the surest way to get one's personal harmonies back in shape, because a natural environment tends to *entrain* our body clocks. And as discussed previously, being quiet and spacious also helps, since the high frequency interference from 'mind chatter' and our noisy surroundings has a very disruptive effect on other more intrinsic rhythms. Meaning and purpose also have a very salubrious effect on health, because a life with direction is not constantly chopping and changing – it is more *coherent*.

Gerta Ital was a German actress who went to study Zen in Japan after World War II. In her book, *On the Way to Satori* (which is a most remarkable story), she laments the passing of the truly isolated monastic settings of old Japan, in which the daily life of the monks was so completely integrated into remote natural settings. Even in the 1960s, when she was living there, such places were being overrun by tourists and the sprawl and noise of modern life.

One of the miracles of the brain is that its activities remain fairly stable despite the welter of stimuli to which it is subject, and as such it is the supreme example of a complex system kept coherent through its rhythmic structure. It has a basic idling frequency, the much-discussed alpha band of around 8Hz, which functions as a 'ready to pay attention' state. Below it are the theta (4Hz) and delta (2Hz) bands, both associated with decreasing arousal and sleep. Above we find the beta band (16Hz+) associated with alertness and attention, and the gamma frequencies (32Hz+) linked to integration of networks across the brain. I have cheated a little with the frequency values, since each band actually covers a range; nonetheless there is a strong suggestion of a harmonic relationship.

The rhythmic structure of the electroencephalogram, however, says little about the age-old problem of the relationship between brain and consciousness. The difficulty of this so-called 'hard question' has not deterred endless theorising, much of which falls into the 'empty barrels' category. Guilio Tononi's writings may be an exception, especially in the light of the discussions so far. His "integrated information theory" proposes that consciousness arises when there is a precise ratio between a neural network's differentiation as a *separate* system, and its integration (i.e. *connection*) with other relevant brain systems. He calls this ratio phi, which is not surprising since he has written a book on the subject of this number. In his article on Tononi's work, Christof Koch ("Crystal Clear on Consciousness") also tells us that, in this theory, the state of a network may be represented as a shape which we can think of as a crystal in high-dimensional space.

At this point the reader may have a 'flashbulb' moment, and recall our previous discussion of Connection/separation. As these current explanatory attempts remind us, it's Connection/separation all the way in and it's Connection/separation all the way out. It is also intriguing that a contemporary information theory of consciousness should invoke crystalline shapes as a mathematical expression of conscious experience. Even so, these theories, however elegant, leave us no closer to bridging the gap between my subjective sense of being and the neural activities that correlate with it. The 'strange loop' of brain and consciousness (in which each seems to be dependent on the other) is just that: very strange, and a mystery that is insoluble at a purely analytic level.

Moreover, theorising on these matters, and discussing the importance of number, ratio and shape, should not encourage us to believe that we are well equipped to understand the dynamic and ever fluctuating nature of process as flow and rhythm. The ups and downs of a two-dimensional chart (or an enneagram) are one thing, but for individuals living in the real world, events seldom follow a readily comprehensible or predictable pattern.

Instruments such as the I Ching or Tarot, by virtue of their harmonic correspondences, may help us tune in to certain trends in our lives, but we must acknowledge that the Whole is always less graspable than we would like it to be from the vantage of our little Part. If Life were controllable, then there would be no real excitement, and we would gain no satisfaction from the inklings of true ignorance that we may acquire with age.

Those of us who keep a diary may also have the unsettling experience of reading back over old entries and finding that ideas which we are cherishing as recent insights were present in our minds decades ago. I had one such instance recently, when I found an essay that I had written at school fifty years ago. It contained a description of the three constitutional types of Sheldon, something in which I thought I had become interested only in early middle age. Hopefully my understanding has now matured and become established at a 'higher octave', but I could be deluded of course. To quote Mark Twain: "History does not repeat itself, but it does rhyme."

This kind of gradual maturing of ideas, skills and life themes suggests a spiral shape to the way we progress in life. This was certainly Jung's conclusion when he observed the individuation process in his patients. It seems necessary for us to periodically lose the thread, so that it can be rediscovered in a deeper or more meaningful way; our local version of the Creator's game of hide and seek. We 'go around the church to find the spire', each time gathering a new perspective. Or we may continue to circumambulate with no apparent result. Sometimes a revelation only comes after much wandering in the desert or walking around Jericho, blowing a trumpet with all our worth.

Culture also seems to progress in this way, with societies spiralling around the 'strange attractors' of collective memes that slowly evolve into higher forms. As with individuals, regression is possible at any time, but the overall result seems to be evolutionary in nature. This sort of process has been organised into a system called *Spiral Dynamics* by the late Professor Clare Graves. The eight spiral tiers of his framework constitute a template which is applicable to the development of individuals, organisations, societies and the human race as a whole. The book *Spiral Dynamics* by Don Beck and Christopher Cowan provides an account which does full justice to the richness of this model, and so I give an outline of the eight stages with apologies for its brevity and inadequacy.

Each level is colour-coded from the very basic beige to the complex and wholistic turquoise:

Beige: Survival is the main issue, getting basic needs met.

Purple: Tribal mentality, individuals are subsumed by the group.

Red: Egocentric orientation with power and domination the main themes.

Blue: Authoritarian organisation with control through common belief systems, regulations and hierarchy.

Orange: Competitive, optimistic, achievement orientated; individuals function within a free-wheeling capitalist society to further material progress.

Green: Egalitarian ideals and the valuing of nurture, consensus and sharing, over 'dog eat dog'.

The final two levels are governed by memes that transcend the mechanics of daily living and the challenge of getting on with one's neighbour. In an echo of Maslow, they are called 'being' as opposed to 'subsistence' value levels:

Yellow: The fact of beingness or conscious existence is valued over materiality. Differences are seen as complementary, and flow and change as intrinsic to the nature of things.

Turquoise: The world is seen as a unity and is more mind than material in nature. Individual selves are both separate from and joined with the whole. Thinking expands into intuitive and multidimensional modes.

Every level contains all previous levels, each of which can be activated should circumstances require it, as in trusting God but tying up your camel.

Graves' system is extremely useful for tracking developments in our global and local culture, but as well as for looking at our personal evolution and noting how we are often conflicted between levels. With luck, we might also notice that however convoluted things may appear in the short term, our lives seem to be moving in an inexorable direction; there seems to be an evolutionary pull, whatever our personal intentions may be. James Hillman might view this as the continual prompting of our inner Daemon, an individual spiritual template that demands expression and fulfilment. The cost of ignoring the inner god is suffering and neurosis. I remember that Jung had an inscription carved outside his retreat to the effect that the Daemon is present whether we summon it or not.

We return to the spiral motif later on, especially in discussing the labyrinth as a practical template for meditation. However, before going any further I would like to have one final word on the subject of time.

When we look at a clock face, it is immediately apparent that we measure time using a sexagesimal (60) based system. We know that this framework goes back to Mesopotamian times, and a simple explanation for its use is that 60 is conveniently divisible by 2, 3, 4, 5, 6, 10 and 12. In the same way, the circle of 60 degrees perfectly accommodates the triangle, square, pentagon and hexagon. This is all well and good, but a more 'cosmic' view arises when we remember our faithful dodecahedron with its 12 pentagonal faces and 60 axes of symmetrical rotation. What do we see on a clock face but 12×5 intervals with hands continuously rotating and sweeping out the sixty directions of its ever-recurring circuit? There is something very delicious in considering that space and time (which are not separable) are both in-formed by a topology that appears in our 3D world as the dodecahedron. For more information on the platonic solids and time, see the work of Randall Carlson.

Time/process is a great mill that grinds slowly but grinds true. This is an expression that I frequently use in connection with the scientific method which plods along, often light years behind intuition, but gets there in the end; like doubting Thomas it has to experience the truth in a very direct and sensual/consensual way. It is the tortoise in the well-known myth, crossing the finish line ahead of intuition's brilliant but erratic speed. So it is with the big truths of society and Creation. What is true, by definition, endures even though it may be deeply hidden for a while. What is false must perish, even though the devil may have his moment in the sun before being swept away by what is real.

Can we say, then, what might be true in the last two chapters? Only in a very tentative and provisional way, anything else would be hubristic. So here are a few concepts and images that I find useful when contemplating The Great Mystery:

Awareness is Light is Awareness. Put another way, the One Substance manifests as Consciousness/Energy (Shiva/Shakti).

Light within itself is timeless, but manifests through waving and spiralling.

Waving and spiralling light (energy and matter) maintain their coherence through the harmony of proportion.

The Laws of Three and Seven express the ways in which the universal dynamic of Connection/separation functions.

Number is basic to Process and Form. Form is Process, Process is Form. And beyond duality and non-duality: Form is Form and Process is Process. The same can be said for the parallel relationship: Connection (addition and multiplication) / separation (subtraction and division).

All Form/Process is, at heart, the zero of Light reflecting Itself through Itself: the Uroboros.

Everything returns or cycles back because everything is One. An act of separation/discrimination divides the One into Two. Three is the connecting and balancing dynamic across the created boundary.

Continuing creation is:

Driven by the One series – dynamic, unpredictable.

Restrained by the Two series – stable, formed.

Balanced by the Three series in a recursive movement of connection.

The Whole and the Part dance in Harmony. The Music plays on, always seeking the key note, but forever dancing off into new and more complex variations.

11

Living in 3D

In the universe there are things that are known, and things that are unknown, and in between there are doors.
William Blake

The universe is VAST. Our sun is one of 200 billion stars in our galaxy and there are probably over 300 billion other galaxies. Light from the most distant celestial objects has been travelling billions of years to reach us at a speed of 300,000km per second. The universe is incomprehensibly huge and, we are told, getting bigger by the moment. And it's 99.9999999…% space. Science and the wonders of our own consciousness have given us a vision that dwarfs the cosmologies of the past, both in grandeur and scale. Yet this modern myth is a poisoned fruit: on the one hand it inspires awe, on the other it seems to relegate us to complete insignificance as we endlessly circle our unremarkable cosmic suburb.

Our traditional reverence for the heavens has become dulled by the pontifications of materialists and reductionists, who see nothing but a soulless universe inexorably winding down under the influence of basic physical forces. This is our contemporary creation myth, one that contextualises, as does Darwinian Theory, all aspects of modern life. But despite the power of this myth and the confidence of those who profess it, the story is full of holes, not the least of which is the fact that most of the matter and energy in the universe appears to be missing. So-called dark matter and energy are thought to be hiding throughout the visible universe, but so far, not a skerrick of the stuff has turned up. The Empress of the night sky continues to be obscured behind invisible veils.

A glaring hole in an otherwise well-established and supported theory often heralds a paradigm shift, and it seems highly likely that we are due for one at any moment. Carl Jung pointed to the fact that our modern age commenced when humans began to withdraw their projections of mythical and archetypal themes from the world around them. The most distant projections, those that had been linked to the heavenly bodies, were the ones that were withdrawn first. Thus the scientific revolution can be traced to Copernicus, Kepler and Galileo and their description of a universe with no discernible divine heaven, and an earth demoted to just another celestial body.

As with contemporary culture, we all have to face the fact that we are not the centre of the universe, but with maturity we may also come to see ourselves as part of life's unity, and thereby gain a new sense of significance and worth. It is this latter sense which allows us to affirm that consciousness is the central fact of existence, and that we are always standing at the centre, both physically and existentially. The reductionists constantly try to push us to the margins by their purely material explanations for awareness, but we must not be seduced by their simplistic arguments. The truth is plain: I am completely at the centre of the Mystery and cannot be reduced to anything less.

Standing at the centre implies 'right relationship' to the six directions around me, and to this end, the rest of our discussions are devoted to exploring the three basic dimensions of space and their significance to self-discovery and the practical matters of living. There are, of course, very elaborate mythologies and practices that centre on spatial models of the universe, but I do not want to digress too far from what is immediately useful. Readers who are interested in exploring some of the more esoteric aspects of spatial thought in the Western corpus may wish to consult Kevin Townley's *The Cube of Space*, a book which brings together concepts from astrology, Kabbalah, sacred geometry, Tarot and more.

The way in which we orientate our body/mind to the reality

of the three dimensions is, in principle, very straightforward. We have to manage up and down, left and right and forward and back. We cannot answer the question as to why there are three dimensions, but we can be clear that each of these three planes imparts unique qualities to our streams of attentional and physical movement through them. Thus, I deal with each of the three dimensions separately, at the same time being cognisant of the dangers of trying to separate out that which cannot be separated.

The important message is: STAY AT THE CENTRE! Our habits of craving and aversion continually drag us away from ourselves; we are all eccentric, literally out of the centre. But it is only at the centre that the still point of this turning world can be felt, as in John Lilly's *Centre of the Cyclone*, a refuge from the craziness of constant movement. You may remember Judith Blackstone's observation that increasing spaciousness coincided with an enhanced sense of solidity. The same is true of centering: the more spacious we become, the more centred we feel, and the more centred we become, the more spacious we feel. Perhaps when a new cosmological paradigm arrives, it will restore the observer/cogniser to her rightful place, firmly at the 'centre which is everywhere'.

We can get some idea about what this view from the centre looks like by listening to the words of 'The Mother' (Mirra Alfassa), as recorded by her secretary, Satprem, in *The Mind of the Cells* (page 23):

> The consciousness floats in this (undulation) with a sensation of eternal peace… And it is very silent, like a movement of waves, with no beginning and no end; it has a condensation like this (vertical gesture), and a condensation like that (horizontal gesture), and it moves by expansion (gesture of pulsating ocean). That is, it contracts and concentrates, then expands and spreads out.

This is very reminiscent of Suzanne Segal's description of the "vastness" in her book *Collision with the Infinite*. She uses the analogy of lying in a bath and only feeling the water when you move. In the same way the human form somehow gives the vastness the possibility of experiencing itself through what she calls undulation.

Water again, flowing, rippling and spinning to feel itself in form.

So let us begin by considering the first axis that always comes to mind when talking of cosmological or spiritual matters:

Heaven and Earth

All religious traditions have cosmogenies which describe heaven(s), earth and hell(s) in a tiered fashion, with good realms inevitably above and infernal ones below. Often these constructs have been derived from earlier shamanic traditions, a particularly good example being the intricacies of the Tibetan world view and their relation to native Bon beliefs.

It was Mircea Eliade who first pointed to the striking similarities between geographically diverse shamanic systems and the process whereby native visionaries travel between worlds on ladders, ropes, vines or spiral stairs. Following in this tradition, Jeremy Narby in his book *The Cosmic Serpent* relates how, during his time with the ayahuasceros of the Peruvian Amazon, he came to believe that these medicine men were deriving their extraordinary knowledge of plants directly from the plants themselves. It seemed that during their visionary states, the shamans had direct access to the information contained in DNA, the spiral molecule which, like a coiled cosmic serpent, is a twisted vine that spans heaven and earth. (If all the DNA molecules in your body were unwound and braided together they would reach to the sun and back nine times.)

To my mind, heaven and earth find their most elegant expression in Chinese philosophy. Hellmut Wilhelm in *Heaven,*

Earth, and Man in the Book of Changes quotes a commentary to Hexagram 15, Ch'ien, Modesty (page 152):

> It is the way of heaven to influence downward and to create light and radiance. It is the way of earth to be lowly and to go upward.
>
> It is the way of heaven to make empty what is full and to give increase to what is modest. It is the way of the earth to change the full and to augment the modest… It is the way of men to hate fullness and to love the modest.

The mediating factor between heaven and earth is Humanity, symbolised by a triangular shape between the yang of heaven and the yin of earth. Sometimes the relationship is rendered in terms of a triangle for Humanity, a square for earth and a circle for heaven; the triangle representing our triune nature (intellectual, emotional and physical) as well as the dynamic of the law of three. Wilhelm points out that in the I Ching, heaven is usually the creative and earth the preserving and formative. However, these relationships are not fixed; if they were, then the position of humans would also be set in stone. The genius of the I Ching, as with Taoism in general, is that it recognises that flexibility and indeterminacy are essential in keeping systems vital and evolving.

Fig. 11 Heaven, Humanity and Earth

More broadly, it is the whole web of organic life, Gaia, which acts as the reconciling force between the energies of heaven (as represented, for example, by the sun) and the dense materiality of earth. The tree is the supreme example of this, drawing up Water and minerals (Earth) from below and combining them, in a magic alchemy, with Air and light (Fire) from above, to create the living protective blanket that keeps our world stable. Humans are organised on similar lines, but are tasked with a different kind of alchemy, the transformation of our base, material nature into consciousness/light.

It is not surprising that diverse cultures should view heaven and earth in similar ways, with heaven representing divine order, perfection, creative force and eternity, while earth is associated with limitation, mortality, mischance and imperfection. As Richard Heath tells us in his many fine books (including *Precessional Time and the Evolution of Consciousness*), our Megalithic and Neolithic ancestors looked to the heavens for both their physical and spiritual bearings. The predictable nature of the celestial movements, and at the same time their awesome unknowability, made heaven the natural frame of reference for ordering both earthly affairs and concerns of the soul. Thus measurement, time and myth come ultimately from the sky.

Another universal story bound up with the polarity of heaven and earth is that of descent and return. Humans seem to naturally intuit their dual nature, and seem always to have puzzled about the relationship between their unchanging sense of I-ness and the obvious fragility and mortality of the body. It makes sense to believe that we have come from somewhere else, and that our destiny is to return there and live as our 'real', undying selves. It also seems to make sense that we have arrived at our present, difficult situation under the influence of some dark force, a malign figure that perhaps rules this world.

We do not have to look very far in myth, fairy tale or religion to find examples of this basic story. In fact it can be argued that all good stories have, as their central plank, the idea of struggling against opposing circumstances to win great rewards: riches, love and most importantly, redemption.

At the beginning of a story, we are typically introduced to the main protagonist (or hero/ine) who finds herself in some sort of dilemma, or to whom something unexpected happens (... "then one day"...). There follows the first major part of the tale in which the protagonist sets out to resolve their difficulty and, as a result, becomes deeply involved in (and identified with) circumstances. In the second part, the nature of opposing forces becomes plain and there is a struggle whose outcome is uncertain. This gives way to the resolution phase in which we discover whether the protagonist has met with success or failure, and all the loose ends are tied up. In short, stories have a beginning, a middle and an end, and we are always hoping for a successful and happy resolution (typically a wedding, if one can be arranged). But without uncertainty there is no excitement and no catharsis.

This threefold narrative archetype has, according to Christopher Booker, seven basic variations (in his *The Seven Basic Plots*). These are: The Quest, Rags to Riches, Overcoming the Monster, Voyage and Return, Comedy, Tragedy, and Rebirth. However, no matter what embroideries are played upon these basic themes, we as the audience are hoping that the hero/ine will come through and garner wisdom, maturity, love or wealth and preferably all four. It cannot be denied that these are all things that we want for ourselves, and it is not hard to see that traditional stories are all about how these aspirations play out across the life cycle, ultimately involving a transcendence of life's inevitable difficulties.

But we are also reminded of Alan Watts' cosmic drama, with God playing hide and seek with Itself, just for the endless excitement of it all. There is often a sense in us that we will just wake up one day and discover that everything is fine, that having *descended* into an entanglement with circumstances, we have *ascended* from sleep and found ourselves freed from its oppressive weight. I first came across this idea as a small child when I read, or perhaps had read to me, Charles Kingsley's *The Water-Babies*. I remember feeling a wonderful sense of exhilaration and freedom when the little chimney sweeps were liberated into the weightlessness and clarity of the water. I can still feel it, although to my continuing regret, I am no swimmer.

Whichever way we attempt to return to our real and native sense of ourselves, it is apparent that the process is one of *recognition*. The hero/ine does not become a different person, rather they mature into what we knew they truly were all along. We know that Cinderella is a princess (of the heart), but we are desperate for this intrinsic goodness to manifest in her outward circumstances as well. And, because the story is about processes in time we can, with Alejandro Jodorowsky (*Metagenealogy*), view the basic dynamic as one between the call of future potential and the weight of the encultured past. This is why waiting is so important. We wait, without expectation, for a movement from the future, from the transcendental whole which is beyond any present imagining. What we are or will be is wholly and radically different from anything our present mindset can fathom.

This theme of evolution as transcendence is also explored by Joseph Chilton Pearce in his many books on psycho-spiritual maturation. He sees that, as evolving humans, we are ready at various critical periods in our development to radically transcend our previous psycho-spiritual stage. One such crucial transition occurs in early adolescence when we may crave a vision of purpose and meaning that will help propel us into adulthood. This is the initiatory vision quest of so many different cultures. Without it, adolescents have to find their own way, which often involves lapsing into conformity, inchoate rebellion or depression.

Another opportunity comes in midlife, a time when, like Dante, we find ourselves in the midst of a dark wood. Studies on happiness and the life cycle tend to indicate that the period of least contentment occurs in the early forties, when involvement with work, money and family is at its peak. Most of us grit our teeth and plough on, spurred by the distant prospect of pensioned retirement. For some, however, called again by their 'soul's code', there is a concerted effort to break free into a more creative direction, one that will hopefully take them back to a self that they recognise as their own.

The trajectory of the prodigal son: departure and return, descent and ascent is fundamentally a circular one, within whose orbit the progress of involution and evolution takes a spiral form. Sometimes we seem to be regressing, but generally there is a forward movement in steps that often seem to have an inevitability born of some mind other than our own. This circular motion is also evident within our immediate physical reality, and so in the next chapter I look at this energetic 'round dance' from a number of different viewpoints: somatic, psychological and spiritual.

12

The Vertical Body

Uprightness and selfhood are really two aspects of the same process.
Jeffrey Maitland

It seems unthinkable that our present mode of self-consciousness could be associated with anything other than a vertical posture. This point is made elegantly and in some depth by Glynda-Lee Hoffman in her book *The Secret Dowry of Eve*. In quoting from a thesis by Rob Hanford, she draws a picture of our primate ancestors as they came down from the trees and began to stand in a progressively more upright fashion on the African savannahs. The upright posture, freely swivelling head and forward facing eyes opened up the vast space of three-dimensional awareness, an openness in which it is impossible not to place oneself (and lose oneself). Our superb stereoscopic vision also allowed the kind of narrow focus that sets up the lines of perspective that predicate subject-object consciousness.

Some other animals, mainly predators, have forward facing eyes like us, but it is hard to imagine how their visual space plays out when their bodies are orientated forward rather than vertically. Owls may appear to be an exception, but they do not have mobile eyes like us – they have to swivel the whole head to look around. Try moving around for a while on all fours and explore your quality of awareness, or alternatively, keep your eyes forward and use only the neck muscles to look around.

The quality of consciousness imparted by verticality is also highlighted when we lie down and tend to lose clarity of thought and a sense of control. Self-awareness and focused cognition seem intrinsically bound up with the vertical posture and with standing at the right angle (90 degrees) in relation to the earth. The upright posture also enables us to easily look up and encompass the infinity of space, something that most of us could profitably do more often.

As well, there is something special about the fact that our bodies and nervous systems are aligned with both gravity and the earth's electromagnetic forces. When we stand upright, our spinal cord is orientated in the same direction as the gravitational force from the earth. Similarly, our whole body is standing in the electromagnetic field that extends between the ionosphere and the earth. The potential difference across this giant capacitor is, on average, over 200,000 volts, with the negative pole being the earth's reservoir of electrons.

Lightning strikes within this electric cavity give rise to electromagnetic stationary waves in the ELF (extremely low frequency) part of the earth's spectrum, the so-called Schumann frequencies, the most well-known of which is at 7.8 Hertz. Much has been made of the correspondence between this frequency and the lower end of the alpha brainwave band, and biofeedback at 7.8 Hertz is often used on neurofeedback machines. Whatever the health implications may be, this resonance of frequency between the brain and the earth is yet another striking illustration of a seamless, rhythmic continuum throughout the ecosphere.

A related phenomenon is described in Lyall Watson's book, *Gifts of Unknown Things*, an account of his sojourn on an Indonesian island in the 1960s. He tells us how, at the beginning of one of the village rituals, the local shaman listened intently to the night sky to determine the exact moment at which a giant gong would initiate the ceremony. During the next 24 hours the gong was sounded 69 times, a frequency which Watson tells us corresponds to the acoustic echo between the earth and the upper atmosphere. He speculates that the sounding of the gong served to enhance and entrain this natural rhythm for the benefit of the rice crop and was evidence of: "... a folded order hidden from view but available to sensibility."

In our present state of knowledge, it is impossible to make precise statements about the relationship between our body's electrical properties and the electromagnetic environment in which we are constantly bathed. Clearly we are electric beings with intense activity centred in the nervous system, heart and active muscles. The electromagnetic fields associated with this activity are extremely weak, however, and there seems to be no overall pattern of polarity in the body as a whole. This goes against the tenets of many traditional and contemporary energy healing systems that describe distinct pathways and polarities in the dynamics of the 'life force'. It also contradicts the now scientifically established fact that most animals at rest prefer to orientate themselves on a North-South Axis. It seems that we naturally want to coherently align ourselves with the earth's electromagnetic lines of force.

The idea of a life force is a very controversial one, but it is a concept with such universal 'street cred' that it deserves some serious consideration. At its heart, literature about the 'life force' principle depends on the subjective experience of those who work directly with the body or who are recipients of such work. It is a feeling of energy movement within and across the body, which can vary in quality from gross sensations such as heat and tingling, to ones that are very subtle and ethereal. Its experience can be accompanied by intuitions and access to information in non-ordinary ways; in other words the 'life force' often seems to be an event in consciousness as much as in the physical world. It is liminal, situated in the hinterlands of the mind/body mystery, yet at the same time very real and immediate.

The importance of considering the idea of a life force, and how it flows, resides in the practicalities of self-regulation and healing, which is why I want to look at two 20th century pioneers in the field of energy research and application.

Leon Ernest Eeman was a British pilot in the First World War who, as a result of a plane crash, was eventually discharged from the Royal Air Force 100% disabled. Conventional medicine seemed to have little to offer for his chronic pain and insomnia and so, as with many health innovators, he decided to find a solution for himself. As a starting point he used Jesus's admonition to heal the sick by the laying on of hands. This led him to consider what it was that flowed between healer and patient, and to find other ways to facilitate the free passage of this healing energy. His crucial discovery lay in noticing that the 'life force' was polarised, somewhat like electricity, with positive poles in the right hand and head, and negative poles in the left hand and feet. A weaker polarity existed between the back (positive) and front (negative) of the body.

To facilitate and balance these flows, Eeman constructed copper circuits to lie on, which connected the head with the left hand, and the base of the spine with the right hand. He used copper on the initial assumption that the force had electrical properties, but came to realise that it was "quasi electromagnetic" in nature; by this he meant that it could be accompanied by measurable electromagnetic phenomena, but was not electromagnetic itself. Many other researchers have arrived at similar conclusions, and in our modern terminology we might say that the 'life force' is an *emergent quality* which arises in the context of biological organisms. As such, it is an expression of the livingness of the system as a whole, and subsumes the electromagnetic, biochemical and other physical aspects of cellular life without being confined to a simple analysis in those terms.

When looking at the body, as with any complex system, we can think in terms of both 'bottom up' and 'top down' information flow. In the therapeutic realm, 'bottom up' treatments use the kind of narrow focus, reductive approaches that involve physical agents and processes, for example, drugs, surgery and some somatic approaches such as myotherapy. Top down methods include stress management and psychotherapy, but can extend into the broad range of healing modalities that rely on intention, visualisation and subtle energy practices such as Reiki, subtle energy technologies and beyond.

Most practitioners who work with living energy seem, over time, to broaden their view of what is actually going on. Eeman was no exception, and as his work progressed he found common cause with homeopathy, radionics and dowsing. In other words, he moved into the area of energy/information/consciousness. If you are interested in an overview of his life and work, a good place to start is *Biocircuits* by Leslie and Terry Patten. You may also find it worthwhile to actually get a set of copper biocircuits or make them yourself. Not everyone seems to find benefit, but any question about their potency was erased from my mind when I lent a set to a friend a few years ago. A strong fire type, he impulsively wired himself up without reading the instructions too carefully. Within a couple of minutes, far from relaxing, he was leaping out of his skin with agitation. He contacted me in disgust, but was amazed when we ascertained that he had used the screens in reverse polarity – a configuration that is occasionally used to arouse people from a dull, energetically flat state! He did not try them again, however; his session had been a bit too disconcerting.

This and other experiences with the screens also taught me something else: that energy balancing methods like this do not work well with low energy states. Depleted individuals have to get their energy back from an outside source such as Nature, or a healer who is able to transmit energy.

Eeman's model of energy is replicated in Randolph Stone's Polarity Therapy, but in a much more elaborate way, and with the benefit of both Eastern and Western concepts. Bruce Burger's book *Esoteric Anatomy* is the best available account, both of Stone's work and the whole subject of subtle energy. Systems such as Polarity Therapy can be complex in their application, but the general model proposed by pioneers such as Eeman or Stone also gives us some simple guidelines for everyday application.

For example, if we are feeling stressed, we often have sensations of pressure in the upper body such as chest tightness or headache, both products of the 'red light reflex'.

We can help to correct this tendency by placing our left hand on the neck and our right hand on the lower back to complete an Eeman circuit. Alternatively and more easily, place the left hand on the forehead and the right over the solar plexus. This drains the pressure downward along the long axis of the body and helps to restore balance. The question of what we are draining remains open. We are simultaneously operating at a number of levels which are not mutually exclusive. Our intention, as an expression of the organism as a whole, initiates processes that range from gross to subtle and which ramify throughout the body.

Similarly, when using the hands for local body healing, there seem to be definite patterns upon which most practitioners agree. The positive polarity of the right hand is best used to treat stasis, congestion, cold and to tonify and get things moving. The cooling left hand is best used over areas that are hot, irritated or swollen. Neither hand can work alone: they have to form a circuit with the opposite polarity placed appropriately to allow a flow of 'life energy' to take place. What is flowing? Life is flowing.

Although a concept such as 'life flowing' is outside the ambit of scientific discourse, there is one area where clear-cut objective measurements can be made, and that is with respect to electrostatic electricity. All electrical systems are ultimately connected to the earth, which acts as the ground or zero reference point for the measurement of voltage. Animals are no exception to this rule, and their electrical systems are usually grounded by their physical contact with the earth. Humans, with their modern use of shoes that have non-conductive soles, are generally not grounded and consequently are subject to the build-up of positive charge. The voltage difference between an insulated human body and the earth can easily be demonstrated by attaching one electrode of a voltmeter to an earthing point while holding the other electrode in the hand. By measuring in this way, it soon becomes apparent that 'ungroundedness' is the rule rather than the exception, and that some environments promote this effect more than others. No prizes for guessing which are the most toxic: densely built urban areas with little plant life and a plethora of electrical and electronic devices.

The potential consequences for health are only now becoming apparent, and there is a burgeoning literature on the subject: Clinton Ober's *Earthing* is an excellent introduction. There is also a variety of aids to help you earth, including shoes, grounding sheets for your bed and grounded pads on which to rest your feet when using a computer or other electronic devices. These earthing aids are often connected to the ground of a house's wiring system, but it is better, in my experience, to attach them to an earthing rod stuck into the ground outside.

There is evidence for the efficacy of these methods right across the spectrum of pathological conditions, but it is largely anecdotal at this stage. We have good reason to believe, however, that there are comprehensible ways in which earthing should work. Much is made these days of the role of chronic inflammation in disease and the contribution of free radicals to the process. A free radical is, in fact, a positively charged molecule that is searching for an electron in order to become stable. In electrical grounding, we draw upon the earth's limitless supply of electrons, and so supply these toxic agents with the neutralising factors that they need. It is a natural antioxidant process, and short-circuits the damaging process of stealing electrons from organic molecules.

Research also tells us that frequent contact with soil organisms helps to make our microbiomes more diverse, with the many health benefits that accrue from having complex communities of microorganisms living in and on us.

Grounding and Balancing

Besides the immediate electrical effects, there are many other benefits from connection with the earth, and these mostly accrue through lying on the ground or from barefoot contact. Warren Grossman's book *To Be Healed By The Earth* is a beautiful account of the healing that comes from closeness to our 'mother'. One only has to spend some time standing with bare feet on cool moss to know that this is good medicine, and that it is operating in a number of ways. I can get quite 'spacey' from doing this, an illustration, I think, of the dynamic polarity between earth and heaven: go deeply into one and the other will inevitably reveal itself.

Grossman also recommends tree hugging and with good reason. Trees bridge the divide between heaven and earth and have the same vertical polarity as humans. Water comes from below and is conducted up to heaven; sunlight comes from above and is converted into tangible substance. We eat of these substances and they are converted into conscious space (at least on a good day). Cooler climate trees seem to be more efficacious for harmonising our energy field, probably because the water flow through their trunks is more significant than in dry climate trees such as eucalypts. As we see later, water is a key to understanding 'bio-energy', and to requote Bioenergetics teacher Gerda Boyesen: "water follows energy and energy follows water".

Although this formulation may seem short on hard scientific detail, there is a direct analogy with the effects of gravity. The relationship between the upright posture and the force of gravity seems an obvious, direct and sometimes painful one, yet the nature of gravity is a complete mystery. We tend to be more confident in our thinking about gravity and the body, however, because the feeling of 'ponderability' is so immediate. Moreover, we could say that the reality of our personal form, our body and the sense of our body, only becomes possible through gravity. As Jeffrey Maitland points out in his superb book *Spacious Body*: "Gravity may be, in fact, the most fundamental condition of form itself."

Maitland's writing is particularly interesting, because his background as a Zen practitioner and philosophy academic has informed his appreciation of the work he does as a Rolfing therapist. Rolfing, as the reader probably knows, is a therapy which aims to re-establish the body's correct relationship to gravity, and in so doing, aims to liberate and harmonise the whole being. Maitland sees uprightness and selfhood as two aspects of the same process, but for most of us, the inevitable traumas and difficulties of life are mirrored in a gradual but inevitable misalignment away from easy and balanced verticality. The effects of the 'red' and 'green' light reflexes play a large part in this, but on a simpler level we can say that our struggle with gravity results from a chronic and excessive frontal attention married to the inevitable left/right asymmetry that is built into our nervous systems.

The 'pull' of the eyes is especially important, with our overly frontal and narrow attention literally tugging the head forward in anticipation of our desires or aversions. The back then has to compensate for this forward weight by tightening and exaggerating the lumbar curve. Ida Rolf aimed to correct this sort of situation by re-establishing a true vertical axis which would endure as a central 'line of gravity'. To effect this, she found that it was important to work with the fascia as well as muscles, and to correct the shortening and thickening that inevitably occurs in the fascial network. A body that has been thus 're-sculpted' to properly align with the vertical no longer has to struggle with gravity in its old restricted way, and exhibits a freedom and ease which often come as a complete revelation to those who have experienced the process.

The idea of attaining a balanced, vertical alignment is also implicit in many other disciplines including Aikido, the Alexander technique and Hatha Yoga. In fact, whenever we talk about 'centering', we are describing our efforts to return to the central line at a balance point between heaven and earth. The Aikido teacher Wendy Palmer describes her personal centering process in the following way. First she asks if the front of her field of sensation and awareness is equal to the back, *and then waits for the sensations that follow the question*. She then repeats the question for left and right and above and below. Importantly *she lets her interest lead her awareness*. There is no preconception or forcing, instead the practitioner takes a more yin approach – enquiring, waiting and receiving.

A vertical spine is also emphasised in many meditative traditions, with the classic posture seated cross-legged, fully upright and, for most Westerners, quite uncomfortable. The usual explanation for this physical aspect of the discipline is that it both maintains alertness and presents the challenge of not avoiding pain. Ainslie Meares concurred with this approach, emphasising the importance of being somewhat physically uncomfortable in one's relaxation practice. This is all very well for those who are fully and unshakably dedicated to their spiritual path, but for many of us a less rigorous posture can still ensure alertness without too much 'slackness' of attention.

There may be an added bonus for those who are able to achieve a steady upright posture while both alert and relaxed. The inventor and consciousness researcher, Itzhak Bentov, pointed out many years ago that mechanical factors may be involved (*Stalking the Wild Pendulum*, 1977). He found that when the breathing becomes very quiet, the pulse of blood flowing from the heart down the aorta forms a coherent standing wave rather than a chaotic interference pattern. It is possible that this resonant wave might, in turn, excite the fluid in the brain ventricles at a low alpha frequency of 7Hz and facilitate brainwave coherence and even kundalini effects. There could also be a parallel with craniosacral work, in which the practitioner waits to feel a coherent pulse along the spinal axis. Heart Rate Variability training is another method that aims to find a resonant 'sweet spot' between breathing and heart rhythm, one that helps to restore autonomic balance.

Whatever the truth of these assertions, there is value I believe in some form of simple balancing routine, both as a matter of course during the day and as a preliminary to meditation/contemplation. Judith Blackstone (in *The Enlightenment Process*) recommends the following sequence:

> Find the centre of the head midway between the ears and initiate the breath from that point. Then find centre points at the level of the heart and about two inches below the navel [which she calls the pelvis centre]. Initiate the breath from both of those points in turn. Next, try to feel all three centres at the same time and initiate breath from all three centres simultaneously. Feel that the vertical core is the centre of pervasive space while inhaling and exhaling.

I find this sequence very useful when combined with the sort of enquiry undertaken by Wendy Palmer. As with all such summaries, however, there is the caveat that these exercises are best used within the context of the originator's whole body of work and personal instruction.

When we return to our vertical core we may observe that there is a constant tendency for our awareness to move upward. Even if we are working to locate the centre of the head, we still may notice a movement from the head's centre in a *forward and upward* direction. To correct this bias, we need to periodically ground by a balancing movement of *back and down*, i.e. attention moves back to the vertical core and down towards the earth. Some simple exercises to facilitate grounded attention are:

Stand erect with (preferably bare) feet on the ground and breathe in and out through the soles of the feet. Imagine fresh (green) earth energy being drawn up into the body on the inhale and stale energy being eliminated on the exhale.

In Buddhist walking meditation one pays careful attention to the sensations of lifting and placing the feet as one walks very slowly and deliberately. This is a very good way of observing the antigravitational pull of the thinking mind as it paces to and fro in its penthouse apartment.

By observing the breath we experience a natural ebb and flow of attention along the vertical axis: with inhalation there is activation of the sympathetic nervous system and a corresponding movement of consciousness upward and forward. With exhalation the opposite is the case, with a natural and relaxing return into the body. Wendy Palmer elaborates on this pattern by suggesting that on the inhalation we imagine a purifying breath that spirals counterclockwise up from the earth, through and around the body and eventually up to heaven. By this means attention moves evenly through the three dimensions. On the out-breath there is a clockwise strengthening spiral that moves from heaven to earth.

Alternatively, concentration on the rising and falling of the abdominal breath may act as a simple anchor to the body's centre of gravity. As well as being the central feature of many meditative approaches, focus on the *hara* is also a key ingredient in a host of physical disciplines from bioenergetics to qigong. More widely, cultivation of the hara has been an intrinsic part of many cultures, most notably in Japan, as outlined in Karlfried Durckheim's book, *Hara*. Rotating 180 degrees around the hara and standing on our heads can be a good way of loosening up the whole body and relieving it of habitual holding patterns. Inverted postures are particularly valued in yoga but be careful, such postures can be hazardous to your neck in particular. Always get proper instruction and supervision when attempting something new like this. Being a slim ectomorph, I am particularly paranoid about my less than robust neck and never let anyone near it unless I have the utmost confidence in them.

Although grounding preferably depends on physical, bodily

sensations, there is always an element of visualisation involved. Thus, when we are feeling the breath moving through our feet, it is hard not to simultaneously see a subtle stream of air passing through our imagined extremity. This is quite natural, and most of us will tend to combine imagery with sensation as we develop our practice. Also, imaging techniques can be simple and effective ways of centering and grounding while 'on the go'. Friedlander and Hemsher, in their book on psychic development (*Psychic Psychology: Energy Skills for Life and Relationships*) describe such exercises in great detail and I refer the reader to their excellent text. I might also add here that relaxing the pelvic floor on the out-breath is an excellent way of 'letting down and letting go' through the whole vertical axis. An important part of the parasympathetic (relaxing) nervous system is distributed from the base of the spine, and so relaxing this area works positively in a number of ways.

Whatever grounding method we use, however, there is a common denominator that involves *returning to the midline and relaxing*. When we relax, attention drops, and like water, finds a natural level. Depending on what our organism needs, our consciousness gravitates to the appropriate location, energy centre or element. I like to think of this process in terms of the play of earth, water, fire, air and ether. Although no one element takes enduring precedence in these interactions, we still see a hierarchical ordering which gives structure and coherence.

Thus, in the body we see a reflection of this sequence starting at earth level, with the incredibly complex, robust and supple arrangement of the foot bones providing the link between the ground and the body's vertical axis. In the lower abdomen we have a predominance of water in the form of the urinary system and the colon (which removes water from the intestinal contents). In the upper abdomen, the liver and proximal digestive tract form a metabolic furnace of chemical transformation, and above them, the respiratory system is constantly stoking the fires below by clearing carbon dioxide and acquiring oxygen. The empty (subjective) space above the shoulders represents ether, the expansive aspect of the senses and consciousness.

The Water Way

The extraordinary thing about living processes is that they combine the elements in a harmonious way: cellular fire is able to burn in water and earth survives the corrosive effects of air. Strictly speaking, entropic processes must inevitably lead to our degeneration and death, but life gets around this through its clever use of energy from the sun and by continually creating new organisms from scratch. And in observing this process of embryogenesis, we are inevitably reminded that life is inextricably linked with the blueness of our planet, with water. Our ancestors evolved in water, we gestate in water and our bodies are mainly composed of water.

We have already outlined the work of Theodor Schwenk and the importance of the forms that arise in fluid media. Schwenk's natural successor, both from a theoretical and practical point of view, was the American dancer and therapist Emilie Conrad (died 2014). It is helpful to know something of Conrad's extraordinary life story before exploring the substance of her work; an interview on conscious-tv.com is a good introduction. Conrad escaped from her abusive father in young adulthood and became a dancer and model. Through happenstance she found herself in Haiti and was soon entranced with Haitian dance, culture and religion. It was here that she had an awakening into the nature of the natural waves and rhythms that govern the life of all organisms. As her insights progressed, she realised that life, as manifest in every aspect of the biosphere, develops and moves in accordance with three processes: pulsing, spiralling and waving. These movements are all properties of fluid media, and as Conrad conceived it, we are living, moving water adapted to land; hence the title of her book: *Life on Land*.

Conrad extended this concept further and proposed that just as the human body has been formed through spiral vortices of water, so too are we in potential resonance with fluid systems everywhere. In this she is completely supported by the work of Schwenk, and by the archetypal ideas implicit in the corpus of sacred geometry touched on earlier in the book. Conrad, however, was not principally a theoretician, and she spent the latter part of her life applying these ideas in a therapeutic way to human dis-ease, particularly trauma and neurological damage. She found that breath and sound were keys to eliciting the body's natural self-regulation and in re-establishing coherent pulsing, waving (i.e. rhythm) and spiralling. The fluidity of motion that she herself exhibited and which she was able to cultivate in others was remarkable, and thankfully we have videos that have vividly preserved the taste and feel of this work.

The idea of water and the patterns intrinsic to it give new meaning to the interface between heaven and earth. Not just humans, but the whole biosphere represent the intelligent working out of patterns of awareness and self-awareness. Water, that mysterious and elusive substance, still a puzzle to science with all its shapeshifting properties, is the mother or matrix within which the codes of life and consciousness can evolve and transform. It is a constant physical and dynamic factor, continually recycling, purifying and restoring itself. When married to the forms of earth, the spirit of fire and the movement of air, its intrinsic patterns become alive and available for the harmonic evolution of awareness.

The spiralling and wave-forming capacities of water are echoed in a number of body structures, most notably that of the spine, which has a snake-like appearance and exemplifies all the capabilities of that animal to twist and flex and pulse. The movement therapist Jalaja Bonheim in her book, *The Serpent and the Wave*, also comments on this similarity and notes how its undulations are manifest in so many of our involuntary movements: intestinal peristalsis, orgasm and the rippling movements of muscles amongst many others. Because it is closely associated with the unwilled aspects of our organic life, it symbolises everything within our bodies and minds that is hidden from the light of consciousness.

Bonheim's description of the snake's earthly and 'dark' side is in stark contrast to the serpent power that moves up the spine and into the transcendental realms of light. This dual nature, which leads to both fear and reverence, is a reminder to spiritual aspirants to pay attention to both faces of their nature: as below, so above. The kundalini imagery is also a vivid metaphor that points us in the right spiritual direction. In our self-involved contracted state, our life force is coiled in upon itself at the base of the spine. In its liberated form it is free to spiral, wave and ascend in resonance with the larger life-fields within which we are imbedded.

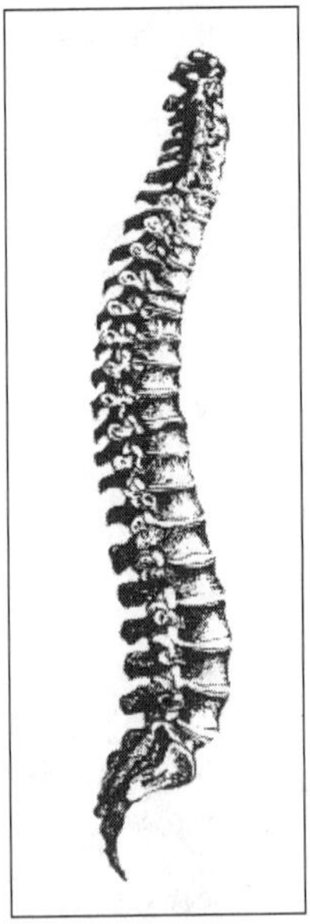

Fig. 12 The Spine in Side View

Before considering this process more deeply, it is worthwhile mentioning Donald Carroll's book: *Sacred Geometry and Spiritual Symbolism*. Carroll spends a good deal of time considering the spine's structure and its numerical properties, particularly in relation to Egyptian symbology. He makes a convincing case that the average length of the spine, around 27.5 inches, was the basis of the 'royal cubit', and was thus the measuring unit for the Great Pyramid. How elegant, if true, that the spine was the measure for that supreme attempt to marry Heaven and Earth in such visible and massive form. And that is saying very little of the endless mysteries that attend that great structure and its esoteric purposes.

Psycho-spiritual Practice and the Vertical Dimension

When we survey religions, myths and the popular imagination, it is evident that there is a tension between a diverging upward movement and a converging downward one; the realms of freedom and happiness are always above and the realms of restriction and suffering are below. Heavens are breezy and light; hells stuffy, dark and often hot. These cosmic maps are mirrored in our personal experiences. Depression, for example, is inevitably accompanied by a slumping toward the ground with eyes downcast. In such circumstances it can be a good idea to look up as often as possible, even do some 'sky gazing' to help lift the spirit. Arnold Mindell, working along similar lines, has an exercise where he asks us to observe from which part of the eye we are actually looking: upper, middle or lower, and then to notice how this correlates with our general state. This, incidentally, does not mean that we move the eye up and down, but rather become aware of where attention is residing in the visual field.

The idea of high and low is also strongly connected with a variety of psychological and moral dimensions. We naturally talk of high moral purpose or lofty intentions in contrast to low cunning or the morals of the gutter. Not surprisingly, psychological studies confirm the 'bleeding obvious', that our spatial sense profoundly affects how we feel and think. Subjects at the University of Minnesota felt freer in rooms with ten foot ceilings than they did in rooms eight feet high. You may chuckle, but this is the way of science: we cannot say that we know something for sure until we actually test it. The same study found that individuals in smaller spaces were more likely to pay attention to detail, a finding that is consistent with the idea that the left brain is separative and analytical in function, as opposed to the right brain with its superior spatial sense that is connective, intuitive and open (more of this in the next chapter).

Other studies show similar findings. People actually do feel better straightening up and raising their gaze. Similarly, being on a physically higher level, either in reality or in imagination, fosters a better mood, greater creativity and more inclusive thinking, the converse also being true. There is also, of course, a shadow side to elevation, with creativity and imagination turning into delusion, well-being into mania and confidence into grandiosity. Jung was particularly conscious of the dangers of psychological inflation when individuals become too removed from their worldly roots. He gives, as an example, the doomed tightrope walker described in *Thus Spoke Zarathustra*. This is an image of Nietzsche's 'Overman' before the inevitable compensatory fall and the philosopher's descent into madness and death.

The close relationship between the vertical dimension and so many of our psycho-spiritual parameters has many roots, not the least of which are the multiple social hierarchies in which we find ourselves. I have already discussed 'Holman's Law' and the pernicious effects on health of being low in a pecking order. However, as this is a pet subject of mine, I want to emphasise again some of the erosive phenomena that arise from the way in which we are locked into tiered structures of power and possession.

First, let us explore what a benign hierarchy looks like as exemplified in the family. Here there is a necessary imbalance of power, influence and resources which, in our ideal family unit, serves only to foster the growth and maturity of the younger members. The watchwords are: guiding (benign limits), allowing (with circumspection), nurturing (but not smothering) and cooperating. In society as a whole, these aspirations were formerly idealised as 'noblesse oblige', the idea that the God-anointed monarch and his/her aristocracy ruled for everyone's benefit. From those to whom much was given, much was expected.

Alas, with what rarity have we seen this ideal enacted. The

poison of power inevitably corrupts those at the top as much as it demoralises those at the bottom. And as Lord Acton so wisely observed, absolute power corrupts absolutely. The winner effect ensures that dominant individuals continue to seek out more conquest in a cycle of addiction, remorselessly driven by all the same internal chemicals that are implicated in drug addiction. Research also tells us that this unholy elixir of 'success' also seems to promote feelings of grandiosity and entitlement, and to drastically diminish the ability to empathise with those below one's acquired station. It is not difficult to see how fascism, fundamentalism or any other mass psychosis arise.

The rest of the story has an inevitable logic about it. The dynamics of the greasy pole suit the male brain like a lock fits a key. Single-mindedness, competitiveness and lack of emotional empathy are all prerequisites for the assumption of power as one's right. Hence the parlous situation of a world that continues to be dominated by the principle of separativeness and appropriation.

Hierarchy is also deeply embedded in the way we perceive and evaluate situations. We are more likely to place value on an item that appears on the top of a list, irrespective of whether it is a political candidate or a brand of baked beans. Similarly, we are generally biased toward individuals who are taller or who appear more confident, irrespective of information that we have been given about their character or performance record. Hence most successful presidential candidates in the last one hundred years have been taller than their opponents. Perhaps in the near future, education on these matters will be part of every school curriculum. Until then, most of us are acting on the basis of unconscious mechanisms of the most primitive sort, a situation that will ensure the continuing and unchallenged hierarchical nature of most of our institutions.

Sadly, we often see the same principles at work in the 'spiritual' realm, not only in the constitution of religious communities, but also in spiritual practice itself. Thus the idea of liberation or attainment is frequently linked to the idea of raising oneself up. In medieval manuscripts we see a ladder to heaven with many an aspirant laboriously climbing, and many a backslider falling from the difficult ascent. The idea of vertical progress through increasingly refined levels of experience is most developed, however, in kundalini yoga. Here the programme is detailed and explicit, with each station along the way (the chakras) a link in the upward thrust toward liberation. It is very appealing to male-type awareness: there is a clear direction, a defined technology and a comprehensible result. Beam me up, Scotty, no more messy entanglements with the body, emotions or other people, it's warp speed to a galaxy far, far away.

Unfortunately the view from ground level is not so impressive. In my many years of observing and participating in matters esoteric, I have come to realise that 'gurus' who work with this kind of energy often fall off the ladder pretty badly. Their spectacular lapses usually take some form of sexual exploitation, which is pretty ironic when we consider that they are abusing the very 'serpent power' that they claim to be transforming. Their transgressions are not surprising when we consider the lopsided nature of these practices and the long shadow that the quest for perfection is liable to cast. It is a situation that Hermann Hesse explored repeatedly in his novels. Thus the aesthete Harry Haller (*Steppenwolf*), the monk Narcissus (*Narcissus and Goldmund*) and the super-intellectual Knecht (*The Glass Bead Game*) are all over-cerebral males on distorted spiritual quests. There is something desiccated and not quite human about them all; their sojourns in the etheric and airy realms need balancing with fire, water and earth: with healthy, relational sexuality, with love and with the everyday.

We see a more balanced approach in Taoist practices which emphasise harmonising with the patterns of nature. This is exemplified in the classic *microcosmic orbit* exercise in which energy is drawn down the front of the body to the perineum and then circulated up through the spine to the head. A detailed account can be found in *Integral Life Practice* by Ken Wilber et al. The importance of the *downward flow* is emphasised by BK Frantzis in Vol. 1 of his *Relaxing into Your Being* series. He sees the ability to allow energy to flow downward as a *very necessary preliminary* to handling upward and other directional flows. His downward dissolving technique, which we encountered earlier, aims to soften and then release areas of frozen energy out into the space beyond the body. This process is an inner alchemy in which the fire of conscious attention melts ice (earth) to water, which in turn is transformed into vapour (air) and released into space (ether). This dissolving process can be an end in itself to promote bodily and emotional health, but also may provide an avenue to accessing the freedom of conscious space itself.

The idea of a downward movement finds a parallel in the evolution of contemporary psychotherapy. In the last twenty years in particular, there has been a trend toward body-centred approaches in a belated acknowledgement of the somatic reality of feelings. Some of this has already been discussed and can be summed up by quoting the title of Professor Bessel van der Kolk's book on trauma: *The Body Keeps the Score*. Our lives are essentially feeling-based, and we access our feeling-toned experiences, difficulties and traumas through internal somatic sensations. It is all very well to talk about ourselves, but if a link cannot be made to our felt senses then no change or real insight is possible. This internal somatic cueing is mediated through the non-dominant hemisphere, and is something that women do much better than men. It is *emotional grounding*, and without it the spiritual wayfarer sets out at his peril.

In the world of shamanism, a parallel process takes the form of journeys to lower worlds and the experience there of chthonic powers, both dangerous and beneficial. Thus, in the Huna system of Hawaii, the lower self, located in the solar plexus, has to be consulted first, before the higher self can act to bring about a desired result.

Using a spiritual path or other means to rise above one's undeveloped side or to avoid the inevitable reverses that life hands us invariably leads to great difficulty or even craziness. This pattern of avoidance and self-destruction is most clearly seen in drug dependence, where a continual attempt to get 'high' progresses to repeated crashes and eventual rock bottom. We might say, then, that a general rule for maturation is: 'in order to go up, first go down'. In other words, we need to come to terms with what is eating us.

Working with both light and shadow ensures balance, as Blake knew:

> Man was made for joy and woe;
> And when this we rightly know
> Thro' the world we safely go.

Viewed like this, working with the chakras, for example, takes on a different complexion. We go *down* to the base chakra to actively encounter our fears and insecurities and to release the bound-up energy there. Subsequent progressive work through the vertical axis aims for balance at the heart centre. The heart point seems to be the natural gravitational resting point of consciousness, a central sun mediating and illuminating both heaven and earth. The alchemy of this marriage is love, the great mystery of Spirit in action, literally making the world go round. The importance of the heart centre is mirrored in the special properties of the physical organ: its unique structure, radiant electromagnetic field and continuously variable rhythm (which is used as a sensitive measure of autonomic balance and health). Readers interested in finding out more can consult the Institute of HeartMath, or Joseph Chiltern Pearce's *The Heart-Mind Matrix*.

Some practitioners on the path may choose to work solely

at the heart level, both physically and metaphorically. For most of us, however, grounding is a necessary accompaniment to our efforts. And whether we are grounding our thoughts, our feelings or our senses, the place to start is always the body. The body *is* our ground and any practice or present-centeredness must include a grounding component. Thus, for random and frequent moments of recollection during the day, one can use simple and brief processes such as:

Feeling the whole body as one.
Feeling/breathing through the feet.
Feeling the sensations of breath at the abdomen.
Softening the gaze and allowing oneself to drop down into the body.

Reginald Ray's *Touching Enlightenment* is a tremendous resource and guide to body-inclusive meditation, as is Tamara Russell's *Mindfulness in Motion*, a collection of simple embodied awareness exercises for everyday use, especially if you are not a devotee of sitting practice.

In many ways our relationship to the body is reminiscent of the way that Jeeves kept his erratic master's feet on the ground. We assume that our conscious selves are calling the shots, but behind the scenes we are completely supported by and dependent upon our somatic reality. Bertie Wooster had the good sense to regularly consult his 'servant'; we should do likewise.

13

A Fearful Symmetry

And Jesus said: "When you give to the poor, let not your left hand know what your right hand is doing..."
Matthew 6:3

Although Jesus is talking on one level about keeping our acts of generosity secret, his admonition also has relevance to the way that we look at the brain/mind. On the one hand, consciousness depends on the coordination of multiple brain circuits to accomplish whatever needs attention in the moment. On the other, the various modules that carry out the brain's many separate functions need to be kept apart enough to get on with their work without interference. This balance of Connection/separation is the crucial fulcrum upon which alert and stable attention depends. Too much connection leads to confusion, overwhelm and even literal seizure. Too much separation, and the organism loses flexibility, creativity and responsiveness.

This balance is also true of every aspect of world-making, and has echoes of Indra's Net, which, with a few modifications, makes a perfectly respectable neurological model. We only have to recognise each jewel as a neuron and allow some connections to go further than others and we have the basis for a fully functioning neural net. Add the capacity to strengthen some connections through repeated use and we bring learning into the mix. *The brain can reflect the world because it is functionally homologous with it.*

As social beings, we are all like neurons in a net of social relationships and participate in the same dance of Connection/separation. For example, Holman's (tongue-in-cheek) Second Law states that the secret of a stable, happy pair bond is:

> *Similar enough to remain Connected ≥ Separate and different enough to remain attracted.*

This is beautifully illustrated by an anecdote in Wendy Palmer's *The Intuitive Body*, in which a friend tells her that the secret of still being very attracted to his wife after many years is that she had never stopped being a mystery to him.

There is a larger lesson here: when existence no longer appears mysterious, then we are probably in a major rut of our own making. Knowledge must be subordinate to The Mystery. Mystery connects through immersion; knowledge constructs itself through acts of distancing, division and discrimination. Knowledge is a necessary and provisional sandcastle on the shore of an infinite sea of Mystery.

Within the Mystery, the Connection/separation dance is played out in every facet of existence, but we see its dynamic most clearly in the nervous system, all the way up from individual nerve cells to the left/right division of the cerebral hemispheres. And in accordance with the maxim from systems theory, that the more complex 'higher' systems subsume but do not replace simpler subsystems, we assume that the L/R hemisphere distinction reflects, refines and amplifies the more basic processes from which it has evolved.

In humans, we usually think of the frontal lobes as occupying the top spot in the decision tree, although a casual glimpse at human society would seem to indicate that frontal functions such as restraint, prosocial behaviour, empathy and sensible decision making are not always the order of the day. The frontal system is also important in modulating the front/back axis of cerebral activity, a topic that is relevant in the next chapter. However, for our present purposes it is the left/right distinction that will take centre stage rather than the more vaunted frontal functions per se.

Our knowledge of the two sides of the brain has steadily

accumulated since the 19th century, and is based largely on the observation of neurologically damaged individuals who have acquired discrete unilateral brain lesions. The picture of very distinct functional differences expanded in the 1960s, when Sperry and others closely observed patients who had had the connection between the hemispheres severed to stop the spread of intractable epileptic seizures. The cutting of the connecting structure, the corpus callosum, allowed selective interrogation of each hemisphere separately, and produced a situation where, in some circumstances, the left hand literally did not know what the right was doing.

Brain imaging techniques have added further to an emerging picture in which the brain is divided laterally into two very distinct functional units with quite different agendas. They constitute the first subordinate set of systems below what we might call whole brain activity, and as such they help modulate the seamless sense of an apparently continuous and unified subjective consciousness. The most obvious difference between these two systems is that the ability to speak and understand words is largely on the left. This is why the left hemisphere has confidently been able to boast, during the course of most scientific discourse on the subject, that it is the 'dominant' hemisphere. In this it has been aided and abetted by another specialty of the left side, namely the systematising methods of science. As a young psychiatrist in the 1970s I certainly grew up with the view that the left hemisphere was the boss, and it is only in recent years that I have achieved a more balanced appraisal of the brain's functional symmetry.

My current understanding has been amplified immeasurably by Iain McGilchrist's definitive work: *The Master and His Emissary*. Please read this book; it is one of the ten books I would take if exiled to a desert island. Not only is there a generous helping of neuroscience, but in the latter half of the book McGilchrist takes us through the evolution of Western culture to demonstrate how the left brain, with its use of reason and language, has hijacked our world view and every aspect of modern life.

Hence the title of his book, which is based on the story of a king whose lands have become too extensive to rule on his own. His sends out his favourite adviser to administer the farther regions of the kingdom. At first things go well, but after a while the emissary begins to think that he can do better at the ruling game than the king himself, and schemes to overthrow his patron. How will it all end? In the case of our present culture the question remains moot. We can only hope that our re-visioning of the two hands of consciousness allows us to move forward in a more balanced way. Since nobody seems to believe anything about humans anymore without a brain scan to back it up, I am approaching this subject under the cover of neuroscience, and in this and every other respect McGilchrist serves us well.

In the table below I have summarised many of the hemispheric differences described in his book and added a few of my own from other sources. This sort of precis and tabulation misses a great deal and omits context. I am giving you a taster so that you will READ THE BOOK. There is also a terrific animation on www.brainpickings.org which serves the same introductory purpose.

From an evolutionary point of view, hemispheric specialisation goes back a long way and it was an Australian research discovery that first showed a distinct functional division among other mammals, even in young chicks. Humans have a visual system in which input from the right visual field of both eyes goes to the L hemisphere and vice versa. Birds have a simpler arrangement whereby all input from the right eye goes to the left hemisphere and vice versa. By covering one eye in chicks, researchers found that the left side of the brain directs foraging and other appetitive behaviour, while the right side looks out for danger. We have the same arrangement with the left frontal lobe, under the influence of dopamine, getting us out of bed and excited about the day.

Well, it gets us out of bed at least. The right side, on the other hand, is harm avoidant and therefore vigilant for anything new or unanticipated in the environment lest it be dangerous.

Table 2 Hemispheric Differences

(See McGilchrist, *The Master and His Emissary*)

	L	R
General	Phenomenon	Noumenon
	Logos	Eros
	Apollonian	Dionysian
	The Art Critic	The Artist
	Pleroma, things (Jung)	Creatura, beings (Jung)
	Concept of self in world (social self, role)	Personal self-sense (somatic, felt self)
	What?	Where? How?
	Objects	Space
	Self-referential	Open to other
	(Virtual world)	(Real world)
	Separate	CONNECT
	Values reduced to utility	Lower values reflect higher
	Linear/segmented	Global/synthetic
	Conformist	Discrepant
	(Not sensitive to change)	(Alert to change)
	Supresses R side	Open to both sides
Attention	Focus/narrow	Broad/global
	(Foveal vision)	(Peripheral, both eyes)

	Processes predictable	Processes new information
		Longer working memory
	Cannot use R style	Can use L style
	Object recognition	Pattern recognition
	Better at simple shapes	Better at complex shapes (Better spatial vision)
	Horizontal	Vertical and depth
	Prefers Red	Prefers Green
Cognition	Literal	Contextual
	Abstraction	Integration
	Utility	What is uniquely present
	Tools, machines, everything made)	
	Stays with the known	Frame shifts
	Non-living (mechanical)	Living, food, music
	Number as absolute	Number as relation
	Confabulate	What is (common sense)
	Certainty (needs to be right)	Tolerates ambiguity
	Language as grasping	Language as personal, poetic
	Denotation	Connotation
	Stays with known (gets stuck easily)	Can frame shift
	Time as sequence of events (before and after)	Time as sense of duration

Interpersonal	People as objects	People as individuals
	Things	People, empathy, inter-subjectivity, emotional expression
	Looks at mouth	Looks at eyes
	Personal 'story'	Inhibits personal view
	Social rules	Gesture and prosody
	Superficial, 'willed' emotions	Emotional, humorous elements of language
	Influence/manipulation	Cooperation, detection of lies/deception
	Language as words	Language as communication
	Word	Image
Emotion	Anger, otherwise neutral	Bonding/empathy emotions
	Appetitive mood (foraging)	Anxious arousal (harm avoidance)
	Optimistic	Pessimistic/realistic
	Parasympathetic	Whole ANS, esp. sympath
	Deliberate malice (Machiavellian)	Restraint
	Morals abstract	Personal moral judgement

Summary	Selection, Systems, Separation	Process, Paradox, Personhood

The vigilant function of the right side also allows it to be *open to what is* and thus the locus of that much sought-after state of mind, *present-centredness*.

The relative balance between the drive to seek new experiences and the instinct to avoid harmful ones is partly the result of our genes, and is a major determinant of temperament: whether we are bold, optimistic and energetic (L side), or anxious, pessimistic and sensitive (R side). The sombre mood of the right brain is probably related to its intrinsic realism; it sees the world as it is and naturally aligns itself with the insights of the Buddha. This is why low mood (but not overt depression) is related to a number of superior cognitive abilities, including better detection of lying, impulse restraint, memory for detail and perceptual acuteness. This should not surprise us, because positivity is always prospective and therefore not essentially related to what is happening now. A majority of humans seem to have a built-in bias toward optimism, and this has been essential, no doubt, to get us through the trials and tribulations of our evolutionary past. However, every tribe or village also needs a decent complement of naysayers to modulate the dangers of unrealistic optimism, hence the survival value of the more melancholic personality.

The openness of the right brain extends to the social realm. There is a receptivity to people as individuals and a general context of relationship, communication and emotional *connection*. Not surprising, then, that our main empathy and face reading circuits are on the right side, and that they begin their interpersonal development at a very early age. Mothers instinctively hold babies on the left side, a phenomenon that was once ascribed to the calming effect of the heartbeat. Although this may well be the case, it is also likely that the child gets a better view of the left side of mum's face, and thus of her signals of reassurance and attachment. The consistent absence of such signals, however, can have disastrous consequences for emotional development, with a lifelong trajectory of unhappiness and interpersonal confusion.

As adults, we also pay more attention to the left side of some-one's face since it gives an insight into their emotional state. At the same time, the right brain is paying attention to the overall context of words and the way in which they are spoken (prosody). In contrast, the left brain understands the meaning of the words and sentences, but has no way of understanding the subtleties of humour, irony or any other emotional flavour. Margaret Thatcher was a classic example of some-one with apparently few empathic skills and a truly dominant left hemisphere. She is reported to have had no sense of humour and had no time for the nuances of human feeling. Her classic remark, that there was no such thing as society, is vivid testimony to the L hemisphere's estranged perspective on the world. Her Chicago School economic policies were also completely consistent with an exclusive emphasis on atomistic, competitive views of wealth distribution.

In times of danger it can be beneficial to cut off feelings and make quick, expedient decisions. Leaders with these black and white qualities appeal to a populace that is going through a difficult period. However, such individuals are not suited to the complexities of modern society where openness to the diversity of others and an ability to negotiate are more useful. The L hemisphere, in contrast to the R, has no ability to consider the livingness of a being, it sees only objects. It is then a small step to treat humans as objects, with the terrible consequences for humanity with which we are all too familiar. The most frightening aspect of this situation is that the L side has the power to suppress the R side of the brain, making it easy for us to 'harden our hearts'. And psychological investigations make it clear that this process is facilitated if we know that the other person is not from our tribe or is lower in a social hierarchy. It is also easier to cut off our empathic responses if we have a more male type of brain, because testosterone facilitates the process of neural compartmentalization.

I come back to sex differences later on, but for now let us return to the basic theme and look again at how the brain operates as a complex system of Connection/separation. The activities of the brain can be summed up in the following simplistic way:

Left Hemisphere: What is it?
Right Hemisphere: Where and How is it?
Limbic System: What does it feel like?
Reptilian Brain: Watch out! and Is it edible?
Frontal Lobes: What to do about it?

The L side separates out and selects a narrow field for attention and denotation, while the right side provides the big picture of context and connotation. Imagine going into a dark room with a soft, diffuse light in your left hand (R hemi) and a narrow, intense torchlight in your right hand (L hemi). You can see the overall shape and pattern of things with your soft, moonlike glow, but you need the torch to examine things in detail. The scientist or rationalist takes only the narrow beam on their journeys into the unknown, and then tries to construct a big picture from the many jigsaw pieces of data that they have collected. Well, that's the theory. In practice, we know that many breakthroughs in scientific knowledge have come through leaps of 'intuitive' insight where a theory has suddenly presented itself in a dream, vision or thought experiment.

With scanning technology we are now in a position to see where such sudden moments of insight arise in the brain. It should not surprise us that when we laboriously work on a problem in a step by step fashion, it is largely the L side that is involved. When an answer just flashes out of 'nowhere', it is the R side that lights up. In practice, working at a problem generally involves both systematic and intuitive processing. The best way to do this is to take frequent breaks from any highly focused task in order to 'decompress'. Relaxation helps restore hemispheric balance, while taking time to open the senses brings more of the R side 'on line'. Enlightened workplaces are now encouraging employees who are stuck on a problem to leave the office and go for a walk (preferably in nature). Nobel laureate Daniel Kahneman describes in his book, *Thinking, Fast and Slow,* how he enjoyed a particularly creative time at Berkeley when he regularly took a leisurely lunchtime walk with his colleague, Amos Tversky. Enjoyable discourse with a friend is something that we know is conducive to lulling the natural wariness of the right side into abeyance, and thus facilitating a good mood.

In thinking about how we use our mental resources, I like the idea that there is only a certain quantity of mental attention at our disposal. If I am aware of my surroundings, I cannot pay so much attention to myself; if I'm concentrating on my somatic reality, there will be less energy for thinking. In the case of concentrated verbal/intellectual work, such as the writing which I am doing at this moment, I cannot expect to see the big picture; I leave that for my more relaxed moments when a spontaneous 'joining of the dots' tends to occur. Walking, bike riding, dozing, meditating, sleeping or daydreaming are all times when things 'click', thanks to the longer neuronal connections in my R brain.

There are also more drastic ways to shut my left brain up for a while. An intense electromagnetic field applied to the L brain will temporarily knock out its inhibiting effect and allow spontaneous insights to arise. This is something for the high novelty seekers amongst us to try; I will be sticking to my more benign and tested methods, including a little alcohol.

In her book *The Possible Human,* Jean Houston draws attention to the incredible number of creative minds, from Catullus onward, that have sought inspiration in alcohol (and other drugs) and often been destroyed by them. The roll-call of casualties becomes even longer when you add syphilis and tuberculosis to the list, both illnesses which may have a 'releasing' effect on the brain. We might also include manic depression, another disorder in which there is hemispheric imbalance. To quote Nietzsche:

> For art to exist, for any sort of aesthetic activity to exist, a certain physiological precondition is indispensable: intoxication.

It is also possible that very creative individuals have more connections between the hemispheres. For example, research suggests that this may be a factor in the genesis of schizophrenia. Sometimes the relatives of individuals with this diagnosis are rather eccentric and socially withdrawn; they have some of the characteristics of the full-blown illness but not the overt florid psychosis. Such schizotypal personalities also tend to score higher on tests of creativity. Brain scanning reveals a thicker connection between the two sides of the brain and a more even distribution of neural activity. The genes that contribute to schizophrenic illnesses are very ancient, and so these findings may explain why they have survived so long: they have provided a creative spark to facilitate our cultural evolution.

Individuals with mixed-handedness may be in a parallel situation. In the past, a straightforward distinction used to be made between L and R handedness, with a number of usually unfavourable health and mental traits associated with the 'sinister' side. We now know that people with strong left-handedness are no different from the right-handed majority with respect to health. Those with mixed-handedness, however, may be more prone to dyslexia, ADHD, Alzheimer dementia and immune problems amongst other things. There is some good news though: mixed-handers seem to be more creative. This has certainly been my observation over the years, but I would add to the problem list: varying degrees of mood instability, anxiety and a general sensitivity to environmental stimuli.

Many such individuals seem to be empathic introverts and thus prone to overstimulation. Because of this susceptibility to over-connectedness, they have to protect themselves by judicious withdrawal and regrouping. They have the opposite problem to social extraverts who need to be constantly connecting to keep their nervous systems awake. The need to spend time alone or in solitary activities tends to give introverts a rich inner world, fertile ground for fiction and philosophy.

The general idea that creativity has to do with enhanced hemispheric crosstalk is also supported by the finding that moving the eyes to and fro in the horizontal plane temporarily enhances some facets of creative thinking. This phenomenon may also have a bearing on the use of techniques such as Eye Movement Desensitisation and Reprocessing (EMDR), in which lateral eye movements are used to extinguish anxiety and trauma responses. Various tapping procedures seem to have similar effects.

Whatever the mechanisms involved, it is clear that we are merely enhancing a process that is already going on all the time. The two hemispheres must be in continuous communication to coordinate the actions of the body as a whole. However, they also seem to take turns depending on the requirements of the moment. Research by Professor Pettigrew at the University of Queensland also suggests that we are born with differing 'switch rates'. Dancers and musicians have more rapid hemispheric alternation than engineers or mathematicians. This makes sense when you consider that mathematics requires prolonged concentration while in systematising mode, whereas dancing requires rapid bilateral communication.

The 'Dance of the Hemispheres' also seems to have a temporal profile. As I described earlier, every two hours or so we need to take a break for a few minutes – the so-called ultradian rhythm (see Ernest Rossi's *The 20 Minute Break*). Such breaks are usually signalled by slight drowsiness or the need for a drink or snack. If we follow these impulses and stop for a short while, we may notice daydreaming or a slightly altered state. These sensations are a sign that either the left hemisphere is taking a breather or that inter-hemispheric calibration is taking place.

These breaks are also times when self-regulatory signals can be 'heard' more easily above the din of our surroundings and the preoccupations of the L brain. No problem is too great or too small to be solved during these 'dreamy' intervals; we may get an inspiration about our next meal, solve a complex intellectual problem or simply remember a phone call we need to make. The brain seems to set priorities and whatever is pressing tends to show up first. Such ordering may not correspond, however, with our L hemisphere's opinion about what is immediately important.

A dramatic example of this process is to be found in the case of Brad Absetz, the subject of Colin Wilson's *Access to Inner Worlds*. Since his youth, Brad had experienced periods when very clear intuitions came to him concerning the sort of direction he should take in life. These sometimes corresponded to periods of extreme lassitude. In his 30s, Brad and his wife adopted a son who later died of cancer. His wife was shattered by the event and subsequently developed what seemed to be a manic-depressive illness.

Brad spent long periods watching over her in a relaxed yet alert state and one day, while in this meditative condition, he noticed spontaneous movements in his arms. He allowed these to develop, and over time, came to realise that he could permit these movements at any time and that they had a coherent, purposeful quality. On the one hand they could express bodily self-regulation, for example selecting food for him with sometimes surprising results. On the other, they produced drawings of complex patterns as well as metal sculptures of enormous variety. Colin Wilson had no doubt about the origin of these creations in the non-dominant R side, and their reflection of the infinite depth of that realm.

The R side's association with our immediate body sense makes it the obvious location for generating the somatic signals by which we make decisions. As Antonio Damasio pointed out in *Descartes' Error*, most of our daily decisions are not made by rational evaluation, but by the quicker route of gut feeling or 'somatic marker' as he calls it. When we meet someone for the first time we respond to them from a *felt sense*. Prejudgements or 'unconscious' affective responses may override the sensation, but our first impression is often correct. Damasio tells us that even simple decisions like making an appointment require the somatic component, because it represents a readily accessed condensate of all our previous experiences of that kind of situation.

Brad's story, amongst others, reminds us that there is an ever-present source of wise information available to us if we can cut through the fog of our emotional hang-ups and prejudices. The source of this wisdom has gone by various names including: essence, objective psyche, true self, soul and others. Ultimately this source is a mystery, and moreover, a mystery which feels as if it originates from an Other. Saying that the source is in the unconscious adds nothing to our understanding and so I simply say that this Other is none other than Life at Large, however you want to name Her.

A particularly dramatic example of right brain mediation is to be found in Jill Bolte Taylor's autobiography: *My Stroke of Insight*. Taylor's experience of being struck down by a massive bleed in her left hemisphere is particularly interesting, because as a brain neuro-anatomist she was able to follow her progress in neurological terms. The immediate effect of the damage to her language centres was a dramatic silence accompanied by feelings of tranquillity and omniscience, a state that she felt must be similar to traditional concepts of Nirvana.

There was also a sense of moving from doing to a condition of pure here and now being, in which she felt her normal boundaries dissolve into a natural state of fluidity and connection. Wonderful as these experiences were, however, they had been predicated on an almost complete incapacity to function in the world. Thus, the most important part of Taylor's story is in the rebuilding process over eight years, in which she learns how to 'reboot' her systematising left brain without it suppressing the more subtle messages of the intuitive right side. For Taylor, a life well lived is one that cultivates compassion and joy, and in which we consciously "step to the right", evaluating situations and people by their energetic feel. Jill Bolte Taylor can also be found on TED.

When I was rereading Taylor's book, I came across Diana Reed Slattery's mind-bending volume *Xenolinguistics*. Those of us who are sufficiently old can remember the frissons of excitement that we felt back in the 60s when we read Timothy Leary, John Lilly and Ram Dass. Psychedelics seemed to offer an unprecedented opportunity to explore and map consciousness: the beautiful and savage land of the internal world. Within only a few years this promise had been drowned out by a tsunami of pseudo-mysticism, misinformation and mental health casualties. Western culture was not ready to "turn on, tune in and drop out", and the inevitable overreaction by 'authorities' put serious research on hold for over thirty years. This hiatus may be one reason that Slattery came to her substance-induced 'psychonautical adventures' rather late in life. We are the benefactors, however, because she brings a wisdom and scholarship which is lacking in much psychedelic literature.

Her review of the field also demonstrates many of the common threads to be found in these kinds of journeys. Particularly striking are the recurrent themes of connection, flow, flux and multidimensionality. The experience of seeing a mesh or web of connecting strands is not unusual, and reminiscent of the sudden perceptual changes described, for example, by Judith Blackstone or Carlos Castaneda. It would be surprising if these experiences were not mediated by the right hemisphere with its longer neuronal connections and 'big picture' functions. And please note that I am not implying that mediation is synonymous with causation; the issue of consciousness and the brain must continue to be outside our current cognitive capacities.

Slattery's account is doubly interesting because she has 'downloaded' a symbolic language from the 'Other' which she calls "Glide". Glide has a special fascination because it is made of waveforms and is capable of a 'yes', 'no' and 'yes and no' type of logic. Not only does 'Glide' have resonances with everything that we have discussed about waves and information, but we can imagine it as a fitting complement to the rigidity of the L brain and its obsession with Aristotelian, black and white logic.

One of the explanations for psychedelic effects is that the various substances involved connect parts of the brain that normally do not easily communicate with one another – often for good reason. It is easy to believe, for example, that the reptilian beings so frequently encountered during ayahuasca trips are at least partly the result of opening up the so-called 'reptilian brain' to conscious experience. Similarly, extraordinary visions and visual effects may result from actually experiencing levels of functioning in the visual cortex that are normally unconscious. Whatever the case, it seems that these 'mind expanding' experiences reveal multiple levels of sensory information before they are highly processed and refined by years of conditioning, filtering and storytelling. In Blake's terminology, the doors of perception are cleansed and we see things as they actually are – infinite. Aldous Huxley seemed to agree when he titled his psychedelic classic: *The Doors of Perception: Heaven and Hell.*

The throttling of direct experience by the systematising and storytelling L brain is our Faustian bargain with reality. It has given us self-consciousness, power, control and knowledge, but at the same time, as with Faust, these Promethean gifts have left us confused, etiolated and dissatisfied. It is hard not to link this alienation from Nature and Reality with our culture's masculine version of power and the concomitant suppression of the feminine. To say as much in academic or political circles, however, is to risk a very unpredictable response. The reason, as the reader no doubt knows, is that in the early 21st century we are very confused about gender.

When there is widespread uncertainty about something as important as sexual identity, then we know for sure that there is fermentation happening in the collective mind, and that the 'two faces' of this sort of dilemma will undoubtedly emerge together. On the one hand, we are probably on the threshold of another cultural step forward in how we understand gender. On the other, we will have to go through an awful lot of nonsense and heartache to get there.

For anyone who doubts our ability to conduct sane contemporary debates about gender, I present this confirmatory and cautionary tale. In 2005 Harvard University hosted a seminar to explore the underrepresentation of women in mathematics and the 'hard sciences' such as physics. The assembled academics discussed a variety of psychological and socio-economic reasons for the disparity, and towards the end, Lawrence Summers, President of Harvard and internationally renowned economist, suggested that there might also be biological factors. His remarks unleashed a firestorm of controversy, particularly amongst various women academics who expressed alarm and despondency at this sort of outmoded sexist comment. Other media heavyweights added their voices to the chorus of protest, with the end result that Summers eventually resigned (for this and other reasons to do with his time at Harvard).

Cool informed debate seemed to be in short supply, and reasoned argument was drowned out by emotional overreaction and political correctness. The reality of the matter is complex, with many psycho-social dimensions involved, but there are biological factors involved and here is one of them: the average mathematical ability of men and women is the same, but the distribution of ability is different. The curve representing the spread of mathematical prowess is broader in men than in women and this means that there will be a few more 'geniuses' among the males, but also more very low performers. Some of the males in the 'genius' class, the Alan Turings of this world, will also exhibit some traits characteristic of the autism spectrum. There is generally no free lunch in Nature: if you use a lot of computing power in one area, then other functions are likely to suffer. All-round geniuses like the economist John Maynard Keynes are rare indeed.

The bitterness and irrationality that surround debates on gender were one reason why Simon Baron-Cohen was hesitant to publish his book *The Essential Difference* which appeared in 2005, just when Summers was dropping his clanger at Harvard. Baron-Cohen's credentials as professor of psychology at Cambridge are impeccable, and so his opinions on the matter of brains and gender are worth considering.

His first and most clarifying step has been to make a distinction between male and female brains, not the bodies in which they are housed. A male brain has a bias toward systematising, whereas a female brain has a bias toward empathising. By *systematising,* Baron-Cohen means the impulse to understand or construct the world in systematic ways. As we have discussed before, the notion of a system refers to anything with a structure governed by rules: a vast territory that might equally apply to setting out a vegetable patch, building an engine or formulating an abstract mathematical formula.

Empathising, on the other hand, consists of reading emotional atmospheres and being able to feel one's way into another person's shoes. It also implies caring about the feelings of others and interacting with feeling-toned communication. Empathy is generally considered to have two components: one which is a more cognitive understanding of how a person is thinking and feeling, and the second is a more affective response, in which the empath actually feels an emotional resonance. Only the former can be learned, the latter seems to be largely innate. On a questionnaire designed to score these qualities of male or female brains, a systematiser answers positively, for example, to questions that ask about wanting to know engine details if buying a car or being able to fix an electrical fault at home. Empathisers, on the other hand, answer positively to questions that ask, for example, about predicting the feelings of others or being distressed at an animal in pain.

Baron-Cohen presents an impressive array of evidence showing that these modes of brain processing are found with differential frequencies in the two sexes, and that they have strong biological roots. For example, male babies prefer to stare at a mobile made of geometrical shapes, whereas female babies would rather stare at a mobile with a facial outline. Baron-Cohen also looks at some of the evolutionary roots underlying this difference: a systematising brain is obviously important for hunting and tracking, and male primates with their deep-rooted programming around dominance and aggression would be ill-served by an empathising side to their nature. Females, on the other hand, require an empathising brain, not only for child-rearing purposes, but also to facilitate stability within the complex networks of tribal relationships.

The inherent bias toward competition/aggression in men and cooperation/nurturing in women is illustrated by two psychological studies. Michele Wirth and Oliver Schultheiss at the University of Michigan were interested in studying the relationship between testosterone (T) and learning. A group of young male subjects had to learn a task that involved tapping out keystroke patterns. After completing a sequence they would be presented with a neutral or angry face flashed *subliminally* on to a screen. Those men with higher salivary T performed better than their lower T colleagues after being exposed to the angry faces. The finding suggests that an aggressive cue acts as a reward to learning in high T men, i.e. they 'get off' on aggression.

Contrast this study with that done by Elainie Madsen and others at the University of St Andrews, who asked a group of men and women to endure pain by squatting against a wall. The longer that they suffered, the greater the reward for a familiar person or charity. Not surprisingly, both sexes were prepared to inflict more pain on themselves for closer relatives. Women, however, spread their generosity more evenly among their relatives and were prepared to suffer more for their best friends. Various explanations for this finding could be provided, although it is likely that, as co-author Robin Dunbar commented: "... females are just more social." I would rephrase that to say that women are more social in a generous way. Men generally like being in groups just as much as women, but the interactions in a male hunting party (at the footy or in a 'man shed') are very different from those found in a group of women friends.

The extreme male brain is exemplified by some individuals on the autism spectrum in whom we find, for example, a very highly developed mathematical or technical facility, but absolutely no capacity to read or respond to the emotions of others. There is no clear-cut parallel example of an extreme female brain, although Baron-Cohen hypothesises that a very empathic female therapist with very little technical capacity might illustrate this type.

Subsequent to the release of his book, Baron-Cohen published further research on the incidence of male and female type brains in men and women. By using questionnaires and setting defined cut-off points, he and his colleagues have been able to classify brains as either male, female or balanced. His results suggest that about one in five men and women have an opposite brain type to their biological sex, but women have twice as many balanced brains as men. With a higher incidence of balanced brains, proportionately more women are going to be skilled in those areas that require negotiation and cooperation, as well as systematising abilities. This suggests that, on average, they will be better managers, better politicians and, it has to be said, generally better at most things. Men, on the other hand, will have a higher proportion of individuals with talent for very specialised, focused skills such as IT, financial analysis and engineering.

To be fair, however, many researchers and thinkers would regard these conclusions as highly contentious and so I refer the reader to an alternative view in the form of Cordelia Fine's work (e.g. *Delusions of Gender*). The September 2017 issue of *Scientific American* on sex and gender also has much food for thought. And at least, we can probably all agree that in our everyday experience, there is a spectrum of 'masculine' and 'feminine' behaviour that can be applied to both sexes. For example, we all know couples where the man is the 'softie' and the woman is the hard-nosed organiser.

What Baron-Cohen does not tackle, however, are the thorny matters of power and aggression, issues that Robert Masters puts at the forefront of his book, *To Be a Man*. Masters makes the simple, but often forgotten, point that our culture is still largely stuck in primitive concepts of masculinity that equate 'being a man' with being tougher, more ruthlessly driven, more competitive, more uncaring and generally unconscious of one's own emotional wounds. This is in contrast to genuine masculine power which comes into being with a true balance of head (rationality, analysis), heart (compassion, love) and guts (resolve, bravery, resilience). Or as a therapist friend of mine with years of experience in the men's movement commented: "Just being a decent human being."

The parallel task for women has been gathering momentum for the past two centuries in Western culture, although women still do not have an equal share of power or financial reward.

Now, however, it is the norm for women to be working in the world, competing and exercising their whole brains in ways that are often superior to men, a situation that was unthinkable just two generations ago. Jung anticipated this development long ago, when he stated that the cultural task in the West lay with women. He could see that, at this point in history, women were more able than men to attain wholeness. Jung's insight was made possible by his discovery that the psyche is bisexual, but with one pole suppressed and underdeveloped in the form of the 'anima' or 'animus'. For Jung, maturity comes with the 'mystical marriage' (see his *Mysterium Coniunctionis*) in which both these aspects of the psyche function in harmony.

This theme is implicit in much of world literature, as Christopher Booker points out in *The Seven Basic Plots*. In an account of male and female principles, that has not in my opinion been bettered, he tells us that the masculine in stories has two aspects: power and order. Power and strength may appear as forces that are dominating, cruel and exploitive, or as disciplined in the service of justice and self-mastery. The sense of order, on the other hand, arises from a desire for frameworks and comprehensibility, and thus a sense of control through organisation. The twin aspects of power and order inevitably give rise to hierarchy, either in a good sense as in the structures of a democratic system, or in the far more common scenarios of inequality and exploitation.

In contrast he sees the female dimension as characterised by selfless feeling, connection-making and the healing of fractured relationships. Thus the feminine is the touchstone for resolving the dramatic tension that arises in any good tale. As we saw earlier, the essence of drama is that a protagonist must confront dark or difficult forces to win a great prize. This opposition usually comes in the form of distorted masculinity with its egocentricity, obsessiveness and callous indifference to sentiment. Over against it we find a female figure who is in need of rescuing or who has to be won in some way. She represents the essence of Life, and the subsequent unfolding drama embodies all that has to be overcome for a final state of union and wholeness to be achieved.

The hero, the heroine and the dark power represent the three basic elements of drama, but they may masquerade in a multitude of forms. If this were not so, drama would be a very predictable business. Thus the hero may have a balanced psyche from the start or may be in the grip of unresolved demons, for example Raskolnikov in *Crime and Punishment*. Similarly the heroine may appear in passive or active form, and may occasionally carry the dark masculine herself, as in *The Taming of the Shrew* or *Emma*. Alternatively the story may be told from the heroine's point of view, which is the case with many of our favourite fairy stories, such as Snow White.

A rich texture is added by a supporting cast of helping and hindering forces who contribute to the build-up of tension until at last we arrive at the final happy and harmonious resolution. We can then all have a good cry and feel a lot better as a result of a much-needed catharsis. Not so in tragedy, of course, where the main protagonists are not able to face themselves in order to undergo the necessary maturing transformation. The feminine principle of LIFE is not embraced or redeemed, and the consequence must inevitably be death. The masculine principle is usually weak from the start (as in *Macbeth*) and not able to undertake the task of individuation, and as a result the feminine must also come to a bad end.

The detective novel is conspicuously absent from the outline of basic plots, and Booker explains that this is because it is just a puzzle and does not meet the requirements of meaningful storytelling. In its purest form, the detective mystery is a diversion for the L brain alone, and as such we might expect its main protagonist to be a rather one-dimensional character. This usually proves to be the case, with most detectives being males whose partners are either non-existent, dead or unwell. These lonely, cut-off males tend to prefer self-medication to healthy self-care and have to be looked after by indulgent housekeepers, friends or admiring women, all of whom are generally kept at arm's length. They are cold, over-cerebral archetypes of the systemising brain.

What do you think an archetype of the R brain might look like?

Booker tells us that the principles that underlie the trajectory of a true story can usually be summed up as moving toward wise authority, harmony, enlightenment and affection and community.

It is not difficult to see these movements as a reflection of the individuation process, both on a personal and collective level. Just as our own journeys aspire to 'whole seeing' and 'whole being', so too does society seem to move in the direction of greater inclusiveness, connectedness, tolerance and equality. The modern democratic project would not be possible without redeeming the feminine and restoring her principles to the centre of public life. It is a work in progress.

It would be easy to assign male and femaleness to the L and R hemispheres respectively, if it were not for the fact that the brain defies simple categories. For example a male's somewhat superior spatial skills are mediated by the R side, and a female's main conduit of connection, language, entails full use of the L verbal centres. Traditionally, however, the left side of the body is associated more with the feminine, and indeed a woman's L breast tends to be slightly fuller. The obverse is true with a man's R testicle generally being larger. These hormonal effects come on at puberty, and it would be surprising if the brain were not similarly affected in an asymmetrical way, just as it had been previously moulded by the surge of testosterone (T) in utero. We are still very much in the dark, however, concerning the complex restructuring of the brain that occurs during adolescence. We do know that T is the elephant (or raging bull) in the room whenever we talk about crime, domestic violence or war. If one constructs a curve in which age is plotted against crime or road accidents, it fits a plot of T levels with uncanny precision, as they surge in adolescence and gradually begin to taper throughout most of adulthood.

The problem is exacerbated by the trend to later marriage. Marital bliss lowers T levels, with further amelioration by oxytocin when children arrive. However, even though men seem to be civilised by women, it is a sad fact that throughout the life cycle, they generally remain more emotionally dependent than women, a function no doubt of their continuing affective immaturity. Thus 70% of relationship separations between heterosexual couples are initiated by the woman, and study after study shows that men derive marked health and longevity benefits from being in a pair bond, but women do not.

But whatever part biological factors may play in these issues, the solutions must be found on a societal level. Studies of baboon colonies in Africa have shown us that if for some reason the dominant males die off, then females can take over very well, and importantly, new young males who join the troupe behave less aggressively. Readers must form their own conclusions from these observations by Robert Sapolsky, although it certainly seems to me that the key to bringing up youngsters is that the prevailing social environment is one of sexual equality, socio-economic equality and a sane competition/cooperation balance. We will go a long way toward these ideals if we focus on modifying toxic hierarchies in all their forms: male and female. This process must start in the home, move on to the primary school playground and culminate in our most august institutions.

Looking at how our politicians perform in *Question Time* reminds us that from kindergarten to old age, the causes of human conflict are monotonously the same – ego, lack of empathy and an inability to see from another's point of view i.e. limited L brain thinking untempered by humanity. Our cultural task is to restore the balance. Given that to change the world we all need to start 'at home', let me go on to consider some of the 'therapeutic' implications of the L-R and male-female dichotomies. The achievement of balance is a lifelong proposition and calls upon all of our capacities for self-reflection and 'right action'. The following list of simple and practical things to consider is not meant to trivialise the very real requirements and challenges of maturation through the life cycle.

Specifically:

1) If you think that you may be generally more male brained, then try to apply the corrective: open up more to receive 'what is' in the moment; come to your senses, listen to others and express to others from a heart level. Have a look at the HeartMath material either at their site or in Joseph Chilton Pearce's *The Biology of Transcendence*. Be less judgemental and practise gratitude and compassion. Cultivate the 'felt sense' of people, places and situations. Consider finding a therapist to help you explore your feelings and somatic reality.
2) If you are more female brained and you get swamped by the feelings and sufferings of others, try to be more detached, not in a hard way, but in a spirit of self-care. Be firm with yourself about disengaging when some-one is draining you. Put a different frame around situations where you feel you have to rescue someone or immerse yourself in another's dilemma. Byron Katie is useful here: is it your business, their business or God's business? If you are not very organised in your life, start making small changes to systematise your affairs more.

   If you are an R biased sensitive temperament, doing puzzles and rote tasks such as multiplication can stimulate the L brain and improve its ability to inhibit excessive R brain generated anxiety; so also can repeatedly screwing up the R side of your face while using a 'squeegy' ball in the R hand. A recent study showed that playing Tetris could ameliorate the acquisition of traumatic memories; an effect, like lateral eye movements (as in EMDR), that possibly results from coordinated hemispheric action. Consider finding a therapist to help with self-exploration.

In general:

3) Be aware of your ultradian cycle and try to actually follow its promptings to take short 'decompression' breaks. Your 'nasal cycle' may be in sync with the ultradian rhythm i.e. the L and R nostrils may be alternately patent every two hours or so. Although this happens with only a minority of people, you can still take advantage of the contralateral innervation of the nostrils by: (a) observing which is the more blocked nostril and thus the more active or stressed hemisphere, and (b) practising alternate nostril breathing to calm and balance your whole system. Many people have a more consistently blocked side which can be evidence of hemispheric imbalance.
4) If you practise any form of bodywork use the opportunity to focus on L-R differences. Yoga is especially beneficial for this kind of awareness. In fact yoga should be treated primarily as an awareness process which aims to cultivate symmetricality in all the three dimensions of space, as well as enhancing sensitivity to the body's energy templates (see *Yoga in the Kashmir Tradition: The Art of Listening*, Billy Doyle).

   Try juggling.
5) If you meditate or simply spend some time resting, notice the L-R difference when you start. This may be particularly

evident with the shoulders. I inevitably find that my R shoulder feels shorter, higher and more cramped than my L, and because I am mixed-handed I imagine that this reflects the fact that I am usually overusing my L brain. Some simple freeing-up movements can begin the balancing process that usually occurs with relaxation. Given, however, that our unilateral handedness imposes marked L-R differences, particularly in the torso, we may not see a complete remediation of the situation.

6) In meditation we can notice other biases. For example, my eyes and sometimes my head tend to drift to the R, a symptom of L brain dominance. Also, with eyes closed there comes a point when we clearly enter chidakasa, the internal visual space. You may notice that, initially at least, that space tends to be to the L or R of your sense of the nose, reflecting contralateral brain dominance. In these circumstances you may simply observe how these phenomena evolve or make a gesture in awareness to feel a balance between L and R sides. If your meditation 'anchor' is the abdominal breath then the process of balancing the three dimensions will usually proceed by itself. When in doubt, don't interfere!
7) Read or write poetry, dance, paint, create. But beware the sort of writing that I am doing at this moment – it is very imbalancing. Anything of a vaguely academic caste can be stressful and harmful to self-regulation. It is a matter of a little goes a long way; once cerebration has achieved a measure of clarity on an issue, leave it alone and come back later when you feel sane again, preferably after a time in Nature.

A psychologist friend told me in all seriousness a few years ago that his PhD had caused him brain damage, and I truly believe that such an outcome is possible on a subtle level. This kind of intellectual effort also has an obsessive quality, little different from any other human addiction.

The L brain delights in wrapping up a story and then tenaciously owning it as part of its maddening world of information, concepts and beliefs. Earlier in the book I quoted a piece from Marion Milner in which she enhanced her perceptions by describing to herself what she was experiencing through the senses. This is a very useful way of employing the chattering mind in the service of the here and now; the process both sharpens attention and prevents the mind wandering off with its current preoccupations.

8) RELAX. When I was growing up in Cornwall I would often hear the expression: 'going water coose', which meant that one was going along like a stream, flowing with the terrain, not getting into a state. Become aware of your dependence on "What next?" and "What if?" Defuse the soap opera that it is daily life.
9) Be with Nature. Receive and Give. What will you do for Mother Earth today? She will always do something for you.

This list is not exhaustive, just some suggestions while you are cultivating the art of being present, embodied and balanced. All sorts of approaches may work for you. IT'S ALL A GREAT EXPERIMENT.

In the next chapter I want to consider how we are constantly pulled out of balance and away from ourselves into the forward dimension, the most enigmatic and ignored of our biases in space. The ideas of above and below and left and right seem reasonably comprehensible in terms of our internal model building, but the front/back dimension has a different quality entirely, and goes to the core of our sense of subjectivity and separateness.

14

Getting Ahead of Myself

No, the mind does not dissolve. In my experience there is a new arrangement of things – the things that were in the front go to the back and the things that were on one side go to the other.
Satyananda (Bernardo Arenas) in *The Teachers of One*

We are constantly moving forward to the next thing, either physically or in our minds. Even when we are supposedly relaxing, there is constant doing; the stories and music that we enjoy are in constant motion toward an end point; our eating, idle pleasures or obsessions all move toward an end point where things stop and we are briefly relieved or satisfied. But the sense of 'enough' is always short-lived; after a brief surcease, we are impelled forward again, sometimes by necessity, but more often by arbitrary cravings and addictions. There is absolutely no rest except in deep sleep.

As Ramana Maharshi explained:

ALL SATISFACTION ARISES FROM THE BRIEF PERIOD OF QUIET THAT FOLLOWS THE ATTAINMENT OF A DESIRE.

It is rather astonishing that this process of constant forward motion toward intrinsically evanescent goals strikes only a few people as a nightmarish scenario, like a train journey to an unknown destination from which you cannot escape. Yet it is embraced by most of us as a natural state of affairs in which it is perfectly possible to be content, even happy. Maybe there is method in this madness; biological life *is*, after all, constant, restless motion, an unending energetic battle against the physical laws that are apparently running down every physical thing in the universe except life. And the majority of humans seem well equipped to cope with this situation by being endowed with the so-called optimism bias that sees unending sunny outcomes when rationality would calculate a bleaker picture.

As I have pointed out before, this is particularly true of extraverts, whose nervous systems impel them to seek out novelty and whose mood reflects this bias in a constant state of hopeful, pleasurable anticipation. *It is the prospect, not the consummation, that provides their motive power.* As that notable commentator Pooh recalled, there was a moment before eating the honey that was better than when he was eating it, but he didn't know what it was called. Once the object of desire is attained, we are off again on another quest, hardly pausing long enough to enjoy the fruits of our labour, driven mad by the future.

The situation for introverts is somewhat different: their aversion to novelty makes forward motion much more difficult for them. They want nothing more than to stop and be quiet while they gather themselves together and summon up enough energy for their next obligatory foray into the day's noisy currents. They are 'serenity seeking' and go through the world with reluctance, one foot on the gas, the other on the brakes. No wonder they are usually tired. Despite their desire for peace and quiet, however, most introverts, being also highly anxious, find that the future constantly looms over them and they become as trapped by prospectivity as everyone else.

There is a name for our continuous march forward – volition, the movement of our bodies and minds into the great space that we see before us. We tend to believe that the sensations arising from this movement are the result of a personal self, exercising choice through the agency of a personal 'will'. Close inspection, however, reveals little evidence for any such independent agent, or any psychological mechanism that we might call volition. There is just forward motion and the sense of self and choice that this movement entrains.

Earlier in the book I started to recount a story from Fred Alan Wolf's *The Dreaming Universe*, in which a physicist closely observed the effects of ketamine on his visual awareness. As his eye muscles became paralysed, his visual field flattened out and became: "hyperdimensional, abstract and dynamic." At the same time any sense of 'I' disappeared, leaving only awareness. After forty-five minutes his eye muscles started to work and a perspective formed with a growing sense of 'I' at its focus. There are parallels to this scenario in the evolution of Western Culture. When the collective 'ego' began its next step forward during the Renaissance, a striking feature of that period's art was the mathematical development of perspective. It was the beginning of a new way of SEEING, one which emphasised an individual view.

The physicist goes on to note that his ego sense continued to grow when he could move his hands and coordinate their action with his eyes, thus giving rise to the simple insight that volition and the 'I' sense are deeply connected. Interestingly, he had little body sense during the experience, just sound and sight, and felt that if he had not been asked to talk about the experiment immediately afterwards, his memories and insights would have disappeared. As Wolf points out, there is a parallel between this account and our normal experience of dreaming. During dream sleep the body is paralysed but the eyes can still move. Thus we have an attenuated sense of a self which, although aware of a dreamscape, has little sense of control over what happens. And because our storytelling critical faculties are asleep, we unquestioningly accept the reality of whatever strange circumstance may be unfolding.

But our constant 'doing' is not confined to moving in physical space; far more pervasive is the continuous internal doing that we call thought. Whether using images or talking to ourselves, we are forever simulating activities from the 'real world'. There is no thought that is not an attenuated action, and scientific studies confirm this: monitoring the subtle electrical activity of muscles shows that as I imagine various scenarios, the relevant muscles in my body respond with sub-threshold activity. Thus practice in imagination is now an accepted part of athletic training and has been shown, for example, to improve muscle performance and strength. How could it be otherwise? We are egos in so far as we are embodied and identified with that embodiment.

Language is especially frontal in its nature, being a series of projectiles thrust into space by the breath. Emilie Conrad, the remarkable dance and somatic therapist, has something particularly apposite to say on this topic in her book *Life on Land*. In studying her own voice, she realised that the forward impulse of language was having a profound effect in shaping the actual tissue of her throat. She realised, as with all actions in the body, that this was a two-edged sword, in which purposiveness was being traded for freedom and flexibility in the tissues themselves. So she then asked herself if it were possible to release the forward thrust and allow the tissues "out of jail" and as a result return to a free and "undifferentiated state". Her goal was eventually achieved by experimenting with very subtle sounds generated in the epiglottal (back) region of the throat.

Conrad also noticed that the tissues of the torso could generally be observed to be pulled forward, even with a person lying down. Coincident with this, breath movements would be absent from the sides and back of the body. This is in line with the idea that our backs lie outside awareness and are thus part of our 'everyday unconscious'. However, in the complementarity that characterises all aspects of somatic function, the contact that we make with the world at the front is predicated on the support that is provided at the back. That support is not just structural, but also comprises the myriad processes that continually organise our integrity as distinct beings. Unfortunately for us, we inevitably neglect these sources of support and nurture, and as a result our hind regions become inflexible and atrophied.

This is most obvious in the spine. As we age, our vertebral column becomes progressively stiffer and its supporting muscles weaker. As a result, the forward currents of our life pull us into a chronic stoop and we end our days pushing around a walking frame gazing at the floor. Our senile posture reveals the real nature of continual prospectivity: it is contractive in nature and leads inevitably to the foetal self-enclosure from which we developed. The remedy is simple: appropriate care for our supportive structures, especially with regard to maintaining flexibility and strength in the mechanisms of extension, for example the extensor muscles of the spine. There is no shortage of methods available, from toning with sound to the techniques of osteopathy and yoga. The main thing is to direct attention to the back, something that can be done on a random basis throughout the day. Remember, energy follows attention and the very act of asking how my rear surfaces and structures feel brings some vitality to those parts. There are more suggestions later for balancing the back with the front.

Indifference to our rear parts is mirrored by an equal disinterest in the vast realm of consciousness that lies behind and beneath the narrow focus of everyday attention. As discussed previously, we are generally operating in a very restricted band of awareness which follows the guidelines and expectations of an equally restricted 'story'. We are generally unaware of the themes and counter-themes in our personal drama, and are equally ignorant of the true nature of moods, feelings, thoughts, perceptions and intuitions that play on the periphery of attention.

Marion Milner, introduced earlier, gives a detailed account of these phenomena in her books: *A Life of One's Own* and *An Experiment in Leisure*. Over many years, Milner observed herself with scrupulous honesty in an attempt to discover for herself what really made her happy. She recorded her observations in diary form and in paintings and drawings. Anyone wanting to know about the true nature of mindfulness should read these works. Milner uses the term 'mindfulness' in the original 1934 edition of *A Life of One's Own* but we could equally describe her activities as self-observation.

I would not dream of trying to describe her conclusions and depriving you of the pleasure of reading her books unsullied by preconception. However, here are two excerpts from *An Experiment in Leisure*:

> I can sink down, out of my head, into a deeper part of my body, usually somewhere in my spine between my shoulder blades, where there are no thoughts, or at least thoughts are only incidental – it produces a most serene sense of happiness, and it is somehow very profane – not that I like it less for that (page 53).

And in reference to this inner feeling which she calls "the inner fact":

> ... this inner fact has sometimes a curious quality of space, an inner spaceless space where all is accomplished... and sometimes when enjoying looking across a wide view of country, I feel there is as much size of universe opening through and behind me as there is out front – a sort of through-the-looking-glass-land (page 53).

The genius of Milner's accounts resides in their total originality and freshness, and in the fact that she was a light on her own path, her own authority. No expert can tell us how to be happy or how our minds work; we are all different. It is only careful and creative self-observation that can inform us and ultimately free us. Consciousness/Life is expansive in all directions, physical, psychological and metaphysical, and shows us as a matter of course the direction in which freedom lies. But we must stop and listen.

The same injunction applies to our culture as a whole, especially our technocracy, whose contempt for the lessons of history borders on the criminal and insane. Not that I was history literate myself until quite late in life. But old age has taught me that the heady and heedless progress of youth leaves a trail of psychological debris and unfinished business which it is the duty of one's later years to clean up. Thus I often now observe memories arising quite spontaneously into my mind of incidents from long ago which can only be described as cringe-worthy in nature, showing me in any number of uncomplimentary lights. I had thought that this phenomenon was simply the latest turn in my ongoing neurosis. However, a friend whom I regard as a paragon of maturity told me a very similar story about herself, and so I concluded that such promptings are a call to chew through various crucial facts about my shadow, and to balance a diminishing prospective view with a realistic appraisal of what I thought was well behind me.

In this effort I am also aided by my dreams, which are relentless in bringing up even the remote past, bidding me look and see things that would otherwise be airbrushed from my account of a life well justified.

I understand now why Jung, later in life, concentrated on his older clients. The process of individuation can either peter out in midlife or take on a greater urgency in a person who is not already stone dead or buried under the weight of their personal and cultural stories. Even those who maintain a flicker of life have to battle an adolescent society that conspicuously lacks wise elders who could lead by example. Perhaps I am being too cynical; of course there are still guides who can help those lost in the dark wood of midlife – maybe the person next door has all you need for the next step.

Keeping a Straight Face

The combination of erect posture and forward motion has both beneficial and problematic aspects. Having our sensitive frontal areas and our sense organs face forward enables us to move into the world with a huge scanner to the fore, picking up vast amounts of multimodal information which is then processed by our large brains. And I am not just talking about first line perceptual data such as vision or hearing; I am also including the feeling senses that we constantly rely on to gauge the complex social and other environments that are in continual flux around us.

But this frontal sensitivity also makes us very vulnerable to the sensory and physical assaults of the everyday world. Women are more susceptible than men in this respect, because breasts are intrinsically sensitive, as well as being a focus for the 'male gaze' and thus male sexual aggression (however attenuated or civilised). Defensive armouring against this vulnerability can start at an early age, a fact first appreciated by the analyst Wilhelm Reich. All frontal structures are involved, but especially the diaphragm and abdominal muscles. Constant or periodic tension in these powerful tissues ensures the gradual stoop toward senility that we discussed earlier. The defensive organisation of the body against attack from the front and above (think of a child's perspective) is, of course, also a whole body development and follows the general form of the 'red light' reflex.

In severe trauma, consciousness retreats away from the periphery altogether and withdraws to a central defensive core, like a medieval army taking refuge in the castle keep and leaving the surrounding villages unprotected. But whatever the degree or chronicity of frontal assault, the essential point is that we have to continually protect our feeling selves from overwhelm because we lead with our vulnerabilities, and it is our points of connection with the world where we are most sensitive.

Nowhere is this more obvious than in the face. If we map how the sensory body is represented in the brain, we find that the face and hands take up a disproportionately large amount of room. This is hardly surprising, since together with the voice they are our portals into the social world, and as such hold all the tensions and strategies that we develop in relation to our fellow humans.

The importance of our 'social face' prompted Douglas Harding (see Chapter 1) in 1967 to write an interesting article for the *Transactional Analysis Bulletin* entitled "The Face Game". He describes how our 'original face', the free *openness* of early childhood, gets filled in with the illusion of personhood and the possession of a head and face. This is largely a social process and one that occupies a good proportion of our brain development. Once we have acquired a face, then there is no limit to the many interpersonal (or is it interfacial?) games that we can play with others. Harding suggests that we go to the root of the problem, see through the unreality of our faces, and thus let all these games wither on the vine of dis-illusion. Failing this 'cut to the chase' approach, however, there are other useful lessons that we can learn from the face's connectivity, not the least of which concerns relaxation.

The fact that our physiognomy occupies so much brain space makes it a 'royal road' into the nervous system. Just smoothing out the brow to the sides and releasing the jaw can have immediate effects. The frown lines between the brows represent a particularly tense area, and it is little wonder that Botox in that region can reduce the incidence of certain headaches. But it is the eyes that carry the greatest load of stress, which is not surprising in view of our earlier discussions of narrow focus and its effects. Vision is by far our most powerful conduit for consciousness, accounting for about one-third of total sensory input, compared to 8% for touch and 3% for hearing. The simplest way to relieve strain in the eye segment of the face is to practise open focus and soften the gaze whenever possible. Ultimately, we want to take the 'frontality' out of looking, something that is discussed at greater length a little later. Like the face and eyes, the hands are another portal into stress relief; just feeling into the sensations of the hand at rest can be a good way of settling into relaxation.

The defensive screen of tension that we all hold in our faces is strengthened immensely by thinking. As Jean Klein repeatedly pointed out, thinking is frontal, and it is this constant activity that acts as a buffer against the impact of the world. In fact, it is such a good defence that we are usually quite dissociated from our sensory reality. Close attention to the *feeling of thinking* reveals a tight sphere of activity in the centre of awareness, creating tension from the neck through to the brow, central face, mouth, jaw and throat. Like a black hole, it exerts a pull on everything that comes into its orbit, swallowing reality into its stale and tense world of knowns. And just as space is bent around those massive cosmic objects, so perception is cramped and distorted around the relentless presence of constant thinking.

I expect that you have had the experience of being outdoors and, for a moment, thinking dies down, leaving three-dimensional reality to rush in with an extraordinary vividness and immediacy. This can be such a shock that thinking and narrow focus promptly kick in and close the experience down. Reality *is* a shock when you are living most of the time in a thought bubble.

The sense that thinking is frontal is partially related to the fact that it reflects integrative activity in our bulging frontal lobes. As well, all the doing functions in the cerebral cortex are anterior to the sensing ones. Thus there is the paradox that in all three dimensions, brain anatomy seems a mirror image of subjective experience. Vision seems right out in front of us, but the visual cortex is at the back of the brain. My extreme left visual field, coming from both eyes, is mediated through the right side of my brain (and vice versa), and my body sense is upside down on the opposite side. No one knows why this should be so, but it is certainly consistent with the idea that there is a broader field of consciousness that relates to the brain from a higher dimensional space and relates to the physical brain in a mirror-like fashion.

Coming to our senses also temporarily reverses the flow of energy which has been guided by our preoccupations and projected out on to objects in the world. There is, for a moment, a pause and an enlivening influx of the world's attention upon us. Receiving such a gift harmonises and restores us, as the body's energies come into synchronisation with the world field. Such moments cannot be caused, but there are things we can do to be more receptive to that Spirit which "bloweth where it listeth."

Reversing the Flow

One of the reasons that prompted me to write this book was the frequency with which I came across accounts of awakening that included comments on the experience of space. This led me to believe that one important aspect of 'liberation' is none other than a perceptual change in the appreciation of dimensionality, an idea that is more concrete than, for example, the concept of transcending the subject-object dichotomy. And although many spiritual aspirants have not arrived at their new perceptions by contemplating space, the alternate approach of bringing attention back to the nature of the observer seems to naturally bring one to that which is still and spacious.

Although there were home-grown varieties, such a process of enquiry was introduced to the West largely through contact with Ramana Maharshi's ashram and his method of asking: "Who or What am I?" Ramana's devotee, Sri Annamalai Swami, comments in David Godman's book, *Living By the Words of Bhagavan*:

> Just keep your attention on the Self twenty-four hours a day. Meditation is not something that should be done in a particular position or a particular time. It is an awareness and an attitude that must persist throughout the day. To be effective, meditation must be continuous.

Self-enquiry brings attention back from objects to the subject; from 'out there in front' to 'back here'. In many ways this procedure is a trick, because the subject can never be an object, can never be located or described in ways that we normally categorise phenomena. If you are a reader of contemporary spiritual literature you probably know this already in an intellectual way. Unfortunately, such knowing has an impairing effect on the koan-like nature of self-enquiry, because it creates another layer of subtle conceptualisation. Nonetheless, the frequent practice of 'coming back' opens us to the still, silent, unchanging backdrop to all experience that initially manifests as *behind* the evanescent world of perceptions, feelings and thoughts.

Jean Klein, the most lucid, I think, of all Advaita commentators, makes this point clear in describing the seeing of a flower. In the absence of thought there is only looking, but you are not aware of the looking until attention returns to its "homeground" in which pure seeing, hearing and touching are arising without the sense of subject and object.

> First you are aware of something and then this something returns to awareness, to its homeground, and what remains is objectless awareness which knows itself by itself.
> (*Transmission of the Flame,* page 10)

And:

> What you are can never be emphasised; it is constantly open, never in conclusion, never in assertion. As soon as you take yourself for somebody, there is contraction, there is localisation, but when you are completely free from the person, you are expanded in space, you are constantly in meditation.
> (*Transmission of the Flame,* page 15)

Flora Courtois gives us a good example of this expansion in her description of an important premonitory experience while sitting in a lecture:

> Sitting in my seat in class one midwinter morning, gazing straight ahead, I suddenly became aware of space in an extraordinary manner, that is, I was equally aware of it behind me, underneath, above, all around and in fact, it seemed to be all through me. This so astounded me that I held my eyes wide open and my breath still for fear of losing this incredible experience.
> (*An Experience of Enlightenment*, pages 39–40)

Courtois is very still and very open, the seeming preconditions of allowing reality to come toward the apparent subject, reversing the flow of grasping, goal-directed attention which Klein pithily refers to as "end-gaining". Klein and Courtois are also both unusual in placing particular emphasis on the visual faculty and our way of using it. Klein is explicit, for example, in advising his students to feel into their eyes, sense them as living and large and to relax them completely. In this way one can locate awareness behind the eyes and away from the "thinking factory" of the forebrain.

Another of his suggestions is to imagine the eyes rolling to the back of the head and resting occipitally at the junction with the upper spine. This is where consciousness energy can build up before it is dispersed toward the forehead and manifested as thinking and intention i.e. before the subject-object dichotomy appears. But one must not make a method of locating the observer at the back. It is another koan, like Herrigel's puzzle at being told to hit a bullseye without intention. Just relax and remain present without strain. Let looking (and the other senses) be. Let yourself be.

You may remember Courtois's account from Chapter 1 in

which she describes how her eyes: "released from their former tension to reach out and see the world outside, were now as free as if they had been blanked out, eliminated altogether." This is an eloquent description of complete 'open focus', with no attempt to use it as a technique or to address a problem or attain any special state – just openness with no sense of a conclusion or end point.

Although no technique can help us be who we already are, balancing our directions can help us be still and focused long enough to revert to what should be a natural state of poise, one in which we can come to our senses and thus come to ourselves. In any process that involves gravitating to our centre, the first step must be to come back from our frontal orientation and locate the body's central axis. From there we can balance front and back, something that had never occurred to me until I read Wendy Palmer's *The Intuitive Body*. Palmer's approach has been discussed before, but let us look again at her method. After asking the question: "Is the front of my (energy) field even to the back?" she goes on to say:

> In asking this question, our attention is drawn to our back, and for a moment more energy is brought to it. The mind is asking the body a question. The answer will usually be "no", but that is not the point of the question: we are asking for a sensate response. In asking the question, our attention and energy have made a shift, and in the process more balance occurs. When the shift occurs in our body, it can emanate into our field.
>
> This practice is different from telling ourselves to straighten up. We are trying to rouse our interest in sensation, not ordering ourselves into a particular state. Rather than giving any direction, we are open to what may occur.
>
> (*The Intuitive Body*, page 25)

Palmer's comment about arousing our interest in sensation is particularly important. We are not ordering our body around, neither are we setting off in any intentional direction. The active question allows a reversal into *receiving and experiencing sensations*. Later in the book, she suggests a practice in which we walk backwards around a track. She comments that after about half a mile, the back begins to "wake up" and we begin to sense a kind of intelligence and presence in our backfield. Later, we can try alternately moving forward and backward until both begin to feel the same. This creates a new sense of spaciousness and wholeness because we are better able to "drop any idea that forward is better." Such a process operates on many levels, and as we move forward more receptively we can also be more active in our appreciation of what has gone before.

We can "wake up" the back because it is a large region of tactile and other sensations. This is well illustrated by experiments in which a grid of tiny probes is placed on the back. They can be made to produce quite detailed patterns of touch on the skin, and these 'pictures' are soon interpreted and understood by the brain in the same way as impulses from the back of the eye (which is basically a highly modified patch of skin).

By becoming more aware of our backs, we open up parts of our brain/mind that have lain dormant, and as a result we can begin to cultivate a body sense and a mindset that are less lopsided. Yoga is replete with such practices, not the least of which is the sequence in yoga nidra in which attention is rotated around the points of contact that our prone body has with the floor. This 'dead pose' is so ideal for relaxation because we are feeling down into the earth with our backs at the same time that attention is also brought into the whole body. All of our normal 'doing' polarities are reversed in the three axes of space. The same posture is also ideal for 'sky gazing'; our groundedness at the back allows an enhanced receptivity to the openness of the visual sky space. This is a particularly good example of balancing polarities: as above, so below.

An enjoyable preliminary to yoga nidra involves simple but very slow stretching and yawning. Flexing the feet and pushing down the heels very slowly initiates this natural lengthening and releasing of the back extensors and a flow of liberated energy along the whole length of the body. From there you can either go into relaxation or, alternatively, tone along the length of the spine with "Ahs" in the lumbar region and lower body, "Ooos" in the thoracic and upper body, and "Mmms" in the cervical area radiating upwards into the head: A-U-M or OM as it is usually rendered.

Most body therapies worth their salt address front and back, left and right, and top and bottom in equal measure, and particularly ensure that extension is a match for the dominant mode of flexion. The sequence in yoga known as sun worship (surya namascar) is a very good exemplar of whole body balancing and an ideal way to start the day.

Much could be said about the many other ways in which we might cultivate a more harmonious relationship between front and back, but ultimately we need to know only one thing: that we have the capacity to sense through 360 degrees and that this potential ability is a real key to spaciousness and a way through to freedom and release. Again I mention the virtues of sitting in a natural aural landscape such as a forest, and tuning in without straining or narrowing focus. In these circumstances it is easier to notice our initial tendency to subtly move toward a sound as it arises i.e. to make a grasping effort, something which is especially awkward for the sounds that arise behind us. As we relax there is the possibility of allowing the sounds to occupy the space of awareness without effort. It is interesting in this connection that paying attention to both distant and near sounds is often an integral part of yoga nidra, although there will generally be few sounds coming from behind, unless the earth is in a particularly grumbly mood that day.

I have said little so far about the space behind us representing the past, the unconscious, or that which is inferior, dangerous or unwholesome. These are mainly shadow areas and may be activated by working with the back and related spaces. As long as we are aware of such a potential, we can deal with these awakenings in ways that have already been discussed. Shadow issues are very basic to our personality and usually revolve around power and ego, survival, self-worth, belonging, sexuality and any combination of these.

Uncompromising feedback about persistent shadow issues is usually available from a life partner or close friend, the reason that such individuals can seldom share in the public adulation of famous figures. Shadow work is a persistent and necessary theme throughout the life cycle, although we seem to become more receptive to the idea of our imperfections as we grow older. Therapy may be useful along the way, but should generally not be a drawn-out process, rather one that can be used on an 'as needed' basis. Some therapists have a more 'precious' view of their craft, and want clients to sign up for a minimum period. I do not subscribe to this practice since it is not client centred and gives the false idea that the therapist knows what's best. Spurious authority creeps in from the start.

Our relationship to a spiritual teacher is somewhat different and a subject that is beyond my present brief. Finding the 'real deal' in a teacher is a challenge and requires great discrimination and maturity. In practice it is a trial and error process, just like life itself, and there are many pitfalls and casualties along the way. One simple guideline: look out for the teacher's shadow issues and expect the same respectful, unassuming behaviour that you would from any civilised person.

And finally I would draw your attention to Marko Pogacnik's fascinating book: *The Universe of the Human Body*. This is a guide to our relationship with Gaia using a variety of intuitively derived exercises to harmonise with the many realms of being that constitute our cosmic home. He refers to that which is located in our back space as the 'causal' realm, and that which is in our front space, the 'manifest' realm. The causal realm is a matrix of archetypal patterns that form a base for everything manifest. It is also the liquid aspect of the universe with beings and realms that are not fixed in form. To gain access to this infinite realm of Life involves breaking down the "Berlin Wall" between front and back spaces. To this end he suggests some simple exercises, but you will need to consult his book for further illumination.

Now that we have covered the three directions along which attention may move, I will try to sum up the idea of centering by way of comments on meditation, that process whereby we return to our "homeground" and therefore back to what is. Hopefully I will not be too definitive, ever mindful of Lao Tzu's stern gaze, and his obvious aversion to saying too much, or ideally, anything at all.

15

At the End of Our Tether

Zazen is not learning to do concentration.
Soto Zen founder Eihei Dogen

Enquiry is the process whereby we come back to ourselves, we are not taking off in any particular direction, we are in our own company. Balancing front and back, left and right, and grounding the whole body sense brings us to our physical centre and a dynamic unity of opposites. Being at the centre naturally creates spaciousness, and in accordance with the law of complementarity, spaciousness brings us to our centre. Jeffrey Maitland (in *Embodied Being*) uses the word Palintonic (from the Greek meaning 'stretched back and forth') to describe the balanced tension around our somatic centre of gravity that is a mark of true health.

We may have some concept that our ultimate centre along the spinal axis should be in the Hara or the Heart Centre or elsewhere, but we need not be concerned about this: we come back to the line of heaven and earth and relax into the whole body with each out-breath, remain alert, and let ourselves be. Occasionally repeating Marion Milner's "I want nothing" may be useful. That is all of it, whether you are sitting quietly or in the midst of things.

If you are aiming to sit still for a while you may need a device to calm yourself down for a few minutes, but after that keep it simple. I like to sit cross-legged on a sofa, looking out on to our garden. In the summer, I sit in the garden – there are seasons to meditation, just like everything else. This works for me while more formal methods do not. I am with Jean Klein (blessed be his memory) when he pointed out that *any method* compromises the natural flexibility and multidimensionality of consciousness. Any method presupposes a goal and 'endgaining'.

John Daido Loori, in his book on shikantaza, comments on the effects of cutting off thoughts with a concentration method:

> It cuts away thoughts the moment they arise, making the mind into a great impenetrable mountain – dead unresponsive.

In contrast, non-thinking, which is the natural openness of 'just sitting':

> ... has no such edges. It is the boundless mind of samadhi which neither holds on to nor lets go of thoughts.
> (*The Art of Just Sitting*, page 135)

The Seer makes the same point to Lars Muhl (in *The O Manuscript*) when he makes a distinction between concentration, which separates and excludes, and attention which sees everything as one "without reservation".

This is not to say that you shouldn't follow a more directive method if it appeals to you. As we have seen earlier in the book, methods vary from those that emphasise a narrow focus to those that are more open, like shikantaza. To my mind, the latter approaches generalise better to everyday mindfulness and to self-observation, but that simply reflects my personal perspective on the matter. It is all a question of experimentation and careful personal evaluation. Try out different practices and take what works for you. For example, Robert Masters, in his book *Emotional Intimacy*, suggests an approach in which we can start with breath counting at the beginning of a session, and then later let go of this method and make no attempt to do anything in particular. The British sage Russel Williams (in *Not I, Not other than I*) recommends several short, ten-minute sessions during the day rather than longer sitting periods.

Be confident in finding your own way.

The 'posture' that I choose for sitting quietly has evolved largely because I have difficulty in relaxing (I am a cerebral, Vata type). If, however, you can easily 'chill out' or even fall asleep, then a more rigorous pose may be appropriate in order to create the optimal balance between alertness and relaxation.

So typically, I make myself comfortable and open my visual space. The natural tendency of the eyes to roam slowly settles down and my gaze gradually becomes fixed on a distant spot. As it does so, the aural landscape becomes more apparent, as does the sense of the whole body as an ill-defined space of feeling/sensation and energetic movement. Thoughts come and go. Attention moves between these modalities, becoming progressively more relaxed as perceptions, feelings and thoughts become manifestations of the overall feeling of Spacious Being, and the relief of resting in Unknowingness.

If I get lost in identification with a mental content, I return to my anchor, the sense of space. Thoughts and their attendant feelings (or perhaps we should say feelings and their attendant thoughts) are like a radio playing in our room. Initially we may be listening to a programme, but as we relax the words seem fainter or further away. The radio continues to play, but is just part of the multidimensional reality of Presence.

At some point I may wish to close my eyes and become more aware of the internal somatic and visual spaces (which tend to blend after a while). I may regularly release the whole body sense on the out-breath. Awareness of a particular mood, feeling or somatic sensation may lead to an exploration along the lines of Focusing or Open Focus body work. Or I may note these for attention on a later occasion. And although my usual preference is to start with opening visual space, I could equally well start with my somatic awareness and expand outward, as in the practices described in Chapter 4.

My sense of the whole body relaxing as one global feeling is very important. Within this space all manner of feelings, energies and images may arise; the whole body, which is everything that is outside the conceptual mind, asserts itself and responds to the infusion of awareness. Shakti responds to Shiva. I can conduct this relationship in many ways, either during the session or later; it is a matter of discrimination.

The important point is to remain flexible: dancing between rigidity and apparent chaos, allowing energies to flow, but between certain defined limits. Meditation is about connection, dialogue and process. Sometimes I may wish to strengthen my focusing ability and confine myself to a particular narrow attentional method, or I may wish to use such a method for a specific purpose such as healing. I may wish to do breath counting just because it feels good. However, in the dance of:

CONNECTION ≥ separation

I try not to lose sight of the fact that my aim is wholeness (which is always already the case). Perfection is something different and the province of, for example, shamatha (concentration) practices that lead to perfect samadhi. Like perfection in any field, the attainment necessarily detracts from other areas of a person's life and from the inclusion of all the 'voices' and 'parts'.

There is another dimension to privileging our somatic reality. As we relax into the whole body sense, we find that our bodily sensations begin to resonate with our other four senses. Whereas before, the tight somatic sense only responded to the surroundings with more tightness, now it is like a pool which ripples and flows with openness and delight at what is being experienced. Sometimes this can leave us too vulnerable to the environment and other people, requiring us to pull ourselves together for a while.

Approaches that open up space to all aspects of our being inevitably allow old structures to fall apart, and practitioners may need various forms of help with this. Friends along the path are an important resource for grounding and contextualising. Teachers and therapists also, but caveat emptor.

After following my personal approach for a while, I was interested to read Alan Wallace's description of the Buddhist practice: "Settling the Mind in its Natural State" as outlined in his book, *The Attention Revolution*. A description of this method provided by the 19th century Dzogchen master Lerab Lingpa points to an eyes-open approach in which awareness is kept spacious "like the sky". Wallace comments that stability of attention arises naturally from the mind at ease; a spacious mind is an easy mind, but also an attentive one, being open to everything.

A related practice also described in the book is "Awareness of Awareness". Padmasambhava's description is as follows:

> While steadily gazing into the space in front of you, without meditating on anything, steadily concentrate your consciousness without wavering, in the space in front of you. Increase the stability of attention and then relax again. Occasionally seek out: "What is that consciousness that is concentrating?" Steadily concentrate again and check it out again. Do that in an alternating fashion. Even if there are problems of laxity and lethargy that will dispel them… (page 133).

This is the same approach as Ramana Maharshi's enquiry method, only with a little more operational definition. Since the subject cannot be an object, the focus of attention is, by default, the process of attention itself.

The advantages of using space as our attentional anchor are, I believe, many and include:

It is very 'ordinary' and not different from everyday

experience.

Space is accessible whatever we are doing, in daily activity or any form of meditation.

It does not exclude or avoid any experiences.

It implies expansion and connection beyond the individual self-sense.

Mention has been made earlier of the two broad 'limbs' of meditation: focused and insight methods, shamatha and vipassana in the Buddhist tradition. Focused methods such as breath following are usually thought of as preliminary training that enables enough stability of attention to allow an examination of the dynamics of mind. However, shamatha can be followed as an end in itself to advanced levels of absorption, characterised by effortless and flawless samadhi. The nine stages of this path are outlined in Alan Wallace's book, but he warns that the advanced stages are only attainable through intense practice in a retreat setting over months and years; not for the faint-hearted. He also points out that such practice is rare in modern times, and thus we have a limited number of personal accounts of the long-term advantages and pitfalls.

We do know from the traditional literature that the attainment of perfect samadhi is strongly reinforcing, not the least because it seems a final solution to suffering and embodiment. Consequently it encourages withdrawal from the world and may not generalise well to everyday living should the person return to a 'normal' life. The story of the guru and the water is a comment on this problem.

Such a criticism should not detract, however, from the credit that is due to those who achieve these higher flights of practice.

Vipassana, on the other hand, aims for a more integrated awakening as a result of insight into the dynamics of mind. In the Buddhist tradition this means that understanding is ultimately about the nature of suffering, impermanence and emptiness of self. Thus the contents of mind need to be scrutinised in these terms, through mindfulness of the body, feelings, thoughts and perceptions.

In the West, insight approaches are evolving away from the rather spare, traditional methods of Southeast Asia or Japan, and moving toward an understanding that is more in line with our modern psychological and cultural mindsets. It is not my intention to survey the field in its current form – this would be impossible, but I can point to some key examples of contemporary thought on these matters.

Jason Siff, for example, advocates a more open attitude to thoughts and feelings in meditation. He points out that to truly understand the dynamics of mind we must observe it while letting it function normally and without any preconceptions about the desirability or otherwise of its contents. He also draws attention to an obvious but ignored fact, that a calm, equanimous mind, as developed by shamatha, may not be the best state from which to develop insight. His Recollective Awareness Method establishes a less controlling relationship toward all the psyche's 'parts' and allows insight and calm to arise naturally by creating an observant space for psychological processes to run their natural course. This facilitates a naturalistic appreciation of the mind in its native state; the meditator is an ecologist, careful not to disturb the flora and fauna, but ever observant.

There is a parallel with some modern psychologies, such as Internal Family Systems Therapy, which does not impose an agenda, but seeks to make space for the various 'parts' to have their say. Restoration of psychic balance gives rise to a natural 'organic' calm.

In the West we have become quite sophisticated in the way we work with feelings, and mindfulness has become an integral part of the therapeutic process. In earlier chapters I discussed how creating space allows feelings to be fully expressed and explored, and that the key to establishing such a therapeutic environment is great trust and safety. Tara Brach is a Buddhist and psychotherapist whose book, *Radical Acceptance,* gives us an intimate look into the world of compassionate healing. Work such as hers reminds us that meditational methods alone are often not enough to deal with chronic psychological suffering. We usually need connection with a healer in a personal and ongoing way as well as support from medication, at least for a while.

I have previously spoken about letting go as primarily an affective (feeling) process and quoted from Tim Burkett's recommendations with regard to working with mental states: if letting go does not work, then let be, and if letting be does not work, then enquire. How we choose to negotiate this injunction is a matter of personal discrimination. Modern Westerners are perhaps more likely to want to enquire and get to the bottom of things, rather than simply letting things be in the knowledge of their ultimate impermanence.

Contemporary therapies are also more likely than in the past to involve the body in awareness work. This is timely, since our psyches have become disembodied in a drastic and worsening way. We have already come across the meditation teacher Reginald Ray who critiques much contemporary Buddhism for the same reason: that it is all too easy to ignore the body in many current meditational approaches. He invokes the Tibetan Vajrayana tradition with its very detailed somatic processes and reminds us that just because the focus is on the body, does not mean that we are engaged any the less in a meditation practice. I was particularly struck by an emphasis on releasing tension down into the earth, as well as taking awareness and the breath down into the earth. This is in contrast with those meditation methods which start by focusing on the breath at the nose or contemplating an internal point at the third eye level.

All of these developments only serve to emphasise that meditation is but a subset of continual self-remembering and self-observation, and that these in turn serve the process of actually living our lives in a fully embodied and relational way. We must not doubt that there are innumerable pathways to self-understanding, and that body, mind and soul (which are not separate) need to be engaged in a balanced way. Such a multidimensional system can be seen in the yoga tradition, with its integrated approach to diet, lifestyle, the body, breathing and mind control. Its weakness in the affective and interpersonal realms has, however, led to rigidity and stasis. Fortunately, yoga disciplines are being infused with new vitality and breadth as a result of contact with Western modes of practice. The results are not always salubrious, but a good contemporary example of East/West integration is Richard Miller's 'iRest' programme, with its very comprehensive development of yoga nidra practices.

Such innovations as 'iRest' are happening in many places and under many guises and are to be welcomed, but at the same time we need to remember that:

> ***Personal discovery and creativity count for a lot.*** There are no foolproof prescriptions for happiness or truth. That is the whole point: liberation is an act of personal creativity, God surprising Her/Himself every time without exception. Be your own authority under the auspices of Grace (always).
>
> ***Coming back to the centre line and grounding in the body is a pretty helpful general heuristic.***

So here are some thoughts on meditation, both in its more formal context, and in the midst of the everyday. Just be aware of the danger of reading other people's thoughts instead of sitting quietly and having your own.

Meditation is:

Waiting and Letting Be.

(Waiting without waiting for anything. Letting be whatever

arises within or without.)
Gratitude.
Feeling the Effortlessness of Space.
Feeling the Effortlessness of Awareness.
Focusing on Opening One's Focus (attending to opening attention).
Alert and Relaxed.
Savouring.
Sitting with Discomfort and Boredom.
Feeling the Natural Energy and Bliss of the Body/Being.
Letting Life Flow (letting the pot simmer).
Integration, Integration, Integration (welcoming all the parts).
Being Al(l)one and All of a Piece.
Nothing, Open to Everything.
Continual Relaxed Alertness of the Whole Body/Mind.
Concentration (separating, being at a centre) and Openness (connecting, being at large).
Coming Home to Oneself.
Recalibrating before Leaving Home and Losing Oneself.
Silence (which is also Space).
Freedom from Intentional (effortful) Focusing. Letting awareness be and noticing each time that intention contracts the field of attention.
Relaxing into the Mystery and Not Knowing How.
Sitting Quietly.
Nothing Special.
Love.
Wondering.
Acquiescing Completely to Sensation.
Spaciousness opening Sensation and Sensation opening Space.
Subordinating Oneself to What Is.
Allowing Sensation to Fill You with Feeling/Sensuality.
Effortless Doing (absorption in the flow of this moment).

Making Effort until the Giving Up of Effort Occurs by Itself.
Complete Receptivity (versus complete activity).
Extinguishing (by non-doing) the Habit of Expectancy.
Seeking the Subject until the Seeker disappears.
Experiencing the Background of Silence while in the midst of things.
Holding Attention Steady until the Illusory Nature of Any Object (or supposed separate entity) Becomes Evident in the Penumbra of Its Background.
Seeing that Experience is Never Two, Always One.
Slowing Movement.
Dwelling in the Heart.
Slowing the Constant Craving of Attention Until Object and Subject Dissolve in Seeing.
Letting Go (or letting It let you let go of you).
Stepping out of Culture Completely (and being left with no foothold from culture, good or bad).
Completely Idiosyncratic.
Being Aware of Narrow Focus.
Allowing the Senses to Function in Their Own Way without Agenda.
Sitting without an Agenda (of any kind).
Being Amazed at Awareness.
Surrendering any Sense of Personal Will or Importance.
RELAXING INTO COMPLETE IGNORANCE.

The following contemplation may be of some help.

Naïve Meditation

Remember when, as a child, you would sneak away and sit beneath your favourite tree in the garden. Whatever was happening in life, you would always feel very good in this special place, just listening and looking. As you grew older, you never lost this habit of getting away and just sitting and feeling how good it was just to be alive, just to be there listening and looking and feeling all sorts of things that you couldn't name.

You have never told anybody about these special times because you feared that they might disappear. Neither have you wanted to understand them in any thinking way – that would certainly destroy them. No, you are just grateful that these blessed moments are given to you, even if sometimes you feel you don't deserve them. You are very grateful.

HARI OM TAT SAT

Epilogue

I pray God to rid me of God.
Meister Eckhart

Now that you have completed this journey, I congratulate you.

So many words consumed, so many concepts and concepts about concepts, so much mental chewing, digestion and elimination.

And now it is important that you give yourself a reward. Here is my suggestion:

Please let go of all these pages and words and concepts. Erase them from your mind, let your brain relax completely and let go.

Let go of the endless cogitation that has gone into this book, the monotonous chirping of cicadas in the frontal regions, the sheer strain of focusing away from the great green world that calls you out to play. Let go.

If you can't let go, just let it be, and hope that it all leaves eventually, as it will, slipping silently into the Mystery.

And if all else fails, then this is what to do: cut through to the core of it all, go straight to the non-dual hub that confounds all thinking and remember Meister Eckhart's phrase: "Isness is God".

And since God is all there is, then:

ALL THERE IS, IS IS.

There is only IS. Nowhere to go but IS, nothing to do or think that is not IS. I IS, YOU IS, IT IS. ONLY IS.

Relaxing into the always IS.

IS the only real, cannot be described.

(Note: "All there is is is" – also the title of an essay by Da Free John in *Do You Know What Anything Is?*)

Appendix 1

Walking on the Earth

Philomena Holman

Even stones have a love, a love that seeks the ground.
Meister Eckhart

Can we look after our Mother Earth? This is a question that should preoccupy us all, asleep though we are to *our only source of nourishment*.

Western psychology has recently graduated from an 'above the neck' approach to a serious consideration of the body, but our next step will hopefully also include Mother Earth, *our only source of sustenance and health*.

As with our own bodies, the Earth is endowed with special organs, senses and energy channels and it behoves us to align ourselves harmoniously with these living dynamics of our home. Thus there is nothing new in finding a special physical location or 'power' spot in which we may feel particularly vital. A simple manifestation of this is seen in the recent finding that most animals (including ourselves) are naturally inclined to rest along a north-south axis.

There is also nothing new in finding personal direction by orientating to the points of the compass; most traditional societies have their version of a medicine wheel in which earth directions are imbued with different qualities in the form of elements, animals, plants and gods. In our Western traditions, the labyrinth is one particular direction finder which has survived Christianity and even been embraced by it.

The great virtue of labyrinths as tools of exploration is their versatility. They are non-denominational and cross over many cultures. They are being built today in all kinds of settings, not just healing centres or churches, but in schools, parks, hospitals and backyards. In all of these places the labyrinth space is used to quieten the mind, delight the senses, encourage meditation, and find direction and balance…

Solvitur Ambulando – It is solved by walking.

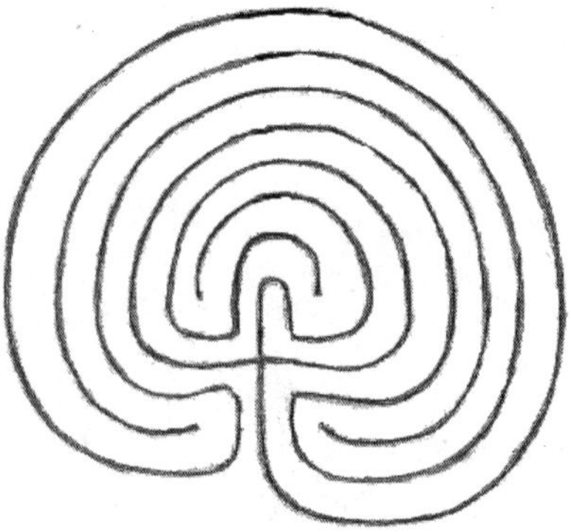

Fig. 13 The Cretan Labyrinth

The integral feature of a labyrinth pattern is its single path which leads circuitously to the centre. There is no confusion as to the direction one walks: even though the path winds continuously to and fro, the way ahead is always in view, unlike in a maze. Mazes are a more recent adaptation of the labyrinth and their intention is to confuse. The labyrinth pattern, by contrast, simply expresses the curves and spirals seen in nature.

In walking the labyrinth, you undertake a simple journey, moving along the winding pathway to the centre or heart. At this halfway point, there is a place of rest, after which you wind your way out again. The physical experience of following a meandering path allows the body to relax into a steady rhythmic pace and frees the mind from focused concentration. The process may induce a soothing trancelike state, where mental and emotional processes flow more readily and enhance creative and expansive experiences.

Many metaphors for scientific and artistic endeavour, as well as everyday problem solving, display this pattern of meandering our way into a question or dilemma, walking around it and finding our way out again. In walking the labyrinth, we mirror this process in a physical way, and thus release narrow mental focus and bodily tension to expand our world in new directions.

The origins of the labyrinth are mysterious. It is certainly a very ancient pattern found in many cultures throughout the world, usually taking a spiral or meandering form. Probably because of its womblike shape, it is sometimes associated with feminine rituals, nature goddesses and mother earth cultures. Throughout history, the pattern has been built in stone and also represented on pottery, decorative tiles, Bronze Age coins and murals.

The uncertain origin of the labyrinth pattern has probably allowed for its adaptation and reinterpretation over millennia. In the Western tradition the most famous early form, traditionally with seven paths, is usually called the classical or Cretan labyrinth, and is based on the ancient myth of the Minotaur. Half-man, half-bull, the monster was said to be imprisoned at the centre of the labyrinth in Crete, which was designed for King Minos by the inventor Daedalus. The Minotaur was finally killed by the legendary Greek hero Theseus, with the help of the Princess Ariadne and her golden thread. The story is given heightened resonance when you visit the labyrinthine buildings and circuitous passageways in the ancient Cretan city of Knossos.

The myth of the Minotaur and the dramatic destinies of the story's protagonists provide a wonderful spiritual and psychological symbolism that helps to explain the labyrinth's continued and varied expressions throughout the centuries. Alongside this mythical tradition of the classical labyrinth, there have always been cultures honouring feminine energies, and in these the labyrinth appears to represent the womb, where entering the mouth, or cave opening, is a journey back into the embrace of Mother Earth.

The labyrinth pattern was adapted in different forms by the Greeks and Romans in early Christian times. Some understood the labyrinth to represent a fortified sacred city, such as Jerusalem or Jericho, with the walls protecting the spiritual wealth at the city's heart, while others saw the labyrinth as representing the cosmos with all its layers of creation.

In medieval times, the Christian cathedrals of Europe often contained images of the labyrinth on walls or in manuscripts, but most famously on pavements. Sometimes, the Minotaur was still represented at the labyrinth's heart, perhaps signifying the devil, but over time the pattern lost its mythical roots and incorporated more Christian symbology.

The most famous and well-preserved of these is at Chartres, and hence they are known as medieval or Chartres labyrinths. Their pattern is often more complex than that of the classical seven-path labyrinth, with the circle divided into quadrants, creating an even more elaborate path system. There are many interpretations of the significance of labyrinths in the overall design of these beautiful cathedrals. Frequently, they are seen as offering pilgrims the opportunity to walk a form of spiritual journey, with all its inevitable twists and turns, winding their way to final salvation at the heart. This response to the labyrinth may have echoed the desire of many pilgrims to visit their true spiritual home in Jerusalem, but which was thwarted by the Crusades.

In walking the labyrinth we can go on our own spiritual pilgrimage to the 'centre' and whatever that holds for us. From a sacred geometrical point of view, we are traversing a flattened torus and as such recreating a universal process of involution and evolution. As with all the processes discussed in this book, the labyrinth is a tool for coming back to our central axis, our own authority as servants of Life. Doing so in harmony with the basic laws of manifestation can only benefit both ourselves and the Earth.

Appendix 2

The Triangular Tarot

First published in *The Magician* (*Journal of The Tarot Guild of Australia*)

December 1999 and Autumn 2000.

A hidden connection is stronger than an obvious one.

Heraclitus

My study of the Tarot turned a significant corner when I realised that its structure is amenable to a triangular representation. The discovery came with the simple revelation that 78 (the number of cards in the tarot) is a triangular number and that the Tarot can be arranged as a perfect triangle with 12 layers of cards. Coincidence perhaps? After all, the Tarot is a mathematical system capable of accepting all manner of explanatory structures, but which, nevertheless, still manages to mysteriously transcend all attempts at linear (and therefore limiting) forms of explanation.

I was intrigued, however, when I realised that other triangular relationships were possible. Using the convention of Case, Maxwell and others (that the Major Arcana consists of 21 cards plus the Fool), it becomes apparent that these 21 cards can also be arranged in a perfect triangle, as can the 28 cards of 2 suites of the Minor Arcana. No doubt these relationships have been noted by many others, but I have not read any comments to this effect in Tarot literature. This seems strange to me, especially in view of the importance attached to triangular numbers by the Pythagoreans and the common acknowledgement of a triangular law working throughout the Tarot.

My further research in this area has brought great benefits to my understanding and so it seemed timely to present some tentative conclusions for Tarot practitioners.

But first, as an introduction to the subject, let me say something about the Tetractys. For the Pythagoreans, number theory has three aspects: arithmetic, geometric and harmonic. The triangular arrangement of the numbers 1 to 10 exhibits these three properties in a simple and profound visual form. See Tarot Figure 1.

Triangular numbers in general and the Tetractys in particular have many interesting properties. Suffice it to say at this point that the Tetractys clearly illustrates:

a. Trinity – a fundamental Pythagorean tenet.
b. Hierarchy.
c. Harmony, for example, the important harmonic relationships 1:2, 2:3, 3:4 are clearly evident.

Most importantly, it illustrates how numbers evolve. In Taoist terms, the One gives rise to Two, Two gives rise to Three, and Three gives rise to the Ten Thousand Things (the province of Manifest Existence, or the Number Four).

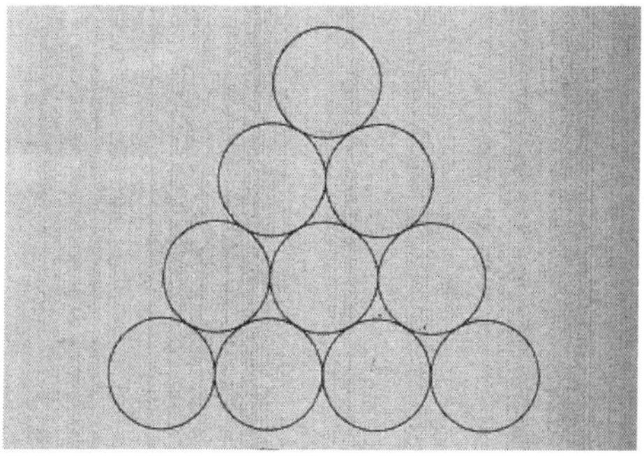

Tarot 1 Figure

Schwaller de Lubicz put this another way – that numbers arise as a manifestation of union between One (Lingam) and Zero (Yoni), both in the sense of the infinitude between Zero and One and in the sense that the number Ten 'sums up' the basic numbers One to Nine.

These concepts seem to apply to the Tarot. For illustrative purposes I want to consider only the Major Arcana and, as stated above, I will follow the convention that 22 cards represent 21 cards plus the Zero card (whose place in the scheme of things I address later).

In working the triangular arrangement of cards I to XXI, I eventually settled upon the structure illustrated in Tarot 2 Figure. I find that this system is immensely rewarding in revealing relationships between the cards and in placing the meaning of individual cards within the context of the whole. In other words, it is useful in taking a systematic rather than a simple linear approach to the Tarot. It will be up to the reader, however, to judge if this scheme has the ring of truth, as judged by aesthetic/intuitive criteria, logical appraisal and practical utility. As with all facets of the Tarot, the arrangement yields insight through contemplation, and within the limitations of this article, I wish only to make a few comments on this system. I ask forgiveness in advance for the necessarily oversimplified nature of my card attributions.

1. This arrangement can be seen as a picture of the 'primal knot' of existence: the individual experiencing herself in a subject (card I) -object (card XXI) relationship to the world. This basic dilemma gives rise to all the circumstances and difficulties that constitute the life cycle and maturational process (cards II–XX).

2. The duality between the 2 sections of the Arcana (I–IX and XII–XXI) represents many different concepts, including:

- The province of consciousness as the passive observer (Purusha) as against the dynamic world of energy and ceaseless flux (Prakriti).
- The individual acting upon the world (centrifugal

movement) and the world acting upon the individual (centripetal movement).
- The realm of (static) eternal principles married to the world of indeterminacy and hazard.
- Top Down versus Bottom Up organisation.

And many more.

Note that each decad is bracketed by images representing One and Zero.

3. The arrangement gives a fresh perspective on the unfolding of the Major Arcana that is not possible in other schema. Thus we see the principle of consciousness (card I) devolving into Psyche (card II) and Soma (card III) or Mind and Nature. The dyad II and III is not an oppositional one; the two female figures clearly imply the principle of complementarity. Incidentally, this is also an illustration of the Forking of the Ways confronting an Initiate. It is only in the third row that we see a true Triad with active (IV), passive (VI) and reconciling (V) cards in which vertical organisation, structure, power and control are reconciled with lateral organisation and heart relationship, through the means of right understanding and guidance.

Row four is clearly the province of the world and action, with an interplay of proactive, goal-directed activity (card VII) and appropriate 'withdrawal and listening' (card IX), mediated by the reconciliation and integration of vital energies (card VIII). Fortune sounds the note of change in this ordered world of the first nine cards. If the two decads are taken to be similar to the two halves of the Yin/Yang symbol, then Fortune and the Hanged Man are like the seeds of reciprocal movement contained within every Yin and Yang trend.

Cards XIII–XXI show patterns that are in many ways parallel to cards I–IX.

The infinite and indivisible matrix of the World devolves

into the complementary relationship between Time (Chronos) and space/energy. This in turn gives rise to a Triad in which the dynamic, as opposed to the stabilising, aspect (IV–VI) of three becomes evident. Finally, sequence XII to XV portrays the obverse of VII–X, i.e. submission of personal will to the Will of God, as the only way of reconciling and tempering the inevitable facts of Death, Evil and Delusion.

4. Interesting patterns emerge if the cards are assigned to Active, Reconciling and Passive aspects in the normal sequential way. Most notable is the fact that I and XXI are linked by a thread of Reconciling cards, either through the sequence II, V, VIII etc or more directly V, XI, XVII. This latter group comprises Prime Numbers only. Prime Numbers are directly related to (or descended from) Unity and it is, I believe, no coincidence that these Reconciling Primes form the central pillar connecting self and the world. This path could be paraphrased: subject/object duality is cut through by living in balance under the graceful tutelage of a spiritual guide. Cards V and XVII also seem particularly appropriate as the central cards in their respective Tetractys formations. I believe that these arrangements also point to the fact that what we normally refer to as the reconciling principle is in fact the modifying action of the whole (unity) upon the opposites, through the process of change.

5. As we depart from the midline we see greater polarities and more 'extreme' states. Polarities exist both within and across decads. Take the Emperor for example. It is balanced by the Lovers, but may dominate this card as in an over-masculinised consciousness. It is in constant interplay with the Tower; structures must constantly be torn down and rebuilt to remain useful, and it is in a contrasting relationship with the Moon – the dark unconscious and the cycles of Nature. (King Canute and the Tide!)

Many other relationships become apparent as one traces the various paths across this figure.

6. The structure of the Tetractys lends itself to multiple triangular hierarchies nested within one another. There are eight such arrangements within the upper Tetractys consisting of either three or six cards. Thus, taking the Emperor again as an example, we see that it 'rules' cards VII and VIII, but is subordinate to cards I and II. The Chariot is not 'ruled' by III, whereas VIII, in common with V and IX, falls under both II and III. The meaning of the respective cards seems to be very consonant with these hierarchic relationships.

7. There is clearly a Septenary Law active throughout the Tarot and the interplay of laws relating to the numbers three and seven is certainly an important part of the Major Arcana, as has been elucidated by Tarot pioneers such as Papus and Case. The double Tetractys reveals both arithmetic and geometric septenary relationships. Can you spot them?

8. The double Tetractys is particularly amenable to the construction of connecting spirals across the decads.

9. It will not be lost on the reader that the two decads are not separate but, like Purusha and Prakriti, are in perpetual embrace. The final form of the figure is thus the Star of David configuration contained in the Zero of the Fool, the non-manifest (Tarot 3 Figure). This gives rise to further relationships between the cards. Justice is placed in the central position over V and VII, as an unambiguous statement of the need for balance in all things.

In summary, this model of the Major Arcana provides a satisfying framework within which to consider the interplay of numerical laws, especially those relating to the integers 2, 3, 7 and 10. It also emphasises the centrality of Primes and provides a visual context with which to contemplate the almost endless arithmetic, geometric, harmonic and symbolic aspects of the Major Arcana.

The Minor Arcana introduce the Tetrad. The overall structure of the Minor Arcana can be treated in the same way as the Major Arcana. We see an interplay between 4 × 7 = 28 'Yang' cards (Wands and Swords) and 28 'Yin' cards (Cups and Discs). These two sets can be arranged in an overlaying triangular form to

Tarot 2 Figure

produce another Star of David. This in turn can be overlain with the Major Arcana, producing a final and satisfying symbolic form of the Tarot which embodies a mathematical reconciliation of the numbers 1 to 10.

Mathematical developments using a triangular matrix, such as the Sierpinski triangle, offer new insights into complexity theories and the interface between order and 'chaos'. The Tarot has probably anticipated these mathematical constructions, but that is a story for another time.

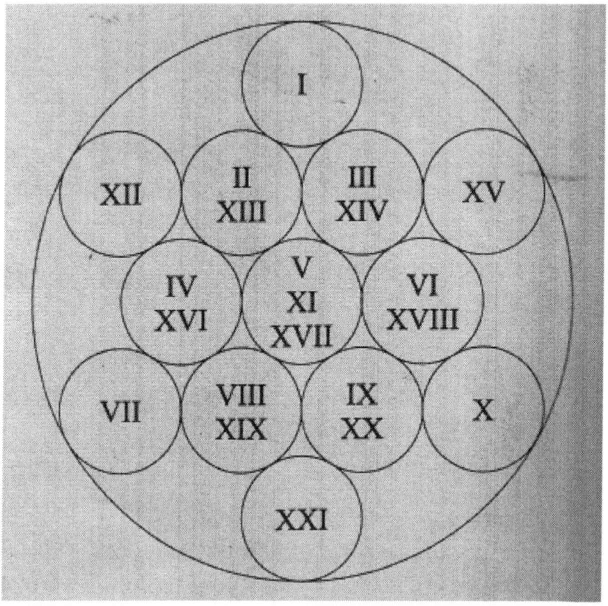

Tarot 3 Figure

Appendix 3

The Geometry of Attention

When I speak of understanding, I mean the mind must have the right perspective, I would say the right geometrical representation of truth. The geometrical representation shows precisely that what we are can never be an object, can never be objectified, represented.
Jean Klein, *Transmission of the Flame*, pages 69–70

Subject and object are concepts. There are no separate subjects or objects, but our usual convention is to talk and think as if there were. That is the context of this discussion.

There is only One: Consciousness/Energy which plays at hide and seek with Itself through the magic of moving within Itself – the vibrating cosmic jelly, praise be the Sound of Its Name.

Consciousness expressing Itself through a human nervous system takes on the form of attention. Attention is directional Consciousness/Energy.

Attention may be solicited by an object: a bird, a face, a thought, a sensation, a feeling. Consciousness identifies with its objects and the Attentional Field 'collapses' on to the object so that only the object exists. The object is like a ***single point***, with any sense of subject or space and its contents being an ill-defined background.

In everyday awareness, attention is constantly moving in the service of desire and aversion, and this "questing beast" creates one objective experience after another. Depending on the level of 'doing' there is a more or less defined sense of personal self, but that sense is still usually subordinate to identification with the constant parade of events. Thinking is simply attenuated doing and produces the same effects, only with internal objects.

The sense of a doer vis a vis an object produces a ***line***, a distancing and a dilemma.

Scanning the environment with an attention that is seeking objects produces a ***flattened cone*** of awareness. At any one moment we are only aware of this thin cone of reality, a few degrees wide, although we sense a broader vista in front of us because this thin cone moves to and fro across the sensory landscape, sending snapshots that are put together into a world picture (like a David Hockney photo montage). This vista is also only a few degrees in height, however, and with little depth of field. It is a very attenuated version of the information that Reality has waiting for us.

Questing, restless attention is only possible with a narrow focus. This foraging-type attention is constantly seeking and moving on till some sort of consummation is attained – in the animal kingdom, usually a bite to eat. It is a torch in the warehouse. Only one sensory modality can be channelled with any clarity at a time.

As we open our attention, by definition there is less movement. Think of the torch gradually turning into an omnidirectional lantern. As the beam widens there is less requirement to move the beam. The view is more comprehensive, if less detailed. With a light that radiates in all directions, all objects are included and there is a greater sense of the overall space around the light. This expanded sense of space and its contents defocuses fragmented reality and enhances the connected whole. There is nothing in awareness except the light itself, the central fact of illumination and consciousness.

Imagine, then, that with this central light continuing to burn, the torch is still available for more detailed and momentary investigations without losing awareness of the centrality of light itself. The torch is not controlled by a subject (it never was) and functions on the basis of the needs of the Whole. When not required, it returns to rest in the central fact of light, which is the infinite ***sphere*** of reality.

The apparent subject is constituted of doing/contraction,

and so the expansion of feeling/sensation/being into complete (spherical) openness 'collapses' any sense of a personal subject or separate object, just as the centre of a circle disappears as anything special (or spatial) after a compass has traced out its circumference.

The paradox of attention is that we need narrow focus to be self-conscious; it has the same distancing effect as language. The emissary looks back at the kingdom from his remote posting and is able to reflect on its nature. The apparent subject-object loop is a distancing phenomenon.

To see through the subject-object delusion we need to examine it, and this too requires distancing. So we start meditation or self-observation/remembering by stabilising narrow attention and slowing its movement. As movement/doing slows, sensation/being becomes more evident.

Distance is produced by the dynamic of directed Consciousness/Energy (which is Attention), and like any energy, it has intensity, coherence and direction. When attention is stabilised and its movement slowed, then its energy becomes amplified and more coherent. Coherent energy waves can nest within the greater coherence of the 'ground state': Consciousness/Energy, the Totality. Then all action is an expression of that emptiness, that expansion, because nested waves can sing together and the Greater can inform the Lesser and the Lesser can sing back. "Eternity in love with the works of time."

With complete openness there is no longer anything that we can call attention. The senses function in a way appropriate to the moment and do not need direction, in the same way that thoughts can continue about their business when they are required. There is only IS and no room for observers or observed.

Note – readers may be interested in the spherical model of consciousness proposed by Wei Wu Wei (Terence Gray) in *Why Lazarus Laughed* or in Arthur Young's *The Geometry of Meaning*.

Appendix 4

Some Things to Do

Be Quiet.
Ms Bray, my primary school teacher

Here are some suggestions for practice, starting with a passage from Russel Williams (*Not I, Not other than I*):

> There is another exercise you can play with: wherever you are, look straight across the room opposite you. It doesn't matter what object you look at – just fix your eyes to the object, and see that there is you and there is that. Be aware of the duality between you and it. Now, without moving your head, or your eyes, take your attention off that object and gradually bring it around to the periphery, so that you become aware of everything around the object, and eventually so that you can see the whole room in your vision...
>
> Now tell me where duality is, and where you are in relation to it. Now there is only the room, with no me (page 89).

Here is an exercise which does for attention what the tension/release method does for muscle relaxation:

Look at your thumb very intently. When you start getting tired, do it for a bit longer and then stop and release. Take a deep breath and let go of any concentration, allow the visual space to open and stay completely alert.

Try something similar with the whole body/mind:

Feel your whole psycho-physical presence all at once and then feel how it is a contraction over against the wide field of Being/Space. Keep concentrating until this becomes too uncomfortable and then: Deep Breath and Let Go.

To do while walking: notice the 3D quality of your surroundings and how objects constantly move in relation to one another (but the openness of the whole visual field does not change). 'Space and back': Open to the spaciousness of your surroundings; then: see in what way thinking inhabits that space; then: be aware of the whole body, its substantiality, its definition; then: tune in to the felt sense of the whole body; then: feel sensation in the body as pure sensation/energy; then: feel the space that permeates the whole body, the same space that is outside the body; then return to the spaciousness of your surroundings.

And finally:

Intone an Ooo... sound with puffed out cheeks. Feel it filling your body and surrounding space. When you stop, listen.

Now experiment with your own discoveries.

Bon Voyage.

Bibliography

Allan, J. *The Healing Energy of Love*. Quest Books, 1986.

Almaas, AH. *The Void*. Shambhala, 1986.

Aron, E. *The Highly Sensitive Person*. Broadway Books, 1996.

Avery, S. *Buddha and the Quantum*. Sentient Publications, 2011.

Baron-Cohen, S. *The Essential Difference*. Penguin, 2004.

Bartholomew, A. *Hidden Nature: The Startling Insights of Viktor Schauberger*. Floris Books, 2003.

Beck, D., Cowan, C. *Spiral Dynamics*. Wiley-Blackwell, 2005.

Bejan, A., Zane, JP. *Design in Nature*. Doubleday, 2012.

Bennett, JG. *Enneagram Studies*. Red Wheel/Weiser, 1983.

Bentov, I. *Stalking the Wild Pendulum*. Destiny Books, 1988.

Blackstone, J. *Belonging Here*. Sounds True, 2012.

Blavatsky, HP. *The Secret Doctrine*. TarcherPerigee, 2016.

Bonheim, J. *The Serpent and the Wave*. Celestial Arts, 1992.

Booker, C. *The Seven Basic Plots*. Continuum, 2004.

Brach, T. *Radical Acceptance*. Bantam, 2004.

Brooks, CVW. *Reclaiming Vitality and Presence: Sensory Awareness as a Practice for Life*. Ed. Lowe, R. and Laeng-Gilliatt, S. North Atlantic Books, 2007.

Burger, B. *Esoteric Anatomy*. North Atlantic Books, 1998.

Burkett, T. *nothing holy about it*. Shambhala, 2015.

Carroll, D. *Sacred Geometry and Spiritual Symbolism*. A. R. E. Press, 2013.

Carse, D. *Perfect Brilliant Stillness*. Non-Duality Press, 2006.

Case, PF. *The Tarot*. TarcherPerigee, 2006.

Chabris, C., Simons, D. *The Invisible Gorilla*. Harmony, 2011.

Chua, A., Rubenfeld, J. *The Triple Package*. Penguin, 2015.

Coates, J. *The Hour Between Dog and Wolf*. Penguin, 2013.

Conrad, E. *Life on Land*. North Atlantic Books, 2007.

Courtland, R. "Dimensions Vanish in Quantum Gravity". *New Scientist*, September 22nd 2010.

Courtois, F. *An Experience of Enlightenment*. Quest, 1986. Republished in *The Hazy Moon of Enlightenment*, Wisdom Publications, 2007.

Csikszentmihalyi, M. *Flow: The Psychology of Optimal Experience*. HarperPerennial, 2008.

Da Free John. *Do You Know What Anything Is?* Dawn Horse Press, 1984.

Damasio, A. *Descartes' Error*. Penguin, 2005.

Doczi, G. *The Power of Limits*. Shambhala, 2010.

Du Sautoy, M. "Grand Designs". *New Scientist*, June 16th 2008.

Durckheim, K. *Hara: The Vital Center of Man*. Inner Traditions, 2004.

Eliade, M. *The Sacred and The Profane*. Harcourt Brace Jovanovich, 1989.

Epstein, G. *Healing Visualizations*. Bantam, 1989.

Fehmi, L. *The Open-Focus Brain*. Trumpeter, 2008.

Fehmi, L. with Robbins, J. *Dissolving Pain*. Trumpeter, 2010.

Fine, C. *Delusions of Gender*. Icon Books, 2005.

Flemons, DG. *Completing Distinctions*. Shambhala, 1991.

Foster, J. *The Wonder of Being*. Non-Duality Press, 2010.

Frantzis, BK. *Relaxing into Your Being: The Water Method of Taoist Meditation Vols. 1 & 2*. North Atlantic Books, 2001.

Friedlander, J., Hemsher, G. *Psychic Psychology*. North Atlantic Books, 2011.

Gendlin, E. *Focusing*. Rider, 2003.

Gendlin, E. *Let Your Body Interpret Your Dreams*. Chiron Publications, 2004.

Ghyka, M. *The Geometry of Art and Life*. Dover, 1977.

Godman, D. *Living By the Words of Bhagavan*. Sri Annamalai Swami Ashram Trust, 1994.

Grossman, W. *To Be Healed By The Earth*. Seven Stories Press, 2007.

Gurdjieff, G. *Beelzebub's Tales to His Grandson*. Penguin, 1999.

Hanna, T. *Somatics*. Da Capo Press, 2004.

Harding, D. *On Having No Head*. The Buddhist Society (UK), 1961.

Harris, JR. *No Two Alike*. W.W. Norton, 2007.

Hartmann, E. *Boundaries in the Mind*. Basic Books, 1991.

Hawkins, David R., MD, PhD. *Letting Go*. Veritas, 2012.

Heath, R. *Precessional Time and the Evolution of Consciousness*. Inner Traditions, 2011.

Herrigel, E. *Zen in the Art of Archery*. Vintage Books, 1999.

Hoffman, G. *The Secret Dowry of Eve*. Park Street Press, 2003.

Houston, J. *The Possible Human*. TarcherPerigee, 1997.

Huizinga, J. *Homo Ludens*. Angelico Press, 2016.

Ingerman, S. *Soul Retrieval*. HarperCollins, 1991.

Ital, G. *On the Way to Satori*. Element Books, 1990.

Jodorowsky, A., Costa, M. *Metagenealogy*. Park Street Press, 2011.

Jung, CG. *Psychological Types*. Princeton University Press, 1976.

Jung, CG. *Mysterium Coniunctionis*. Princeton University Press, 1977.

Kahneman, D. *Thinking, Fast and Slow*. Farrar, Straus and Giroux, 2013.

Kaku, M. "The Power of Staring". *New Scientist,* April 16th 2005.

Kapleau, P. *The Three Pillars of Zen*. Anchor, 1989.

Katie, B. *Loving What Is*. Three Rivers Press, 2003.

Kavanagh, J. *A Little Book of Unknowing*. Christian Alternative, 2014.

Keeney, B. *Shaking Medicine*. Destiny, 2007.

Klein, J. *Transmission of the Flame*. Third Millennium Publications, 1990.

Klein, N. *This Changes Everything*. Simon and Schuster, 2015.

Koch, C. "Crystal Clear on Consciousness". *New Scientist,* April 14th 2012.

Laughlin, RB. *A Different Universe*. Basic Books, 2006.

Levenson, L. *Keys to the Ultimate Freedom*. Sedona Institute, 1993.

Loori, JD. *The Art of Just Sitting*. Wisdom Books, 2002.

Lundy, M. *Quadrivium*. Walker Books, 2010.

Madsen, EA et al. "Kinship and altruism: A cross-cultural experimental study". *British Journal of Psychology*, 98:339–359, 2007.

Maitland, J. *Embodied Being*. North Atlantic Books, 2016.

Maitland, J. *Spacious Body*. North Atlantic Books, 1995.

Marvelly, P. *The Teachers of One*. Watkins Publishing, 2002.

Masters, R. *To Be a Man*. Sounds True, 2015.

Masters, R. *Emotional Intimacy*. Sounds True, 2013.

McGilchrist, I. *The Master and His Emissary*. Yale University Press, 2012.

Meares, A. *Relief Without Drugs*. Souvenir Press, 1994.

Melchizedek, D. *The Ancient Secret of the Flower of Life*. Light Technology Publishing, 1999.

Merali, K. "Is This a Theory of Everything?" *New Scientist*, November 17th 2007.

Merali, K. "Our Finite, Wrap-around Universe". *New Scientist*, January 12th 2008.

Merrell-Wolff, F. *Pathways Through to Space* and *The Philosophy of Consciousness Without an Object* published together as *Experience and Philosophy*. State University of New York Press, 1994.

Michell, J. with Brown, A. *How the World Is Made*. Figure drawn by Allan Brown. Thames and Hudson Ltd., London, 2008.

Miller, R., Schoomaker, E. *The iRest Program for Healing PTSD*. New Harbinger, 2015.

Miller, WR and C'de Baca, J. *Quantum Change*. Guilford Press, 2001.

Milner, M. *A Life of One's Own*. Routledge, 2011.

Milner, M. *An Experiment in Leisure*. Routledge, 2011.

Mindell, A. *Earth-Based Psychology*. Independent Publishers Group, 2007.

Muhl, L. *The O Manuscript*. Watkins Books, 2013.

Narby, J. *The Cosmic Serpent*. Jeremy Tarcher, 1999.

Noble, D. *The Music of Life*. Oxford University Press, 2008.

Ober, C. *Earthing*. Basic Health Publications, 2014.
Palmer, W. *The Intuitive Body*. North Atlantic Books, 1999.
Papus. *The Tarot of the Bohemians*. Wilshire Books, 1982.
Parsons, T. *Invitation to Awaken*. Inner Directions, 2004.
Patten, T., Patten, L. *Biocircuits*. HJ Kramer, 1988.
Pearce, JC. *Exploring the Crack in the Cosmic Egg*. Inner Traditions International and Bear & Company, 2014.
Pearce, JC. *The Heart-Mind Matrix*. Park Street Press, 2012.
Plichta, P. *God's Secret Formula*. Element, 1996.
Pogacnik, M. *The Universe of the Human Body*. Lindisfarne Books, 2016.
Prechter, R. *The Wave Principle of Human Social Behavior*. Elliott Wave International, 2013.
Pugh, D. & Pugh, N. *Unveiling Creation: Eight is the Key*. Sunstar, 1999.
Red Hawk. *Self Remembering*. Hohm Press, 2015.
Reich, W. *Listen, Little Man!* Farrer, Straus, Giroux, 1974.
Roberts, B. *The Experience of No-Self*. State University of New York Press, 1993.
Rossi, E. *The 20 Minute Break*. Jeremy Tarcher, 1991.
Sapolsky, R. *A Primate's Memoir*. Scribner, 2002.
Satprem. *The Mind of the Cells*. Institute for Evolutionary Research, 1982.
Scheff, T. *Catharsis in Healing, Ritual, and Drama*. iUniverse, 2001.
Schwaller de Lubicz, RA. *A Study of Numbers*. Inner Traditions, 1985.
Schwartz, R. *Internal Family Systems Therapy*. Guilford Press, 1997.
Schwenk, T. *Sensitive Chaos*. Rudolf Steiner Press, 1996.
Scientific American: Special Issue: Sex and Gender, September 2017.
Segal, S. *Collision with the Infinite*. Blue Dove Press, 1996.
Siff, J. *Thoughts Are Not the Enemy*. Shambhala, 2014.
Slattery, DR. *Xenolinguistics*. Evolver Editions, 2016.
Smith, R. *Gurdjieff: Cosmic Secrets*. The Dog, 1993.

Subagh Singh Khalsa. *Anatomy of Miracles*. Simran & Seva Publishing, 2015.

Sumner, G. *Body Intelligence Meditation*. Singing Dragon, 2014.

Svoboda, R. *Prakriti*. Lotus Press, 1998.

Tarthang Tulku. *Time, Space and Knowledge*. Dharma Publishing, 1997.

Tavris, C., Aronson, E. *Mistakes Were Made (but not by me)*. Mariner Books, 2015.

Taylor, JB. *My Stroke of Insight*. Penguin, 2009.

Tenen, S. *The Alphabet That Changed the World*. North Atlantic Books, 2011.

Tononi, G. *Phi: A Voyage from the Brain to the Soul*. Pantheon, 2012.

Townley, K. *The Cube of Space*. Archive Press, 1993.

van der Kolk, B. *The Body Keeps the Score*. Penguin, 2015.

Van Dusen, W. *The Natural Depth in Man*. Swedenborg Foundation, 1979.

Vollmar, K. *The Secret of Enneagrams*. Element, 1997.

Wallace, BA. *The Attention Revolution*. Wisdom Publication, 2006.

Walter, K. *Tao of Chaos*. Element, 1996.

Watson, L. *Gifts of Unknown Things*. Destiny Books, 1991.

Watts, A. *Tao: The Watercourse Way*. Pantheon, 1975.

Watts, A. *Cosmic Drama*. Celestial Arts, 1975.

Watts, D. *Six Degrees*. W.W. Norton, 2004.

Wei Wu Wei. *Why Lazarus Laughed*. Sentient Publications, 2003.

Welwood, J. *Toward a Psychology of Awakening*. Shambhala, 2000.

Wilhelm, H. *Heaven, Earth, and Man in the Book of Changes*. University of Washington Press, 1979.

Williams, C. "Daydream Believer". *New Scientist*, May 26th 2017.

Williams, R. *Not I, Not other than I*. O-Books (John Hunt), 2016.

Wilson, C. *Access to Inner Worlds*. Celestial Arts, 1990.

Wirth, M., Schultheiss, O. "Basal testosterone moderates responses to anger faces in humans". *Physiology & Behavior*, 90: 496–505, 2007.

Wolf, FA. *The Dreaming Universe*. Simon & Schuster, 1994.

Wolf, FA. *Time Loops and Space Twists*. Hierophant, 2011.

Young, A. *The Geometry of Meaning*. Robert Briggs Associates, 1976.

Young, A. *The Reflexive Universe*. Robert Briggs Associates, 1976.

Zak, P. *The Moral Molecule*. Plume, 2013.

Zeff, T. *The Highly Sensitive Person's Survival Guide*. New Harbinger, 2004.

Acknowledgements

More than thanks go to my dear wife, Philomena, whose beautiful presence, patience, forbearance and considerable editorial skills have made this work possible. I promise not to do it again. Thanks as well to my daughters, Rosa and Zoe, whose own academic journeys, and other significant accomplishments, have put this small work into perspective.

To friends Ash Hauser, Ewald Einoder and David Tacey who can all be relied upon for a good chat on 'higher matters'. And to Jenny Werbeloff, who has been enthusiastic from the start about the basic idea of Living Space.

For permissions, I am particularly grateful to Richard Lang and the Shollond Trust for the Douglas Harding material, Abbot Wendy Egyoko Nakao at the Zen Center of Los Angeles for the Flora Courtois quotes, Emma Edwards for the extracts from *Transmission of the Flame* and The Franklin Merrell-Wolff Foundation for the *Pathways* and *Philosophy* quotes.

Thank you, Letitia Allan, for our lovely conversation about healing in the Spirit and also to David Godman (*Living By the Words of Bhagavan*), Susan Hawkins (*Letting Go*), Fred Alan Wolf (*The Dreaming Universe*) and the Institute for Evolutionary Research for the words of the 'Mother'.

I am also very grateful for permissions and sources from the following publishers: Quest Books (HP Blavatsky), Shambhala (AH Almaas, T. Burkett, L. Fehmi, J. Welwood), Sounds True (J. Blackstone), Princeton University Press (H. Wilhelm), North Atlantic Books (CVW Brooks, J. Maitland, W. Palmer), John Hunt (J. Kavanagh, R. Williams), Hohm Press (Red Hawk), Thames and Hudson (Figure 5), Routledge (M. Milner), Inner Traditions International and Bear & Company (JC Pearce), Dharma Publishing (Tarthang Tulku), Watkins Books (P. Marvelly) and Wisdom Publications (JD Loori, BA Wallace).

Last but not least to John Hunt Publishing whose encouragement has kept me working when many alternative ways of spending my time seemed more attractive.

Index

BOOKS

O-BOOKS

SPIRITUALITY

O is a symbol of the world, of oneness and unity; this eye represents knowledge and insight. We publish titles on general spirituality and living a spiritual life. We aim to inform and help you on your own journey in this life.

If you have enjoyed this book, why not tell other readers by posting a review on your preferred book site? Recent bestsellers from O-Books are:

Heart of Tantric Sex

Diana Richardson

Revealing Eastern secrets of deep love and intimacy to Western couples.

Paperback: 978-1-90381-637-0 ebook: 978-1-84694-637-0

Crystal Prescriptions

The A-Z guide to over 1,200 symptoms and their healing crystals

Judy Hall

The first in the popular series of six books, this handy little guide is packed as tight as a pill-bottle with crystal remedies for ailments.

Paperback: 978-1-90504-740-6 ebook: 978-1-84694-629-5

Take Me To Truth
Undoing the Ego
Nouk Sanchez, Tomas Vieira
The best-selling step-by-step book on shedding the Ego, using the teachings of *A Course In Miracles*.
Paperback: 978-1-84694-050-7 ebook: 978-1-84694-654-7

The 7 Myths about Love...Actually!
The journey from your HEAD to the HEART of your SOUL
Mike George
Smashes all the myths about LOVE.
Paperback: 978-1-84694-288-4 ebook: 978-1-84694-682-0

The Holy Spirit's Interpretation of the New Testament
A course in Understanding and Acceptance
Regina Dawn Akers
Following on from the strength of *A Course In Miracles,* NTI teaches us how to experience the love and oneness of God.
Paperback: 978-1-84694-085-9 ebook: 978-1-78099-083-5

The Message of A Course In Miracles
A translation of the text in plain language
Elizabeth A. Cronkhite
A translation of *A Course in Miracles* into plain, everyday language for anyone seeking inner peace. The companion volume, *Practicing A Course In Miracles*, offers practical lessons and mentoring.
Paperback: 978-1-84694-319-5 ebook: 978-1-84694-642-4

Rising in Love

My Wild and Crazy Ride to Here and Now, with Amma, the Hugging Saint

Ram Das Batchelder

Rising in Love conveys an author's extraordinary journey of spiritual awakening with the Guru, Amma.

Paperback: 978-1-78279-687-9 ebook: 978-1-78279-686-2

Thinker's Guide to God

Peter Vardy

An introduction to key issues in the philosophy of religion.

Paperback: 978-1-90381-622-6

Your Simple Path

Find happiness in every step

Ian Tucker

A guide to helping us reconnect with what is really important in our lives.

Paperback: 978-1-78279-349-6 ebook: 978-1-78279-348-9

365 Days of Wisdom

Daily Messages To Inspire You Through The Year

Dadi Janki

Daily messages which cool the mind, warm the heart and guide you along your journey.

Paperback: 978-1-84694-863-3 ebook: 978-1-84694-864-0

Body of Wisdom

Women's Spiritual Power and How it Serves

Hilary Hart

Bringing together the dreams and experiences of women across the world with today's most visionary spiritual teachers.

Paperback: 978-1-78099-696-7 ebook: 978-1-78099-695-0

Dying to Be Free

From Enforced Secrecy to Near Death to True Transformation

Hannah Robinson

After an unexpected accident and near-death experience, Hannah Robinson found herself radically transforming her life, while a remarkable new insight altered her relationship with her father, a practising Catholic priest.

Paperback: 978-1-78535-254-6 ebook: 978-1-78535-255-3

The Ecology of the Soul

A Manual of Peace, Power and Personal Growth for Real People in the Real World

Aidan Walker

Balance your own inner Ecology of the Soul to regain your natural state of peace, power and wellbeing.

Paperback: 978-1-78279-850-7 ebook: 978-1-78279-849-1

Not I, Not other than I

The Life and Teachings of Russel Williams

Steve Taylor, Russel Williams

The miraculous life and inspiring teachings of one of the World's greatest living Sages.

Paperback: 978-1-78279-729-6 ebook: 978-1-78279-728-9

On the Other Side of Love

A Woman's Unconventional Journey Towards Wisdom

Muriel Maufroy

When life has lost all meaning, what do you do?

Paperback: 978-1-78535-281-2 ebook: 978-1-78535-282-9

Practicing A Course In Miracles

A Translation of the Workbook in Plain Language and With Mentoring Notes

Elizabeth A. Cronkhite

The practical second and third volumes of The Plain-Language *A Course In Miracles*.

Paperback: 978-1-84694-403-1 ebook: 978-1-78099-072-9

Quantum Bliss

The Quantum Mechanics of Happiness, Abundance, and Health

George S. Mentz

Quantum Bliss is the breakthrough summary of success and spirituality secrets that customers have been waiting for.

Paperback: 978-1-78535-203-4 ebook: 978-1-78535-204-1

The Upside Down Mountain

Mags MacKean

A must-read for anyone weary of chasing success and happiness – one woman's inspirational journey swapping the uphill slog for the downhill slope.

Paperback: 978-1-78535-171-6 ebook: 978-1-78535-172-3

Your Personal Tuning Fork

The Endocrine System

Deborah Bates

Discover your body's health secret, the endocrine system, and 'twang' your way to sustainable health!

Paperback: 978-1-84694-503-8 ebook: 978-1-78099-697-4

Readers of ebooks can buy or view any of these bestsellers by clicking on the live link in the title. Most titles are published in paperback and as an ebook. Paperbacks are available in traditional bookshops. Both print and ebook formats are available online.

Find more titles and sign up to our readers' newsletter at http://www.johnhuntpublishing.com/mind-body-spirit

Follow us on Facebook at https://www.facebook.com/OBooks/ and Twitter at https://twitter.com/obooks